STRUCTURED LITERACY INTERVENTIONS

The Guilford Series on Intensive Instruction

Sharon Vaughn, *Editor*

This series presents innovative ways to improve learning outcomes for K–12 students with challenging academic and behavioral needs. Books in the series explain the principles of intensive intervention and provide evidence-based teaching practices for learners who require differentiated instruction. Grounded in current research, volumes include user-friendly features such as sample lessons, examples of daily schedules, case studies, classroom vignettes, and reproducible tools.

Essentials of Intensive Intervention
Rebecca Zumeta Edmonds, Allison Gruner Gandhi, and Louis Danielson

Intensive Reading Interventions for the Elementary Grades
Jeanne Wanzek, Stephanie Al Otaiba, and Kristen L. McMaster

Intensifying Mathematics Interventions for Struggling Students
Edited by Diane Pedrotty Bryant

Literacy Coaching in the Secondary Grades: Helping Teachers Meet the Needs of All Students
Jade Wexler, Elizabeth Swanson, and Alexandra Shelton

Structured Literacy Interventions: Teaching Students with Reading Difficulties, K–6
Edited by Louise Spear-Swerling

Structured Literacy Interventions

Teaching Students with Reading Difficulties, Grades K–6

edited by

Louise Spear-Swerling

Series Editor's Note by Sharon Vaughn

THE GUILFORD PRESS
New York London

A Division of Guilford Publications, Inc.
370 Seventh Avenue, Suite 1200, New York, NY 10001
www.guilford.com

Printed in the United States of America

This book is printed on acid-free paper.

Last digit is print number: 9 8 7 6 5 4

Library of Congress Cataloging-in-Publication Data

Names: Spear-Swerling, Louise, editor.
Title: Structured literacy interventions : teaching students with reading difficulties, grades K–6 / edited by Louise Spear-Swerling.
Description: New York, N.Y. : The Guilford Press, [2022] | Series: The Guilford series on intensive instruction | Includes bibliographical references and index.
Identifiers: LCCN 2021025312 | ISBN 9781462548781 (paperback) | ISBN 9781462548798 (cloth)
Subjects: LCSH: Reading—Remedial teaching. | Reading (Elementary) | Reading disability. | Response to intervention (Learning disabled children)
Classification: LCC LB1050.5 .S86 2022 | DDC 372.4—dc23
LC record available at *https://lccn.loc.gov/2021025312*

About the Editor

Louise Spear-Swerling, PhD, is Professor Emerita in the Department of Special Education at Southern Connecticut State University. Her research interests focus on children's reading development and literacy difficulties, as well as teacher knowledge for reading instruction; she has presented and published widely on these topics. Dr. Spear-Swerling is the author of two previous books on reading difficulties and is an editorial board member for several journals, including *Annals of Dyslexia, Teaching Exceptional Children,* and *Reading Psychology*. A former special educator at the elementary level, Dr. Spear-Swerling prepared both general and special education teacher candidates to teach reading using structured literacy approaches for many years. She consults often for K–12 schools, primarily on cases involving students with severe or persistent literacy difficulties and ways to improve their achievement.

Contributors

Stephanie Al Otaiba, PhD, Department of Teaching and Learning, Simmons School of Education and Human Development, Southern Methodist University, Dallas, Texas

Jill H. Allor, EdD, Department of Teaching and Learning, Simmons School of Education and Human Development, Southern Methodist University, Dallas, Texas

Erin Munce Anderson, MEd, College of Education, University of Washington, Seattle, Washington

Christy R. Austin, PhD, Department of Educational Psychology, University of Utah, Salt Lake City, Utah

Michael D. Coyne, PhD, Department of Educational Psychology, Neag School of Education, University of Connecticut, Storrs, Connecticut

Charles Winthrop Haynes, EdD, Department of Communication Sciences and Disorders, School of Health and Rehabilitation Sciences, MGH Institute of Health Professions, Boston, Massachusetts

Roxanne F. Hudson, PhD, College of Education, University of Washington, Seattle, Washington

Devin M. Kearns, PhD, Department of Educational Psychology, Neag School of Education, University of Connecticut, Storrs, Connecticut

Shannon L. Kelley, MAT, Department of Educational Psychology, Neag School of Education, University of Connecticut, Storrs, Connecticut

Susan Lambrecht Smith, PhD, Department of Communication Sciences and Disorders, School of Health and Rehabilitation Sciences, MGH Institute of Health Professions, Boston, Massachusetts

Susan M. Loftus-Rattan, PhD, School of Education, Duquesne University, Pittsburgh, Pennsylvania

Cheryl P. Lyon, MAT, Department of Educational Psychology, Neag School of Education, University of Connecticut, Storrs, Connecticut

Melissa McGraw, MEd, College of Education, University of Washington, Seattle, Washington

Donna D. Merritt, PhD, independent consultant, Mansfield Center, Connecticut

Louisa C. Moats, EdD, Moats Associates Consulting, Inc., Sun Valley, Idaho

Rebecca Ray, MA, College of Education, University of Washington, Seattle, Washington

Louise Spear-Swerling, PhD, Department of Special Education, Southern Connecticut State University, New Haven, Connecticut

Elizabeth A. Stevens, PhD, Department of Learning Sciences, Georgia State University, Atlanta, Georgia

Jennifer Stewart, PhD, Department of Teaching and Learning, Simmons School of Education and Human Development, Southern Methodist University, Dallas, Texas

Alison Wilhelm, MEd, College of Education, University of Washington, Seattle, Washington

Richard P. Zipoli, PhD, Department of Communication Disorders, Southern Connecticut State University, New Haven, Connecticut

Series Editor's Note

Are you wondering whether there is a knowledge-to-practice guide available to assist you in implementing Structured Literacy (SL) approaches to teaching students with reading difficulties? Are you perhaps also secretly wanting to understand what SL actually is and how it differs from other instructional approaches to teaching students with dyslexia and related reading difficulties? Well, join a growing group of educators who are eager to better understand and implement approaches to SL. Fortunately for us, Louise Spear-Swerling has come to the rescue. In reading her book, I learned not only what SL is but also clear ideas for implementing it as part of teacher-education programs as well as instruction with students.

Spear-Swerling has assembled an all-star team to take us step-by-step through both understanding what the elements of SL are and how to implement them with students who have dyslexia. What I like so much about this volume is the way the organizational structure of the book identifies each of the components of SL and unpacks it so neatly. The provision of step-by-step lessons that allow us to watch each element of SL come to life through our reading is remarkable. After reading this book, I know more about SL and, even more important, I know more about how to integrate it into my instruction.

The book launches with an overview of SL and how it aligns with the reader profiles of students with reading difficulties. Since many schools are using multi-tiered systems of support (MTSS) approaches, the first chapter recognizes how structured literacy might fit into an MTSS model. Most important, the chapter removes the mystery of SL and reveals how the components can be utilized in reading instruction and intensive reading intervention. What I like about the introductory chapter is that we learn that SL is represented in many approaches to reading instruction, and we are also provided with clear examples of approaches that are incompatible with SL.

The robust knowledge and practice learning continue throughout all of the chapters. If you are like me, you will appreciate the application activities at the end of each chapter. These are much like the real-world issues with which we grapple every day. As you scroll through the table of contents you will recognize that each chapter addresses one of the key elements of SL, with knowledge-to-practice foci throughout and application activities to assure that what we are learning can be applied to our daily decision making. The figures and tables sprinkled within each chapter organize key information in readily accessible ways. I found this volume to be an essential source of knowledge to practice application of SL. Considering the emphasis on finding effective ways to provide instruction for students with dyslexia and related reading difficulties, I think you will find this book to be an extremely valuable knowledge and practice source that you will return to many times. I strongly suspect that you will be telling your colleagues, "You just have to get this book—it's more than worth it!"

SHARON VAUGHN, PhD

Preface

When I was growing up in the late 1950s and 1960s, reading difficulties were not well understood. Formal avenues for extra help were limited to special education or expensive private tutoring. Those avenues tended to be hampered by a lack of knowledge about the nature of different reading problems and the most effective ways to help poor readers. Thankfully, this situation has changed dramatically in my lifetime. Scientific knowledge about reading has exploded, especially in the past couple of decades, and continues to grow at a rapid pace.

One important set of research findings involves the value of certain features of instruction—such as highly explicit, systematic teaching and prompt corrective feedback—in meeting the needs of at-risk readers and those with disabilities. In the past couple of years, Structured Literacy (SL) approaches (International Dyslexia Association, 2019, 2020), which combine these features of effective instruction, have generated strong interest. SL approaches are grounded not only in important components of literacy, such as phonics and spelling, but also in key components of language, including morphology, syntax, and semantics. While the value of explicit, systematic teaching, especially of foundational skills, such as decoding, has been recognized in the research and special education communities for many years (e.g., Engelmann, 1969; Gillingham & Stillman, 1970), SL approaches are also informed by a broader set of research findings about language and literacy that have arisen somewhat more recently. The comprehensive nature of SL approaches makes them useful for many types of poor readers—not only those with dyslexia and other difficulties in foundational skills, but also those with problems involving vocabulary, comprehension, and writing.

In this book, *Structured Literacy* is conceptualized as an umbrella term encompassing a variety of intervention methods, instructional approaches, and commercial programs—that is, SL is defined in relation to research-supported, effective features of instruction, rather than narrowly focused on particular programs or methods. This broad focus is essential. First, despite the overall research support for explicit, systematic teaching, there is also recognition among researchers (e.g., Compton, Miller, Elleman, & Steacy, 2014; Kilpatrick, 2015) of the limitations of many traditional programs and methods, such as those emphasizing verbalization of extensive phonics rules, in helping students with the most serious reading problems. An approach that incorporates recent research findings, and that also attends to emerging research, is critical for improving systems of intervention for these students on an ongoing basis. Furthermore, a narrow, rigid focus on specific programs or methods can be very problematic for schools—for example, some programs may impose constraints for which there are not good empirical justifications, such as requirements for hundreds of hours of practicum training for interventionists.

In addition to focusing on SL approaches to intervention, this volume is organized around common poor-reader profiles that have been identified in research (e.g., Catts, Adlof, & Weismer, 2006; Catts, Compton, Tomblin, & Bridges, 2012; Leach, Scarborough, & Rescorla, 2003; Lesaux & Kieffer, 2010). After Catts and colleagues, we term these profiles *specific word recognition difficulties* (SWRD), problems that center on word reading; *specific reading comprehension difficulties* (SRCD), problems that center on language comprehension; and *mixed reading difficulties* (MRD), problems involving both word reading and language comprehension. Poor-reader profiles are educationally useful for understanding many reading difficulties, both those associated with disabilities, such as dyslexia or autism spectrum disorders, and those associated with experiential factors, such as limited exposure to English. Information about poor-reader profiles can help practitioners target interventions appropriately for individual children, and this information also addresses the practical needs of most educators, who typically work with a range of poor readers, not just one profile of reading difficulty.

The chapters in this volume are written by experts who are well known as researchers but who are also highly skilled at writing for practitioners. The primary audience for this book is practitioners who teach struggling readers at the kindergarten through grade 6 level, including general educators, special educators, reading specialists, and interventionists. School leaders who manage systems of intervention, such as principals and directors of special education, as well as teacher educators, will also find the book helpful. Chapters are written to be maximally useful to all of these groups, with a strong foundation of research summarized in each chapter, but with a concentration on translating research into practice, including case studies, sample intervention activities, and lesson plans. Each chapter includes application activities at the end to check for and extend readers' understanding.

In Chapter 1, I introduce the main themes of the book. This chapter discusses in detail the key features of SL approaches and contrasts SL with non-SL approaches. It also reviews research on the three common poor-reader profiles, with an explanation of how information about these profiles can be helpful to readers of the book.

In Chapter 2, Stephanie Al Otaiba, Jill Allor, and Jennifer Stewart discuss SL interventions for phonological awareness and phonics. This chapter addresses skills for decoding one-syllable words, including examples of useful assessments and effective intervention activities, as well as a discussion of dialect-informed instruction. In addition, these authors provide information about important web-based resources for teachers on evidence-based interventions in reading. This chapter, as well as the next three, are especially useful for poor readers whose difficulties are based at least partly in decoding, those with a profile of SWRD or MRD.

Chapter 3, by Devin Kearns, Cheryl Lyon, and Shannon Kelley, discusses SL interventions for reading long words, beyond the one-syllable stage. Research-based interventions that use syllable information and those employing morphology-related strategies are explained in detail. These authors also discuss important supporting practices for multisyllabic word decoding, such as teaching flexibility and providing adequate practice.

In Chapter 4, Louisa Moats explains why learning to spell in English is difficult for many children, including most poor readers. She presents SL approaches for teaching spelling from the initial stages of spelling development involving simple one-syllable words, through much more complex types of words, including multisyllabic words. She also explains insights gained from recent research about how to teach spelling of words containing odd or less predictable spellings (i.e., phonetically irregular words).

Chapter 5 addresses SL approaches to reading fluency intervention. In this chapter, Roxanne Hudson, Erin Anderson, Melissa McGraw, Rebecca Ray, and Alison Wilhelm describe the three elements of reading fluency and how to assess each element. Their discussion of interventions focuses on children whose fluency difficulties are based partly or entirely in poor decoding, those with SWRD or MRD. They explain how repeated reading, as well as phrase-cueing interventions, may be useful for these children, with sample lesson plans for both types of interventions.

Chapter 6, by Michael Coyne and Susan Loftus-Rattan, discusses research-based interventions for vocabulary. This chapter emphasizes a broad program of vocabulary development that is especially important for poor or at-risk readers with generalized vocabulary weaknesses, whether these weaknesses stem from intrinsic learning difficulties or lack of exposure to words. These authors provide a step-by-step explanation of how to teach vocabulary using an SL approach, including how to decide on specific words to teach. They also explain how their vocabulary activities can be tailored for older poor readers with SWRD who cannot read grade-level text due to poor decoding, but who can benefit from grade-appropriate oral language activities to continue building their vocabulary knowledge.

In Chapter 7, on oral language comprehension interventions, Richard Zipoli and Donna Merritt focus on poor readers with a profile of either SRCD or MRD, profiles that typically include oral language comprehension weaknesses. They provide a detailed discussion of research-based SL interventions at the sentence level and at the discourse level, for narrative language. They also explain how to provide these interventions in the context of and with transfer to children's reading, as well as the importance of targeting related language skills, such as inferencing.

Chapter 8, by Elizabeth Stevens and Christy Austin, addresses SL interventions for reading comprehension. The chapter is organized around research-based practices to use before reading, during reading, and after reading, with an emphasis on informational text and students with a profile of SRCD. Chapter 8 describes research-based practices for areas such as building background knowledge, generating main ideas, and summarization, as well as explicit teaching of text-specific vocabulary words that children need to learn in order to understand a particular text.

Chapter 9, by Susan Lambrecht Smith and Charles Haynes, presents a comprehensive approach to SL intervention in written expression, including intervention at multiple levels: words, sentences, micro-discourse (two or three related sentences), and paragraphs. The chapter includes detailed application of the chapter content to the specific case of a student with dyslexia but can also be applied to poor readers with other reading profiles.

In Chapter 10, I discuss multicomponent SL interventions—interventions that address both word reading and comprehension—for students with MRD. These interventions draw upon much of the content of previous chapters and apply it to three specific examples of poor readers with varying needs in decoding and language comprehension. Issues in designing multicomponent interventions are discussed, and sample lesson plans for each poor reader are provided.

SL approaches are a valuable way to design and improve interventions for children with a variety of reading problems. All of the contributors to this volume hope that it will help practitioners substantially increase the effectiveness of their teaching and reach a much broader range of struggling readers.

REFERENCES

Catts, H. W., Adlof, S. M., & Weismer, S. E. (2006). Language deficits in poor comprehenders: A case for the simple view of reading. *Journal of Speech, Language, and Hearing Research, 49*(2), 278–293.

Catts, H. W., Compton, D. L., Tomblin, J. B., & Bridges, M. S. (2012). Prevalence and nature of late-emerging poor readers. *Journal of Educational Psychology, 104*(2), 166–181.

Compton, D. L., Miller, A. C., Elleman, A. M., & Steacy, L. M. (2014). Have we forsaken reading theory in the name of "quick fix" interventions for children with reading disability? *Scientific Studies of Reading, 18*(1), 55–73.

Engelmann, S. (1969). *Preventing failure in the primary grades.* Chicago: Science Research Associates.

Gillingham, A., & Stillman, B. (1970). *Remedial training for children with specific language disability.* Cambridge, MA: Educators' Publishing Service.

International Dyslexia Association. (2019). *Structured literacy: An introductory guide.* Newark, DE: Author.

International Dyslexia Association. (2020). *Structured literacy: Effective instruction for children with dyslexia and related reading difficulties.* Newark, DE: Author.

Kilpatrick, D. A. (2015). *Essentials of assessing, preventing, and overcoming reading difficulties.* Hoboken, NJ: Wiley.

Leach, J. M., Scarborough, H. S., & Rescorla, L. (2003). Late-emerging reading disabilities. *Journal of Educational Psychology, 95,* 211–224.

Lesaux, N. K., & Kieffer, M. J. (2010). Exploring sources of reading comprehension difficulties among language minority learners and their classmates in early adolescence. *American Educational Research Journal, 47,* 596–632.

Acknowledgments

By its nature, an edited book presents a different set of demands than does authoring a book on one's own. So, first, I would like to thank the individual chapter contributors, who agreed to lend their formidable expertise to this project, as well as to write their chapters in ways that would be especially useful to practitioners and that would result in a coherent whole. Many thanks are also due to Sharon Vaughn for her valuable guidance at the outset of this work and her perceptive feedback on individual chapters, as well as to Rochelle Serwator and Katherine Sommer at The Guilford Press for all their help throughout the process of preparing the manuscript.

My work with teachers, school administrators, parents, and children has long informed my writing. That was certainly true for this book. I am most grateful to all of these individuals for sharing their experiences with me and enabling me to continue to learn from them. Finally, heartfelt thanks go to my husband, daughter, and son. They have demonstrated an unfailing support of my work, along with an interest in hearing the details of it, and they have provided many helpful insights.

Contents

Purchasers of this book can print enlarged copies of the reproducible materials at *www.guilford.com/spear-swerling-forms* for personal use or use with students (see copyright page for details).

CHAPTER 1

An Introduction to Structured Literacy and Poor-Reader Profiles

Louise Spear-Swerling

Ms. Cuffe, a district administrator for a highly diverse suburban school district, was dismayed. The district was strongly committed to a response-to-intervention (RTI) model, sometimes termed *multi-tiered systems of support* (MTSS). Among other features, this model provides universal screening of all children for reading difficulties, with early intervention for at-risk and struggling readers, and with increased intensity of intervention for children who do not respond adequately to initial interventions. However, recent data from the intervention programs across elementary schools in Ms. Cuffe's district indicated that the outcomes of intervention were often poor. Many students made limited progress despite months or even years of intervention. Others appeared to make progress initially but failed to build reading fluency or struggled with other areas of literacy, such as written expression, later on. Ms. Cuffe had particular concerns that the interventions in use in the district schools were not consistent with research findings on the needs of poor readers. She had done some reading about Structured Literacy (SL) approaches to intervention, as well as observed SL interventions in a neighboring town. Ms. Cuffe thought that these interventions might be much more effective for the struggling readers in her district than the ones currently in use. In a meeting with a group of the district's K–6 literacy interventionists, she broached the idea of implementing SL.

Several of the literacy interventionists were doubtful. "Isn't Structured Literacy all about phonics?" said one. "Some of our poor readers do need phonics, but many of them need a focus primarily on comprehension, especially those in grades 4, 5, and 6. How is Structured Literacy going to do anything for those children?"

"Yes," chimed in a second educator. "Isn't Structured Literacy mainly for kids with dyslexia?"

"I really don't like the idea of using just one program for all students," said another, shaking her head. "Poor readers have different needs."

The topic of this book involves SL interventions for children with reading difficulties. As the different chapters in the book illustrate—and as Ms. Cuffe was eventually able to convince the literacy interventionists in her meeting—SL approaches do not involve just one particular commercial program or method, and they are not only for students with one type of reading difficulty or disability. Nor are they only about teaching phonics. *Structured Literacy* is an umbrella term for a range of interventions that share certain instructional features and content. These interventions can be highly effective for a variety of struggling readers, including those whose difficulties center on comprehension, as well as decoding. SL interventions include teaching not only foundational literacy skills, such as phonemic awareness, phonics, and spelling, but also higher-level components of literacy, such as reading comprehension and written expression.

SL interventions can be valuable tools for many types of practitioners, including reading specialists, RTI/MTSS interventionists, special educators, and classroom teachers. Information about these interventions can also assist professionals who are involved in planning or overseeing systems of interventions, such as Ms. Cuffe. This chapter provides a foundation for the remainder of the book, by discussing the content and key features of SL, by differentiating SL from other commonly used approaches to reading instruction, and by explaining common profiles of reading difficulties. Knowledge of common poor-reader profiles is very useful for targeting interventions appropriately and can help readers of this book determine which chapters are particularly relevant for a given poor reader.

CONTENT AND KEY FEATURES OF SL

The term *Structured Literacy* was adopted by the International Dyslexia Association (IDA; 2019, 2020) to describe a set of instructional approaches and interventions with certain characteristics. The content of SL involves literacy-related skills and components of oral language that play key roles in literacy development and figure prominently in various types of literacy difficulties (Berninger et al., 2006; Fletcher, Lyon, Fuchs, & Barnes, 2019; Foorman et al., 2016; National Reading Panel [NRP], 2000; Seidenberg, 2017). The content of SL includes:

- *phonemic awareness,* awareness of individual sounds (phonemes) in spoken words and the ability to manipulate these sounds;
- *phonics,* knowledge of letter–sound (grapheme–phoneme) correspondences in English and the ability to apply this knowledge in decoding unfamiliar printed words;
- *orthography,* knowledge about common spelling patterns in English;
- *morphology,* knowledge about meaningful word parts, such as roots, prefixes, and suffixes;

- *syntax*, or sentence structure; and
- *semantics*, meaning at the level of words (i.e., vocabulary), sentences, and longer discourse, such as paragraphs and longer text.

The fact that IDA introduced the term *Structured Literacy* might lead some educators to conclude that these approaches are intended uniquely for students with dyslexia, a type of learning disability that centers on problems in learning to decode and spell printed words (Fletcher et al., 2019). SL interventions can certainly benefit these children. However, SL interventions are not intended solely for this student population, and they can be effective for many other poor readers as well. Individual SL interventions may differ from one another in some ways—for example, in the extent to which they incorporate multisensory activities, such as repeated tracing and saying of letter sounds or printed words. However, all SL approaches share a core set of instructional features, which are summarized in Table 1.1.

First, all SL interventions emphasize explicit, systematic instruction. *Explicit* means that important skills are taught directly, with modeling and clear explanation by the teacher; children are not expected to learn important skills solely from exposure or induction. Clear explanation is concise and avoids excessive wordiness. *Systematic* means that there is a planned sequence of instruction, one that gradually progresses from simpler to more complex skills. Children learn to decode and spell consonant–vowel–consonant (CVC) words, such as *map* and *fit*, before learning to decode or spell incrementally more difficult short vowel words, such as *branch* and *twist*, and certainly before complex two-syllable or multisyllabic words. Likewise, in the domain of writing, children learn to write correct sentences before being expected to produce lengthy pieces of writing. Systematic teaching does not mean that teachers must always adhere rigidly to a sequence, without the capacity to make adaptations to meet individual students' needs. However, having a clear scope and sequence can help promote efficiency of instruction (Fletcher et al., 2019) and ensure that children attain the prerequisites they need to learn more advanced skills.

Attention to prerequisite skills is a key feature of SL interventions, not only in relation to children's progress through a planned sequence of skills but also in the planning of everyday instructional activities. For instance, in explaining the meaning of new vocabulary words or of a syntactically complex sentence, SL teachers avoid using language that children may not understand. SL teachers also provide prompt, targeted feedback to children's mistakes. When children are reading a text, teachers ask questions during the reading, instead of waiting only until the end, so that potential misunderstandings can be addressed right away; in writing activities, teachers provide feedback that is specific and unambiguous, so that children are not confused about how to make revisions.

SL approaches emphasize planned, purposeful selections of instructional examples, tasks, and texts. These selections attempt to avoid unnecessary confusion, enhance students' chances of success, and maximize progress. To put it another way, SL approaches emphasize "instructional design that minimizes the learning challenge" (Fletcher et al., 2019, p. 101), again seeking the most efficient, as well as effective, instruction.

TABLE 1.1. Features of Structured Literacy

Feature	What it means	Example(s)
Explicit teaching	Key skills are directly taught, modeled, and clearly explained by the teacher	Teacher clearly models and explains how to segment a simple word into phonemes; how to apply a comprehension strategy, such as summarization
Systematic teaching	Instruction follows a planned, logical sequence, simple to complex	Children learn how to spell simple consonant–vowel–consonant words before spelling short vowel words with consonant blends; how to write correct sentences before writing paragraphs
Attention to prerequisite skills	Instruction considers prior skills needed to complete or understand a more advanced task	In teaching the meaning of a new vocabulary word, teacher uses clear definitions with words children will know
Targeted, unambiguous, prompt feedback	Teacher provides timely feedback to children's mistakes that helps children correct errors and avoid similar mistakes in the future	Teacher asks questions during children's text reading, with prompt clarification of misunderstandings as needed
Planned, purposeful choices of examples, tasks, and texts	Examples of words, instructional tasks, and texts for reading/writing are carefully chosen to fit children's current skills and avoid confusion	Phonics activities avoid the use of phonetically irregular words; children with limited decoding skills read phonetically controlled (decodable) texts
Synthetic-phonics approach at grapheme–phoneme level for initial phonics and spelling instruction	Initial approach emphasizes grapheme–phoneme correspondences and blending rather than larger units (e.g., whole words, onset–rime)	Children learn to decode a word, such as *shack,* by learning phonemes associated with the graphemes *sh, a,* and *ck,* and how to blend the phonemes into the correct word
Consistent application of skills and teaching for transfer	Children are expected to apply skills they have learned to varied and increasingly complex tasks, with tasks chosen to facilitate application of those skills	During oral reading of text, teacher draws children's attention to decoding errors and has child correct them; in writing activities, children are expected to spell previously learned words correctly
Data-based decision making	Assessments are used on a continuing basis to target interventions, monitor progress, and make needed adjustments	Assessments help a teacher target the specific comprehension weaknesses of a poor comprehender

Efficiency matters when students are behind and progress must be accelerated. Suppose, for instance, that a teacher is presenting a phonics lesson on one-syllable words with a closed pattern. These are words that have a single vowel and end in a consonant, such as *lap, inch,* and *stuck,* in which the vowel has a short sound. In this activity, an SL teacher avoids using examples that are phonetically irregular (e.g., *what* and *of*), as well as regular words containing vowel patterns that children have not yet learned, such as *charm* and *light.* Such words are likely to create confusion because they do not have a short vowel sound. These types of words will eventually be taught, of course, but in a planned, systematic way that minimizes potential confusion.

As another example, in SL interventions, children at the beginning levels of decoding usually read phonetically controlled (decodable) texts—texts emphasizing certain phonics patterns that children have been taught. Decodable texts provide children with practice in applying phonics skills and help to build fluency. These texts also discourage a habit of guessing at words that may develop when a child is reading texts with many difficult-to-decode words and with pictures that encourage guessing. For children whose reading problems center on comprehension rather than decoding, texts are also chosen in a purposeful way—for instance, to facilitate application of a particular comprehension strategy that children have been taught (e.g., summarization) or to ensure that the vocabulary and background knowledge demands of the text are a reasonable match for the child's skills—not too easy, not too difficult.

SL approaches not only teach phonics skills explicitly and systematically; typically, they emphasize a particular approach to teaching phonics, a synthetic-phonics approach beginning at the grapheme–phoneme level. This approach focuses initially on having children learn grapheme–phoneme correspondences—that is, relationships between individual letters or letter patterns (graphemes) and phonemes, or the smallest unit of speech sound in a word. Children also learn how to blend phonemes into a whole word, using an instructional sequence that begins with the simplest, easiest-to-blend words (e.g., *sun*) and progresses gradually through more difficult word patterns. To decode a word such as *shack,* children would learn that the *sh* grapheme corresponds to the phoneme /sh/, the grapheme *a* to short /a/ as in *at,* and the grapheme *ck* to /k/, as well as how to blend those phonemes to form the spoken word *shack.*

Synthetic phonics at the grapheme–phoneme level does not mean teaching all words through letter-by-letter decoding, which does not work well for most English words. Even at the beginning of phonics instruction, children must learn grapheme–phoneme correspondences for some common letter patterns, such as *sh, th, ck,* and so on. The point is that initial phonics instruction is at the phoneme level, not at the whole-word level (e.g., inducing phonics relationships from word families, such as *shack, back, pack*), and not at the onset–rime level (e.g., learning larger intrasyllabic units, such as *sh, tr, bl, -ack, -ap, -ick, -ip,* and blending those larger parts). In this approach, as in other phonics approaches, children must eventually learn to attend to larger letter patterns in words, including common morphemes (e.g., suffixes such as *-ing, -ed, -ful*). However, the *initial* approach to decoding unfamiliar printed words emphasizes grapheme–phoneme-level correspondences, which forces close attention to the internal details of words, and which also facilitates integration of phonemic awareness instruction, as explained in detail by Al Otaiba, Allor, and Stewart (Chapter 2, this volume).

Another important feature of SL is an emphasis on consistent application of learned skills to a variety of tasks, including more advanced types of tasks over time, and with these tasks chosen in ways to facilitate such application. Sometimes this feature is termed "teaching for transfer" (Wanzek, Al Otaiba, & McMaster, 2020, pp. 6–7). For example, SL teachers do not ignore errors in a child's oral text reading simply because they fit the context (e.g., *a* for *the*, *this* for *that*, or *mom* for *mother*). Instead, teachers encourage careful attention to the print and application of phonics skills. Texts must also be selected in a purposeful way, to match children's current level of phonics skills—if texts contain numerous words that children cannot decode, children have few options but to guess. Some review of previously taught skills is always a part of SL lessons, but cumulative review is also built into SL interventions in a comprehensive way, through consistent application of learned skills to a variety of tasks and purposeful selections of examples, tasks, and texts.

Finally, appropriate assessment is essential to SL interventions. SL approaches use data-based decision making. They employ appropriate assessments to identify reading problems early, to target interventions correctly, to monitor children's progress, and to refine and adjust interventions as needed, on an ongoing basis. For example, with poor readers whose difficulties center on reading comprehension, SL teachers use assessment to clarify individual children's specific difficulties within the domain of comprehension, such as vocabulary, background knowledge, syntax, or understanding of text structure. This information is then used to plan initial intervention, with ongoing monitoring of children's progress in reading comprehension and adjustments in intervention if a student is failing to progress adequately.

Although multiple interventions fall under the umbrella of SL, some approaches to instruction and intervention are not compatible with SL. These include approaches that emphasize allocating substantial amounts of classroom or intervention time to independent work or having children choose most of their own instructional tasks and texts; these practices make explicit, systematic teaching difficult at best. Similarly, approaches with a heavily constructivist orientation that emphasize having children induce important skills and concepts with little or no explicit, systematic teaching, are generally incompatible with SL. SL approaches are also incompatible with the three cueing systems model of reading (e.g., Clay, 1994; Goodman, 1976), which has been influential in teacher education and early reading instruction (see Hanford, 2019). This model maintains that, rather than attending closely to all the letters in a word, good readers use semantic (meaning) and syntactic (sentence structure) cues, in conjunction with partial letter cues, such as the first and last letter of a word, to read words. As discussed further in the next section, research does not support the three cueing systems model of reading, and many practices associated with it are problematic, especially for poor readers.

Archer and Hughes (2011) point out that explicit, systematic teaching is sometimes cast as boring, soulless instruction that does not engage children or inspire the motivation to read and write. Motivation and engagement are indeed important. Even the best intervention cannot be successful if the teacher is unable to engage the students' attention. Moreover, struggling readers can gain many long-term benefits from being motivated to read independently for enjoyment, such as increases in fluency, vocabulary, and background knowledge (Mol & Bus, 2011). However, helping poor readers succeed in literacy is vital to motivating them, because repeated failure is not motivating to most people. SL interventions can be implemented in ways that are not only effective and efficient but also highly engaging. Children can use manipulatives, such as counters and letter tiles, to learn about phonemic awareness and phonics skills; they can use word cards to sort various patterns to learn about spelling; and they can develop their writing skills in the context of rich, engaging oral discussions. The chapters that follow provide many examples of SL interventions that can be highly motivating and engaging to struggling students.

RESEARCH SUPPORT FOR SL

Content

Numerous research studies, literature reviews, and meta-analyses (Berninger et al., 2006; Foorman et al., 2016; NRP, 2000; Seidenberg, 2017; Stanovich, 2000) provide strong support for the content of SL approaches. This research has established that learning to read and write is based heavily in language processes, such as phonemic awareness, syntactic competence, vocabulary knowledge, and broad oral language comprehension. These studies have also shown that good word recognition skills are an essential foundation for text reading fluency and more advanced reading comprehension. Contrary to the claims of the three cueing systems model, the development of proficient reading is not a matter of learning to use context cues in conjunction with partial letter cues to read words. Rather, progress in early reading is driven by close attention to letter sequences in printed words and the development of highly accurate, automatic word reading (NRP, 2000; Seidenberg, 2017; Stanovich, 2000). Although some poor decoders may be able to compensate for their decoding problems by relying on sentence or picture context, especially at early grade levels, this strategy does not work well as children advance in school and the texts become more demanding (Spear-Swerling, 2015). It is important for teachers to recognize a pattern of overreliance on context—for example, a child who frequently guesses at words based only on the first few letters and sentence context or pictures—as a sign of risk in reading (Moats & Foorman, 2003).

Written English involves a complex orthography in which letters and sounds have a largely consistent, but not always transparent, relationship. English orthography contrasts with Spanish and some other alphabetic orthographies, in which there is a mostly one-to-one mapping between letters and sounds. The letter *a* in Spanish almost always corresponds to the sound heard in *taco*, but in English, the letter *a* can correspond to varied sounds, including the short sound as in *cat*, the long sound as in *cake*, a schwa sound as in *ago*, and so forth. These sounds are quite predictable in most English words, but they require attention to letter patterns and their position in words, as opposed to letter-by-letter decoding. As an example, the *a* in *cake* has a long sound (i.e., says its name) because it is part of a vowel–consonant–final *e* (VC*e*) pattern that ends the word. Despite some exceptions, such as *done*, most one-syllable words with a *vce* pattern follow the same generalization as *cake*, with the first vowel long and the final *e* silent. Likewise, a given sound in English, such as long /a/, frequently can be represented by multiple spellings, not only *a*–consonant–*e* as in *cake* but also the single letter *a* as in *table*, *ay* as in *play*, *ai* as in *train*, *ei* as in *vein*, and others, a characteristic that makes English spelling particularly challenging to struggling students.

Written English represents morphological as well as grapheme–phoneme relationships. For instance, although the letter *s* most often says /s/, when *s* is indicating a plural—as in *dogs*, *bones*, and *pins*—it is sometimes pronounced /z/. Even in the very early stages of learning, children have to understand these basic morphological relationships in order not to misspell the word *dogs* as *dogz* and *pins* as *pinz*. At advanced stages of reading and spelling, attending to common roots, affixes, and other aspects of morphology becomes even more important. Without some understanding of morphology, a child might reasonably spell *healthy* as *helthy* and *psychology* as *sikology*. All of these types of knowledge—phonics, orthography, and morphology—are essential in order for children to attain advanced levels of word recognition and spelling in English (Moats, 2020; Seidenberg, 2017).

A widely referenced scientific model of reading development, one that includes the abilities and types of knowledge discussed above, is the simple view of reading (Hoover & Gough, 1990). This model emphasizes that two broad factors are important to reading comprehension: word recognition and oral language comprehension. The word recognition factor taps skills such as phonemic awareness, which is required to grasp the alphabetic principle and begin to develop skills for decoding unfamiliar words, phonics knowledge, orthographic knowledge, and morphology. The oral language comprehension factor taps areas such as vocabulary, syntax, background knowledge, and discourse comprehension. To have good reading comprehension, a child must have good abilities in both word recognition and oral language comprehension. Conversely, reading difficulties are commonly based in one, or both, factors. The individual component abilities required for skilled reading also interact, and some contribute to both factors in the simple view. For example, morphology plays a role in vocabulary development, as well as in word reading and spelling (Carlisle, 2010). Developing highly skilled reading requires building fluent use and coordination of a wide range of reading-related abilities over many years (Scarborough, 2002).

Instructional Features

Features of SL involving explicit and systematic teaching, prompt and targeted feedback, and data-based decision making are highly consistent with research on effective methods of intervention for poor and at-risk readers in general (Archer & Hughes, 2011; Fletcher et al., 2019; Gersten et al., 2008; NRP, 2000). They also reflect research findings on effective ways to intensify interventions for poor readers who are not responding sufficiently to initial interventions (Wanzek et al., 2020). These features of intervention can enhance children's progress in various components of reading, as well as written expression. For example, research supports not only explicit teaching of foundational reading skills, such as phonemic awareness and phonics (Foorman et al., 2016; NRP, 2000), but also of certain research-based reading comprehension strategies (e.g., activating prior knowledge, questioning, and summarization) and of text structure (e.g., teaching the structure of narrative texts, as well as various informational text structures) (NRP, 2000; Shanahan et al., 2010). In written expression, studies support the explicit teaching of foundational writing skills, such as handwriting, spelling, and sentence structure, as well as important writing processes, including planning and revision (Graham et al., 2012).

Poor readers with experientially based reading problems, as well as those with intrinsic learning difficulties or disabilities, can benefit from features of SL, such as explicit, systematic teaching. For instance, English learners who are poor readers benefit from appropriately targeted interventions that combine explicit teaching of foundational reading skills with explicit teaching of English vocabulary and other language skills (Baker et al., 2014). However, students with severe and persistent reading disabilities typically require substantially more intensity of intervention than do other poor readers (Fletcher et al., 2019; Vaughn, Denton, & Fletcher, 2010). Greater intensity of intervention is often operationalized in terms of more intervention time, a smaller group size, and greater frequency of progress monitoring, although it can also include other variables, such as increasing the amount of instructional scaffolding provided by the teacher and opportunities for practice (Fuchs, Fuchs, & Stecker, 2010).

As noted in Table 1.1, SL approaches generally use a particular approach to phonics instruction, a synthetic-phonics approach with initial instruction at the grapheme–phoneme level. The meta-analysis of the NRP (2000) found clear benefits for explicit, systematic phonics teaching as compared to no or incidental phonics teaching but was not able to differentiate the effectiveness of various systematic phonics approaches. However, post-NRP research has found greater benefits for synthetic-phonics approaches in which initial instruction starts at the grapheme–phoneme level, as compared to other phonics approaches (Brady, 2011, 2020; Christensen & Bowey, 2005). In particular, synthetic–phonics approaches at the grapheme–phoneme level appear to yield greater benefits than other phonics approaches for more demanding reading and spelling tasks, such as children's accuracy and speed of reading transfer (i.e., unfamiliar) words (Brady, 2011). Also, synthetic-phonics approaches at the grapheme–phoneme level incorporate phoneme blending and segmentation—phonemic awareness skills known to be important to the development of decoding and spelling skills—whereas with other types of phonics approaches, supplementary phonemic awareness training may be needed (Johnston & Watson, 2004). If necessary, children may begin phonemic awareness instruction by using cubes or other counters without letters, but as they learn letters and develop skill in identifying the initial phoneme in a word, and then all phonemes in simple words, they transition to using letter tiles to represent phonemes.

There is widespread agreement among researchers that opportunities for children to apply their developing decoding skills in reading appropriate texts is a key aspect of effective intervention (Fletcher et al., 2019; Kilpatrick, 2015). Therefore, in addition to synthetic-phonics intervention, poor readers with needs in this area should also have ample practice in text reading, including reading aloud with the guidance of a teacher who provides targeted feedback to their decoding mistakes.

SOME SAMPLE SL AND NON-SL PRACTICES

This section of the chapter provides several detailed examples of specific SL practices and contrasts them with some non-SL practices—including those common in three cueing systems approaches—for the same areas of literacy (see also Moats, 2017, 2020; Spear-Swerling, 2018).

Decodable and Predictable Texts

Decodable texts are used as part of SL interventions, especially with children whose problems involve specific word recognition difficulties (SWRD) and mixed reading difficulties (MRD), and who are at relatively early stages of decoding. Predictable texts are not used in SL interventions. Figure 1.1 contrasts the first few pages of a sample decodable text with the initial pages of a sample predictable text.

Both texts in Figure 1.1 are intended for children at beginning reading levels, who would generally be learning to decode the simplest word type: CVC words. For each text, the figure indicates how pictures are used to enhance comprehension or motivation, as well as the types of words used in the text, including CVC words, high-frequency

Decodable text	**Predictable text**
Ben has a tan cat. The cat is Max. [picture of smiling boy with cat]	Good morning! It's time to have breakfast. What does Nicholas want to eat? [picture of smiling boy at table]
Ben has a lot of fun with Max. [picture of Ben and Max playing]	He can eat oatmeal. [picture of bowl of oatmeal]
Max likes to sit on a red rug in the den. [picture of Max on the rug]	He can eat waffles. [picture of waffles on a plate]
A big bug is on the rug near Max. [picture of bug]	He can eat bacon. [picture of bacon on a plate]
Max sees the bug run by him. [picture of Max looking startled]	He can eat scrambled eggs. [picture of scrambled eggs on a plate]
CVC words: *Ben, has, tan, cat, is, Max, lot, fun, sit, on, red, rug, in, den, big, bug, run, him* High-frequency words (not CVC): *a, the, of, with, likes, to, near, sees, by* Other words: (no other words)	CVC word: *can* High-frequency words (not CVC): *good, morning, it's, time, to, have, breakfast, what, does, want, eat, he* Other words: *Nicholas, oatmeal, waffles, bacon, scrambled, eggs*

FIGURE 1.1. Examples of decodable text and predictable text.

words other than those with a CVC pattern, and additional words that do not fit into either of these first two categories. Even the decodable text employs some words that do not have a CVC pattern (e.g., *see, the*) because it is virtually impossible to write English sentences without some of these words. However, most words in the decodable text are CVC (or VC), providing children with practice in the decoding skills they are learning. Also, the decodable text has pictures, but these are not selected to enable guessing at words instead of decoding.

In contrast, the predictable text has very few CVC words and includes many words that beginners would not be able to decode, such as *breakfast, oatmeal, scrambled,* and *bacon.* The repetition of the phrase "He can eat" might help children learn these high-frequency words, but it would not provide practice in applying decoding skills, especially for children whose decoding skills are weak. The pictures encourage guessing instead of close attention to letter sequences in words, which may convey a misleading message to poor decoders about what to attend to when reading, and which may make poor readers appear to be decoding successfully when they actually are not doing so.

SL and Non-SL Activities for Word Reading and Spelling

Figure 1.2 provides an example of a grapheme–phoneme mapping activity that is often employed in SL interventions, either through the type of written grid shown in the figure, or through the use of letter tiles or cards with grapheme–phoneme-level correspondences, not just the 26 letters of the alphabet. For instance, the phoneme /sh/ is represented with a single tile or within a single box, not with separate tiles or boxes for *s* and *h*.

The activity involves giving children a chain of words in which single-phoneme changes are made in unpredictable places in the word, not only the first letter of a word. If the activity is used for decoding, the teacher writes or forms the words with letter tiles, one word at a time; if it is intended for spelling, the teacher dictates the words in sequence and the children write them or use tiles to spell them. Words are carefully chosen to fit the patterns children have been taught. The words shown in Figure 1.2 would be appropriate for children who have learned to decode CVC words, as well as short vowel words with consonant blends and digraphs. The teacher avoids words that

s	i	p		
s	a	p		
s	n	a	p	
s	l	a	p	
f	l	a	p	
f	l	a	sh	
f	l	u	sh	

FIGURE 1.2. Sample grapheme–phoneme mapping activity.

are irregular (e.g., *was*) or that have patterns children have not yet learned. For example, *sip* to *sir* would not be appropriate because *sir* involves a vowel-*r* pattern and does not have a short vowel.

This activity, if implemented well, helps children learn to attend closely to the internal details of words (McCandliss, Beck, Sandak, & Perfetti, 2003) and can be done in a brisk, game-like fashion, which many children find engaging. Many more words than the examples shown in Figure 1.2 could potentially be part of a 10- to 15-minute activity—*flush* to *slush*, *slush* to *slug*, *slug* to *slog*, and so on—providing children with ample practice decoding unfamiliar words in an enjoyable way.

Contrast the SL activity in Figure 1.2 with the sample non-SL activity in Figure 1.3. This activity is a word configuration activity that involves looking at word shapes. It is sometimes used for spelling as well as reading. In this activity, children write the words shown at the top of the figure in the appropriate set of boxes. For instance, the word *saw* is supposed to be written in the set of boxes on the lower left of the figure, because *saw* has three letters, none of which are tall letters, like *t* or *f*. The word *for*, which has one tall letter followed by two shorter ones, is supposed to be written in the set of boxes shown in the upper left of the figure. Words used in this type of activity are often high-frequency words.

Word configuration activities do not draw children's attention to letter patterns in words; rather, they draw attention to the outer shape of words, which is essentially useless for reading or spelling words in English (e.g., *for* has the same outer shape as *too, tea, fan, box, ham, den,* and myriad other words). Besides failing to develop children's phonics skills, these activities may inadvertently lead children to focus on the wrong property of words—their shape—instead of the property that is most important: the sequence of letters within the word.

Examples of Feedback in SL and Non-SL Approaches

The clear, targeted feedback that students receive in SL approaches contrasts with the type of feedback frequently given in non-SL approaches. Figure 1.4 provides a few examples of this kind of feedback in several domains of literacy: spelling, oral reading of text, and written expression.

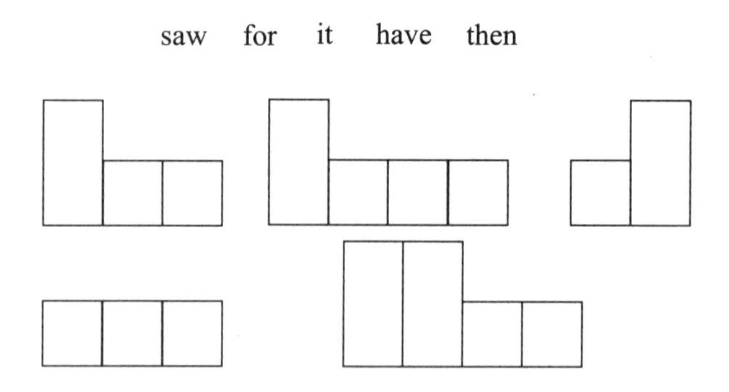

FIGURE 1.3. Sample word configuration activity.

Component area/child's error	Example of SL teacher's feedback	Examples of non-SL feedback
Spelling/A child misspells the word *making* as *makeing*	"What's the base word? Right, *make*; remember the rule for adding *-ing* to this kind of word. What do you need to do? Yes, take out the *e*. So, how do you spell *making*?"	"Take out the *e* in the word"; or teacher provides excessively wordy feedback (e.g., "What is the base word of *making*? Right, *make*. What's the syllable type of *make*? Yes, *make* is a magic *e* word because it has a vowel–consonant–*e* pattern with a long vowel and a silent *e*. Tell me the rule for adding *-ing* to a magic *e* base word. What do you have to do when you add *-ing* to these words?").
Oral reading of text/In the sentence *Mark likes to torture his little sister with his bad singing,* a child reads *torture* as *torment* and then just keeps reading, with no attempt to self-correct	Teacher immediately points to the *-ture* in the printed word *torture*; if child does not self-correct, teacher says, while pointing to *-ture,* "this says /cher/"; when the child decodes *torture* correctly, the teacher says, "Well done! Now just reread that sentence."	"Torture." (Teacher simply tells the child the word, without pointing to it or having the child reread); or teacher ignores the error because it fits the context and does not greatly alter the meaning.
Written expression, sentence structure/In a piece of descriptive writing, a child has many short, repetitive sentences, such as *The puppy is brown. It is little. It has floppy ears. It has huge paws. It likes to bark. Its name is Lucky.*	"The writing would sound better if you combined some of these short sentences. Remember our sentence combining. How can you combine the first three sentences? Excellent. *The little brown puppy has floppy ears.* Now try to do the same thing with some of your other sentences."	"Revise for sentence structure"; or "Try to revise so that there aren't so many short sentences."

FIGURE 1.4. Examples of feedback in SL and non-SL approaches.

As Figure 1.4 shows, in SL approaches, the feedback is not only clear and specific but also facilitates the student's ability to transfer a skill to other tasks in the future. For the child's misspelling of *making,* the teacher reminds the child of a relevant spelling rule that has been taught; for the child who writes short, choppy sentences, the teacher reminds the child of the utility of sentence combining. This kind of feedback is more useful than simply telling the child the correct spelling of a word or noting problems with sentence structure in a piece of writing. It is much more useful than no feedback at all, as in the example of a teacher ignoring a child's decoding error in reading *torment* for *torture.* In each case, the SL feedback ends with the child giving the correct response and experiencing success.

It is important to avoid excessive wordiness in giving feedback, which may be unintentionally confusing. In the second example of non-SL feedback for the misspelling of *making,* the teacher steps the child through a lengthy sequence of identifying the syllable type of the base word and reciting a rule for adding the ending. This lengthy sequence could be appropriate in a few specific situations (e.g., a child is making the same type of error repeatedly). In general, however, it is best to avoid unduly long-winded feedback because it may fail to keep the child's attention, be difficult for a child with language weaknesses to process, or may distract the child from looking carefully at the pattern in the printed word. Helpful feedback may vary further depending on the specific task, type of response, and other variables (see Archer & Hughes, 2011, for a thorough discussion of the type of feedback typical of SL approaches).

Figure 1.5 summarizes some key practices used in SL approaches with those common in three cueing systems approaches to assessing and teaching reading.

COMMON POOR-READER PROFILES

Poor-reader profiles relate to the simple view of reading (Hoover & Gough, 1990) discussed in a previous section of this chapter. Poor readers can have difficulties with word recognition, coupled with average or better oral language comprehension; or the opposite profile, average word recognition coupled with weaknesses in language comprehension; or they can have weaknesses in both word recognition and language comprehension. Table 1.2 displays three common poor-reader profiles that have been documented in numerous studies and literature reviews (e.g., Capin, Cho, Miciak, Roberts,

Practice	Three cueing systems	Structured literacy
Phonics instruction	Phonics is taught but not explicitly or systematically, and often with a larger-unit approach (e.g., word families)	Explicit, systematic phonics teaching, with initial grapheme–phoneme approach
Assessment of oral text reading	Contextually appropriate errors (e.g., *a* for *the*, *mom* for *mother*) may not be counted	Nearly all word-reading errors are counted, with a few exceptions (e.g., self-corrections, mispronunciations due to articulation or foreign accent)
Texts used in initial reading instruction	Predictable texts that encourage use of pictures and sentence context to aid in reading words	Decodable texts that give practice in applying learned phonics skills and that do not facilitate guessing
Teacher feedback to oral reading errors	Contextually appropriate errors may be ignored; feedback may encourage guessing from context cues rather than close attention to letter sequences in words	Errors not ignored; feedback encourages attention to letter sequences and application of decoding skills *first*, then checking to ensure the word makes sense
Early identification of reading problems	Key abilities, such as phonemic awareness and decoding, may not be appropriately assessed; overreliance on context to compensate for poor decoding often not recognized as a sign of reading difficulties	Key abilities, such as phonemic awareness and decoding, are well assessed; overreliance on context to read words is recognized as common in poor decoders and a sign of risk

FIGURE 1.5. Some practices in three cueing systems and SL approaches.

& Vaughn, 2021; Catts, Adolf, & Weismer, 2006; Catts, Compton, Tomblin, & Bridges, 2012; Leach, Scarborough, & Rescorla, 2003; Lesaux & Kieffer, 2010; Norbury & Nation, 2011; Spear-Swerling, 2004, 2015). For all profiles, children's difficulties may range from mild to severe.

The profile shown in the first row of Table 1.2 involves SWRD, so termed because these poor-readers' difficulties are specific to word recognition and do not involve language comprehension. Weaknesses in word recognition are usually phonological in nature, relating to phonemic awareness, phonics, and decoding of unfamiliar words. Because these skills underlie spelling as well as word reading, weaknesses in spelling are also typical of SWRD. These students have at least average oral language comprehension and vocabulary knowledge, and they generally perform well on oral comprehension tasks, such as oral questions during teacher read-alouds of grade-appropriate

TABLE 1.2. Common Poor-Reader Profiles

Profile	Description	Potential focus of SL interventions
Specific word recognition difficulties (SWRD)	• Word recognition skills below average, usually due to poor phonemic awareness and/or poor phonics skills • Broad oral language comprehension and vocabulary at least average • Reading comprehension at least average in texts child can decode well • Poor reading comprehension and poor fluency based entirely in word reading	• Phonemic awareness • Phonics • Automaticity of word reading • Spelling/written expression • Text fluency (word accuracy/automaticity focus)
Specific reading comprehension difficulties (SRCD)	• Word recognition skills, including phonics and phonemic awareness, at least average • Reading comprehension below average despite good word reading, often due to a specific weakness in oral language area(s), such as vocabulary, syntax, background knowledge, inferencing, or pragmatics • Any fluency weaknesses based entirely in language comprehension, not word reading	• Individual students' specific weaknesses in language comprehension (e.g., vocabulary, syntax, inferencing) • Text fluency (prosody/language comprehension focus) • Reading comprehension • Written expression
Mixed reading difficulties (MRD)	• Word recognition skills below average, usually due to poor phonemic awareness and/or poor phonics skills • Reading comprehension also weak, beyond what can be accounted for by poor word reading (e.g., students have poor reading comprehension even in some texts they can decode well) • Specific oral language weaknesses (e.g., vocabulary, syntax) contribute to reading comprehension problems that are due to a combination of word recognition and language comprehension weaknesses • Reading fluency often poor due to a combination of word recognition and language comprehension weaknesses	• Phonemic awareness • Phonics • Automaticity of word reading • Spelling • Text fluency • Individual students' specific weaknesses in language comprehension (e.g., vocabulary, syntax, inferencing) • Reading comprehension • Written expression

books. When children with SWRD read texts that they can decode well, their reading comprehension is good. Problems with reading fluency and reading comprehension in students with SWRD relate entirely to problems with accuracy or automaticity of word recognition.

Specific reading comprehension difficulties (SRCD), shown in the second row of Table 1.2, involve the opposite pattern. Children with SRCD have average or better word recognition skills, including at least average phonological skills. Despite their good word reading, however, they have problems in reading comprehension. Their difficulties in reading comprehension usually involve weaknesses in one or more areas of oral language comprehension (Catts et al., 2006; Nation, 2005), such as vocabulary, background knowledge, syntax, discourse structure, inferencing, or pragmatic language; other specific cognitive weaknesses, such as in executive function or working memory, may also negatively impact their reading comprehension (Cutting, Materek, Cole, Levine, & Mahone, 2009; Fletcher et al., 2019; Wagner, Beal, Zirps, & Spencer, 2021). The language weaknesses of students with SRCD are often relatively mild, with students' weaknesses not severe enough to make them eligible for speech/language services (Nation, 2005). However, as these students advance in school and the texts they are expected to read become more demanding in terms of comprehension, even mild weaknesses in language comprehension may begin to impact reading comprehension (Scarborough, 2005).

Students with SRCD tend to display some similar difficulties in both listening and reading. If a student with SRCD has limitations in vocabulary knowledge, those problems tend to manifest whether they are listening to a teacher read a story or reading it themselves. In addition, these difficulties often affect written expression, as well as reading comprehension. For example, weak vocabulary knowledge may impact word choice and elaboration in a student's writing. When students with SRCD have poor reading fluency, those difficulties are not based in word recognition difficulties; rather, children with SRCD might read slowly because of difficulty understanding what they are reading.

The third profile of poor reading involves MRD, in which students have below-average word recognition, as well as reading comprehension problems that exceed what can be explained by poor word recognition alone. A student with MRD who has weaknesses in vocabulary might display poor reading comprehension even when reading text that he or she can decode well, because of the added influence of not knowing the meanings of words. In students with MRD, poor reading comprehension and poor reading fluency reflect a combination of weaknesses in word recognition and language comprehension. As is true for some poor readers with SRCD, poor reading in some students with MRD may also be influenced by specific cognitive weaknesses in areas such as executive function and working memory (Cutting et al., 2009; Fletcher et al., 2019; Wagner et al., 2021).

An important point about poor-reader profiles is that, by themselves, they do not provide information about underlying causality. Poor readers might have a profile of SWRD because they have an intrinsic disability, such as dyslexia, or because of inadequate classroom reading instruction with no explicit teaching of phonemic awareness or phonics. Poor readers with a profile of SRCD might have an intrinsic disability, such as a language disorder or high-functioning autism (Norbury & Nation, 2011), or their reading difficulties might relate entirely to limited exposure to English. Nonetheless, the profile is very useful as a starting point for planning interventions. A child with SWRD who reads slowly due to poor word recognition might benefit from fluency interventions aimed at accuracy and automaticity of word reading, but these fluency interventions are not likely to help a student with SRCD, whose reading difficulties are not based in word reading.

The prevalence of different poor-reader profiles has varied across research studies, depending on variables such as the age and demographic background of the participants, the specific measures used to determine the profile, specific criteria for defining groups, and other aspects of study methodology. In a mostly middle-class sample, Leach and colleagues (2003) found that SWRD and MRD were far more common in children identified as poor readers in the primary grades than SRCD—however, among children identified as poor readers in grades 4 and 5, about one-third of poor readers displayed SRCD. Catts and colleagues (2012) also found late-emerging poor readers, typically defined as poor reading first manifesting after grade 3, to be heterogeneous in profile, with 36% having a profile of SWRD, 52% SRCD, and 12% MRD.

In contrast to Leach and colleagues (2003) and Catts and colleagues (2012), Lesaux and Kieffer (2010) studied sixth-grade poor readers and found virtually none with SWRD. However, their sample included many English learners and children from low-socioeconomic status (SES) backgrounds, and vocabulary weaknesses were widespread in their sample, so children with word-reading difficulties, about 21% of the sample, displayed MRD, not SWRD. In a more recent study involving fourth graders with severe reading comprehension difficulties, as well as a substantial proportion of English learners, Capin and colleagues (2021) found that virtually all of the poor readers had a profile of MRD, although there was some variability across children in relative weakness of word recognition versus language comprehension.

Overall, research on poor-reader profiles supports the idea that significant problems in word reading persist in many older poor readers, as well as the value of multicomponent interventions, a topic addressed in the final chapter of this volume. Because individual children may manifest any of the three profiles, appropriate assessment of component reading and language skills is essential.

The far right-hand column of Table 1.2 summarizes the potential focus of SL interventions for students with different profiles of poor reading. Not every area listed is necessarily relevant for a given student. For instance, an older child with SWRD might still need work on automaticity of word recognition, spelling, and text-reading fluency, but not on phonemic awareness or basic phonics skills. Also, children with different profiles might need a different focus in text-fluency interventions. Those with SRCD are unlikely to benefit from a fluency intervention that targets word reading but might benefit from one targeting prosody of text reading, such as the phrase cueing intervention described in detail in Chapter 5 (Hudson, Anderson, McGraw, Ray, & Wilhelm, this volume), especially if it is combined with intervention addressing their underlying comprehension weaknesses.

For children with SRCD and MRD, whose reading difficulties include comprehension, it is important to try to determine individual students' specific weakness(es) within that domain, such as vocabulary, syntax, inferencing, and so on. It should also be remembered that individual poor-readers' specific language weaknesses will manifest in their written expression, as well as their reading comprehension. If a poor reader has difficulties with syntax, for example, those difficulties will tend to affect his or her ability to write correct sentences, as well as read them.

Information in Table 1.2 may help readers of this volume determine which chapters are especially appropriate for a particular student or group of students with whom they are intervening.

SUMMARY

The content of Structured Literacy involves key language and literacy-related skills needed for learning to read and write, including phonemic awareness, phonics, orthographic knowledge, morphology, syntax, and semantics. Central features of SL interventions include highly explicit, systematic teaching of important skills and concepts, with attention to prerequisite skills; the provision of prompt, clear, targeted feedback; planned, purposeful selections of instructional examples, tasks, and texts; the use of a synthetic-phonics approach at the grapheme–phoneme level in initial phonics and spelling intervention; teaching for transfer; and data-based decision making. SL interventions can be effective with children who have a range of reading problems involving comprehension, as well as foundational skills: those with SWRD, SRCD, and MRD.

APPLICATION ACTIVITIES

Activity 1

An interventionist working with a group of second-grade poor decoders is introducing the magic *e* (ME) rule: the generalization that in a word with a *vce* pattern, the first vowel will be long and the *e* will be silent. The children know all long vowel sounds and have already learned to decode a wide variety of one-syllable, short vowel words. Which of the following sets of words would be best for the interventionist to use as examples of ME words? Explain your answer in relation to each set of words.

Set A: *ape, chime, blade, some, lose, stripe*
Set B: *tape, poke, prince, cube, hope, dance*
Set C: *rope, bride, use, shake, cone, ate*
Set D: *cake, wide, rode, cube, tame, save*

ANSWER

Set A is not a good example set because it has two phonetically irregular words in it: *some* and *lose*. Set D is restricted to four-letter words, which may cause children to incorrectly infer that ME words always have four letters. Set B contains the words *prince* and *dance,* which (though they end in a silent *e*) do not conform to the *vce* pattern and do not have a long vowel. The best choice is Set C, which provides varied and appropriate examples of ME words, including ME words that do not start with any consonants (e.g., *use, ate*).

Activity 2

Lola is a sixth-grade poor reader with a profile of SWRD, who has struggled with decoding since first grade. She has had several years of highly structured phonics interventions, and she can now accurately decode all one-syllable word patterns, as well as a wide range of two-syllable patterns, such as words with common suffixes (e.g., *needing, likely*), words with consonant-*le* (e.g., *candle, staple*), and words with a *vccv* pattern (e.g., *rabbit, lantern*). She has some ability to decode multisyllabic words but still needs work in this area. Her primary intervention needs to involve further work on decoding of multisyllabic words, spelling, and text-reading fluency. Does Lola need to read decodable text in her intervention?

ANSWER

Lola should not need decodable text in the sense of text that is phonetically controlled to specific word patterns, because at this point she can consistently decode a variety of one-syllable and two-syllable words, and even some multisyllabic words. These skills should enable her to function well in uncontrolled texts, such as curriculum materials and trade books. However, it is important that texts used in her intervention be ones that she can read with a high degree of accuracy, so that she can build fluency and understand what she is reading. Therefore, texts for intervention should be at Lola's instructional level, which may be below her grade placement (grade 6).

Activity 3

Lewis is a fifth grader who was thought to be doing well in reading during his first few years of school. He consistently met both accuracy and rate benchmarks for oral reading fluency on the screening and progress monitoring assessments that his school used in grades K–3. He also had good spelling and writing skills. However, last year, in the middle of fourth grade, Lewis's teacher and parents became concerned about his reading, and he has been referred for intervention. The main concerns about Lewis involve his comprehension of the texts used in grade 5, especially his ability to answer inferencing types of questions and to grasp the key points of a text. Lewis's teacher notices these problems in oral class discussions, as well as when Lewis is reading. Lewis is also having some difficulties in written expression. His foundational writing skills are strong, including his spelling and handwriting, but he has great difficulty elaborating answers; he will often produce only a sentence or two of writing, when a much longer response is expected. In addition, his writing shows numerous weaknesses in sentence structure and organization. Based on this description, does Lewis's profile of reading difficulties sound like SWRD, SRCD, or MRD? Justify your answer.

ANSWER

Lewis's profile appears to be that of a student with SRCD. If he consistently met accuracy and rate benchmarks for oral reading fluency in the early grades, and if his spelling is strong, this makes SWRD or MRD unlikely, because there does not appear to be a phonological or word recognition component to his literacy difficulties. Likewise, his written expression problems appear to be connected to broad language skills, not phonology. It would be important to probe the nature of Lewis's comprehension and writing weaknesses further in assessment, to clarify these issues and to help plan intervention.

REFERENCES

Archer, A. L., & Hughes, C. A. (2011). *Explicit instruction: Effective and efficient teaching.* New York: Guilford Press.

Baker, S., Lesaux, N., Jayanthi, M., Dimino, J., Proctor, C. P., Morris, J., et al. (2014). Teaching academic content and literacy to English learners in elementary and middle school (NCEE 2014-4012). Washington, DC: National Center for Education Evaluation and Regional Assistance, Institute of Education Sciences, U.S. Department of Education. Retrieved from *http://ies.ed.gov/ncee/wwc/publications_reviews.aspx*

Berninger, V. W., Abbott, R. D., Jones, J., Gould, L., Anderson-Youngstrom, M., Shimada, S., et al. (2006). Early development of language by hand: Composing, reading, listening, and speaking connections; three letter-writing modes; and fast mapping in spelling. *Developmental Neuropsychology, 29,* 61–92.

Brady, S. (2011). Efficacy of phonics teaching for reading outcomes: Indications from post-NRP research. In S. Brady, D. Braze, & C. Fowler (Eds.), *Explaining individual differences in reading: Theory and evidence* (pp. 69–96). New York: Psychology Press.

Brady, S. (2020). Strategies used in education for resisting and rejecting the science of reading. *Reading League Journal, 1,* 33–40.

Capin, P., Cho, E., Miciak, J., Roberts, G., & Vaughn, S. (2021). Examining the reading and cognitive profiles of students with significant reading comprehension difficulties. *Learning Disabilities Quarterly, 44,* 183–196.

Carlisle, J. F. (2010). An integrative review of the effects of instruction in morphological awareness on literacy achievement. *Reading Research Quarterly, 45,* 464–487.

Catts, H. W., Adlof, S. M., & Weismer, S. E. (2006). Language deficits in poor comprehenders: A case for the simple view of reading. *Journal of Speech, Language, and Hearing Research, 49*(2), 278–293.

Catts, H. W., Compton, D. L., Tomblin, J. B., & Bridges, M. S. (2012). Prevalence and nature of late-emerging poor readers. *Journal of Educational Psychology, 104*(2), 166–181.

Christensen, C. A., & Bowey, J. A. (2005). The efficacy of orthographic rime, grapheme–phoneme correspondence, and implicit phonics approaches to teaching decoding skills. *Scientific Studies of Reading, 9*(4), 327–349.

Clay, M. M. (1994). *Reading recovery: A guidebook for teachers in training.* Portsmouth, NH: Heinemann.

Cutting, L. E., Materek, A., Cole, C., Levine, T., & Mahone, E. M. (2009). Effects of fluency, oral language, and executive function on reading comprehension performance. *Annals of Dyslexia, 59,* 34–54.

Fletcher, J. M., Lyon, G. R., Fuchs, L. S., & Barnes, M. A. (2019). *Learning disabilities: From identification to intervention* (2nd ed.). New York: Guilford Press.

Foorman, B., Beyler, N., Borradaile, K., Coyne, M., Denton, C. A., Dimino, J., et al. (2016). *Foundational skills to support reading for understanding in kindergarten through 3rd grade* (NCEE 2016-4008). Washington, DC: U.S. Department of Education. Institute of Education Sciences, National Center for Education Evaluation and Regional Assistance.

Fuchs, D., Fuchs, L. S., & Stecker, P. M. (2010). The "blurring" of special education in a new continuum of general education placements and services. *Exceptional Children, 76,* 301–323.

Gersten, R., Compton, D., Connor, C. M., Dimino, J., Santoro, L., Linan-Thompson, S., & Tilly, W. D. (2008). *Assisting students struggling with reading: Response to Intervention and multi-tier intervention for reading in the primary grades. A practice guide* (NCEE 2009-4045). Washington, DC: National Center for Education Evaluation and Regional Assistance, Institute of Education Sciences, U.S. Department of Education. Retrieved from *http://ies.ed.gov/ncee/wwc/publications/practiceguides/*

Goodman, K. S. (1976). Reading: A psycholinguistic guessing game. In H. Singer & R. Ruddell (Eds.), *Theoretical models and processes of reading* (pp. 497–508). Newark, DE: International Reading Association.

Graham, S., Bollinger, A., Booth Olson, C., D'Aoust, C., MacArthur, C., McCutchen, D., et al. (2012). *Teaching elementary school students to be effective writers: A practice guide* (NCEE 2012-4058). Washington, DC: National Center for Education Evaluation and Regional Assistance, Institute of Education Sciences, U.S. Department of Education. Retrieved from *http://ies.ed.gov/ncee/wwc/publications_reviews.aspx#pubsearch*

Hanford, E. (2019, August 22). At a loss for words. Retrieved from *www.apmreports.org/story/2019/08/22/whats-wrong-how-schools-teach-reading*

Hoover, W. A., & Gough, P. B. (1990). The simple view of reading. *Reading and Writing: An Interdisciplinary Journal, 2,* 127–160.

International Dyslexia Association. (2019). *Structured literacy: An introductory guide.* Newark, DE: Author.

International Dyslexia Association. (2020). *Structured literacy: Effective instruction for children with dyslexia and related reading difficulties.* Newark, DE: Author.

Johnston, R. S., & Watson, J. E. (2004). Accelerating the development of reading, spelling and phonemic awareness skills in initial readers. *Reading and Writing, 17,* 327–357.

Kilpatrick, D. A. (2015). *Essentials of assessing, preventing, and overcoming reading difficulties.* Hoboken, NJ: Wiley.

Leach, J. M., Scarborough, H. S., & Rescorla, L. (2003). Late-emerging reading disabilities. *Journal of Educational Psychology, 95,* 211–224.

Lesaux, N. K., & Kieffer, M. J. (2010). Exploring sources of reading comprehension difficulties among language minority learners and their classmates in early adolescence. *American Educational Research Journal, 47,* 596–632.

McCandliss, B., Beck, I. L., Sandak, R., & Perfetti, C. (2003). Focusing attention on decoding for children with poor reading skills: Design and preliminary tests of the word building intervention. *Scientific Studies of Reading, 7,* 75–104.

Moats, L. C. (2017). Can prevailing approaches to reading instruction accomplish the goals of RTI? *Perspectives on Language and Literacy, 43,* 15–22.

Moats, L. C. (2020). *Speech to print: Language essentials for teachers* (3rd ed.). Baltimore: Brookes.

Moats, L. C., & Foorman, B. R. (2003). Measuring teachers' content knowledge of language and reading. *Annals of Dyslexia, 53,* 23–45.

Mol, S. E., & Bus, A. G. (2011). To read or not to read: A meta-analysis of print exposure from infancy to early adulthood. *Psychological Bulletin, 137,* 267–296.

Nation, K. (2005). Children's reading comprehension difficulties. In M. J. Snowling & C. Hulme (Eds.), *The science of reading: A handbook* (pp. 248–266). Oxford, UK: Blackwell.

National Reading Panel. (2000). *Teaching children to read: An evidence-based assessment of the scientific research literature on reading and its implications for reading instruction.* Washington, DC: National Institutes of Health.

Norbury, C., & Nation, K. (2011). Understanding variability in reading comprehension in adolescents with autism spectrum disorders: Interactions with language status and decoding skill. *Scientific Studies of Reading, 15,* 191–210.

Scarborough, H. S. (2002). Connecting early language and literacy to later reading (dis)abilities: Evidence, theory, and practice. In S. B. Neuman & D. K. Dickinson (Eds.), *Handbook of early literacy research* (pp. 97–125). New York: Guilford Press.

Scarborough, H. S. (2005). Developmental relationships between language and reading: Reconciling a beautiful hypothesis with some ugly facts. In H. W. Catts & A. Kamhi (Eds.), *The connections between language and reading disabilities* (pp. 3–24). Mahwah, NJ: Erlbaum.

Seidenberg, M. (2017). *Language at the speed of sight.* New York: Basic Books.

Shanahan, T., Callison, K., Carriere, C., Duke, N. K., Pearson, P. D., Schatschneider, C., et al. (2010). *Improving reading comprehension in kindergarten through 3rd grade: A practice guide* (NCEE 2010-4038). Washington, DC: National Center for Education Evaluation and Regional Assistance, Institute of Education Sciences, U.S. Department of Education. Retrieved from *whatworks.ed.gov/publications/practiceguides*

Spear-Swerling, L. (2004). Fourth-graders' performance on a state-mandated assessment involving two different measures of reading comprehension. *Reading Psychology, 25,* 121–148.

Spear-Swerling, L. (2015). *The power of RTI and reading profiles: A blueprint for solving reading problems.* Baltimore: Brookes.

Spear-Swerling, L. (2018). Structured literacy and typical literacy practices: Understanding differences to create instructional opportunities. *Teaching Exceptional Children, 51,* 201–211.

Stanovich, K. E. (2000). *Progress in understanding reading: Scientific foundations and new frontiers.* New York: Guilford Press.

Vaughn, S., Denton, C. A., & Fletcher, J. M. (2010). Why intensive interventions are necessary for students with severe reading difficulties. *Psychology in the Schools, 47,* 432–444.

Wagner, R. K., Beal, B., Zirps, F. A., & Spencer, M. (2021). A model-based meta-analytic examination of specific reading comprehension deficit: How prevalent is it and does the simple view of reading account for it? *Annals of Dyslexia, 71,* 260–281.

Wanzek, J., Al Otaiba, S., & McMaster, K. L. (2020). *Intensive reading interventions for the elementary grades.* New York: Guilford Press.

CHAPTER 2

Structured Literacy Interventions for Phonemic Awareness and Basic Word Recognition Skills

Stephanie Al Otaiba
Jill H. Allor
Jennifer Stewart

Ms. Baker, a first-grade teacher, is concerned about Maria, who scored in the high-need range on a computerized literacy screening measure her district uses for response to intervention (RTI) to determine which students are on grade level and which students need more intensive intervention. She followed up by administering the CUBED assessment (described later in the chapter; Language Dynamics Group, 2018). Based on these assessments and her observation of Maria during instruction, Ms. Baker realizes that Maria knows the sounds of many letters and is able to orally segment the initial sound of a spoken word. She can also blend the first consonant sound in a word and a rime (i.e., the rest of the word) to form a word—for example, /f/ /an/ or /s/ /at/. However, unlike her classmates, Maria is still unable to sound out simple consonant–vowel–consonant (CVC) words by phoneme, such as /s/ /a/ / t/, even though Ms. Baker has been teaching these skills and most of her students are learning them (see Table 2.1 for examples of assessment items and supporting evidence).

Ms. Ortiz, a third-grade teacher, is concerned about Tim, who scored in the high-need range on a literacy screening measure her district uses to inform RTI implementation. She followed up by administering the CUBED progress monitoring (Language Dynamics Group, 2018). Based on these assessments and her observation of Tim during instruction, Tim is able to identify short vowel words that begin with blends, but struggles with the silent-*e* word patterns and vowel teams. Given these serious deficits in word recognition, Ms. Ortiz is not surprised that Tim does not read fluently. She is troubled that the core reading program she is using focuses mainly on comprehension, and does not offer many explicit instructional activities for teaching word recognition. Even though Tim can understand when a text is read to him, Ms. Ortiz is worried that he cannot read fluently enough to comprehend content-area texts for social studies or science by himself, and these have been his favorite subjects in school. He is starting to lose motivation for reading and this appears related to frustration with himself, as he often refers to himself as "stupid"

TABLE 2.1. Descriptions of Student Performance and Supporting Assessment Data

Description of student performance	Supporting assessment data/example
	Maria, first grade
Letter-sound knowledge • Knows the sounds of many letters (i.e., correctly says letter sound when she sees the letter)	• Provided 58 correct letter sounds in 2 minutes with no errors • Performs well on letter-sound practice during instruction
Phonological awareness (segmenting) • Consistently identifies the first sound in words	• Ms. Baker: What is the first sound you hear in the word *boat*? • Maria: /b/
Phonological awareness (blending) • Consistently blends onsets and rimes	• Ms. Baker: Listen. /j/ /et/ What word? • Maria: *jet*
Sight word identification • Does not correctly identify any basic high-frequency words	• Unable to correctly identify any of the first five words on the assessment: *the, a, to, his, I* • Does not attempt to read any words during small-group instruction
	Tim, third grade
Decoding • Consistently reads short vowel words correctly, but struggles with silent-*e* pattern and vowel teams	• Reads four CCVC nonsense words (e.g., *plet*) correctly • Reads one of four silent-*e* nonsense words (e.g., *nabe*) correctly • During oral reading practice, Tim consistently reads short vowel words correctly and some high-frequency words but needs support to decode silent-*e*-pattern words (e.g., *same*) and other vowel team words (e.g., *seed, rain*) • In his writing, Tim consistently spells short vowel words correctly
Fluency • Does not read fluently	• Reads 50 words per minute with poor prosody on grade-appropriate text (i.e., expression and intonation) • Reads below the expected benchmark of 88 wpm • Meets criteria for the high-risk category
Comprehension • Listening comprehension is strong • Reading comprehension is poor	• Listening retell score of 35 (grade-level benchmark of 27) • Reading retell score of 15 (score of 16 or below is considered high risk)

Note. wpm, words per minute.

when he is struggling. Tim struggles with reading comprehension, but his oral language and listening comprehension are relatively stronger. (See Table 2.1 for evidence of these conclusions.)

The purpose of this chapter is to increase practitioners' knowledge, ability, and self-efficacy for accelerating the reading performance of students like Maria and Tim, who have not yet developed the foundational literacy skills of basic phonemic awareness and word recognition skills. By practitioners, we include a variety of teachers, including reading specialists and other general and special education teachers who plan and deliver intervention for elementary-age students. We also envision that this chapter may support school and district administrators who hire faculty, plan professional development opportunities, select core reading curriculum and reading intervention programs, and supervise instruction and intervention implementation. First, we discuss the research on typical development of phonemic awareness and word recognition so that teachers understand more about how Maria and Tim compare to typically developing readers. Second, we synthesize the research on effective instruction and intervention. Third, we summarize research on assessments to inform instruction and intervention. Fourth, we explain how teachers can apply this research to accelerate reading performance. Fifth, we summarize the main implications of the chapter. And finally, we provide several application activities that relate to accelerating reading performance for students like Maria and Tim.

RESEARCH ON DEVELOPMENT OF PHONEMIC AWARENESS AND WORD RECOGNITION

In this chapter, we are guided by a framework known as the Simple View of Reading (Gough & Tunmer, 1986), which helps explain that reading is the product of two sets of skills: code-focused and meaning-focused skills. Foundational code-focused skills include phonological and phonemic awareness, letter–sound correspondence, phonics (including decoding and encoding, or spelling), and word recognition. Meaning-focused skills include vocabulary and comprehension. Although the meaning-focused skills are not our focus in this chapter, reading with understanding, or comprehension, is the ultimate goal of reading and code-focused skills that should be linked to meaning (Castles, Rastle, & Nation, 2018). Both sets of skills are encompassed within the Structured Literacy (SL) skills that are emphasized in the International Dyslexia Association's (IDA) Knowledge and Practice Standards (*https://dyslexiaida.org/knowledge-and-practices*). SL instructional approaches are consistent with the broader research base for explicitly and systematically teaching the structure of language across the domains of listening, speaking, reading, and writing (e.g., National Reading Panel [NRP], 2000). As we describe the developmental process of acquiring reading, we emphasize that learning to read is not as natural as learning to speak, and must be taught explicitly (Castles et al., 2018; Ehri, 2005, 2017).

What Are Phonological and Phonemic Awareness and How Do These Skills Develop?

Whereas phonological awareness is a broad term that encompasses awareness of chunks of sounds in speech, phonemic awareness refers to awareness of the individual sounds (phonemes) in words (e.g., NRP, 2000). Young children develop these skills gradually, beginning with larger chunks of sounds, such as words in sentences or syllables in words (e.g., the *sis* in *sister*). Then, they begin to identify, or discern, the first sound in a word (which may be referred to as the onset) from the rest of the word (the rime)—for example, the /c/ in *cat*. Eventually, they learn to blend each sound to form a word, so for example, /mmm/ /o/ /mmm/. They also learn that a word like *cat* can be broken down, or segmented, into three sounds: /c/ /a/ /t/. By kindergarten a key aspect of teaching SL involves instruction in phonemic awareness because students need to hear and manipulate individual sounds and to link these sounds to letters and words in order to develop word reading and spelling (e.g., Brady, 2020). The most critical skills for explicit instruction for beginning readers include phoneme identity, phoneme blending, and phoneme segmentation, along with systematic instruction showing students how these skills connect spoken language to letters, words, and text. The need for such instruction, particularly for students with dyslexia or other reading disabilities, should extend until mastery. As students progress through elementary school, they develop more complex levels of phonemic manipulation. For example, students may realize that *funny* pronounced backward is *enough*. Within multisyllabic words, students may also learn that the difference between *preview* and *review* is only one sound, but that sound is part of a prefix, and changing this morpheme, or unit of meaning, modifies what the word communicates.

What Are Basic Word Recognition Skills and How Do These Skills Develop?

Children typically develop letter-sound knowledge as they are developing phonological and phonemic awareness; these skills gradually become intertwined as children establish their understanding of the alphabetic principle, which is when they bring these two skills together to read simple words (e.g., Ehri, 2000; NRP, 2000; Snow, Burns, & Griffin, 1998). Children need to learn how the sounds in a word are blended together to pronounce a word and also how to represent, or spell, each sound in a word. They also develop concepts of print—how these skills develop may differ based on language. For example, in English and Spanish, we read from left to right. By contrast, the Arabic alphabetic language is printed from right to left. Other languages, such as Chinese, Japanese, and Korean, are logographic, or character based, with characters representing units of meaning.

Once children understand the alphabetic principle and concepts of print, they learn more word recognition skills, which include decoding and irregular word-reading skills that most children achieve by the end of first grade. These skills include letter sounds,

CVC words (e.g., *bat*), words with consonant blends and digraphs (e.g., the /bl/ in *blend* and the /ph/ in *digraph*), silent-*e* words (*bike*), and words with vowel teams (e.g., the *ea* in *team*). Both Maria and Tim, despite their grade differences, need explicit instruction to accelerate their word recognition skills. They also need support for learning to read words automatically and quickly that are spelled with less-common patterns, including irregularly spelled words (e.g., *the* or *friend*). They also need practice to read fluently in texts of various genres. Beyond basic word recognition, children need support for recognizing more and more patterns, recognizing high frequency irregular (sight words) automatically, developing flexible decoding while reading irregular words, and learning about multisyllabic words, including word structures that represent morphemes, or units of meaning (e.g., prefixes, suffixes, root words).

As children become more experienced, they map letter-sound patterns to read words more automatically, and begin to store more connections among patterns and word meanings in their brains, which facilitates what is known as the self-teaching mechanism (e.g., Seidenberg, 2017; Share, 1995). For example, as Maria learns the alphabetic principle and can decode short vowel words, she may start to spontaneously apply that knowledge to read other, unfamiliar words. Researchers also refer to these connections as "orthographic representations" or "orthographic mapping"—with more practice, students develop complete representations and are then able to recognize words instantly (Ehri, 2017). Reading that is less effortful and more fluent allows children to focus more on constructing meaning within a text (e.g., Perfetti, 1985; Seidenberg, 2017). Students like Maria and Tim have not yet developed this level of automaticity, efficiency, or fluency. Once they are more fluent, they will also be more likely to self-correct if they recognize that a word did not make sense, which further enables the self-teaching mechanism (Share, 1995). Tim's teacher may help him identify and stop when a word that he has read does not make sense and then reread a phrase, sentence, or paragraph. She might teach him strategies that show him how to be flexible in testing different pronunciations, particularly when a word may have a vowel or vowel combination that does not follow a common phonics rule, including words that are high frequency but somewhat irregular such as *have*, *friend*, or *was* and less frequent irregular words such as *aisle* or *treasure* (Kearns, Rogers, Koriakin, & Al Ghanem, 2016; Lovett, Lacernza, & Borden, 2000; Savage, Georgiou, Parrila, & Maiorino, 2018; Steacy, Elleman, Lovett, & Compton; Tunmer & Chapman, 2012).

Teachers who understand reading development and use SL approaches help their students to learn to decode words and to understand that good readers do not just memorize every word, nor are they just good "guessers." Table 2.2 provides helpful resources to learn more about SL approaches. Table 2.3 provides a partial list of programs with explicit and systematic approaches for intervention in phonology and word recognition.

Teachers need to recognize when students get off the path toward efficient and fluent reading, and struggle because they employ less efficient word-reading strategies, such as overrelying on the first sound, pictures, or context to guess a word (e.g., Spear-Swerling & Sternberg, 1996). Teachers also need to be mindful about their students from

TABLE 2.2. **Examples of Resources for Teachers about Explicit and Systematic Phonological Awareness and Word Reading Instruction**

Resource	Author or original funding agency	Key features	Website
What Works Clearinghouse (WWC): Intervention Reports and Practice Guides	Institute of Education Sciences through the Department of Education	• Provides reviews of effectiveness for individual reading programs, and guides for implementing evidence-based academic and behavioral interventions across K–12.	• Foundational Reading Skills: *ies.ed.gov/ncee/wwc/PracticeGuide/21* • RTI Assistance: *ies.ed.gov/ncee/wwc/PracticeGuide/3*
Professional Learning Communities (PLC) Facilitator's Guide	Regional Educational Laboratory (REL) Southeast	• Support guide for the implementation of WWC recommendations for foundational reading skills.	• *ies.ed.gov/ncee/edlabs/projects/project.asp?projectID=4541*
IRIS Center	IRIS Center Peabody College	• Provides free online resources about evidence-based instructional practices, particularly for struggling learners and those with disabilities. • Provides online resources for implementing Peer-Assisted Learning Strategies (PALS).	• *iris.peabody.vanderbilt.edu/module/dbi1* • *iris.peabody.vanderbilt.edu/module/dbi2* • *iris.peabody.vanderbilt.edu/module/pals26*
Florida Center for Reading Research (FCRR)	Florida State University	• Conducts research, disseminates information on evidence-based practices, and provides student center activities for classroom instruction.	• *fcrr.org*
UFLI Virtual Teaching Resource Hub	University of Florida Literacy Institute (UFLI)	• Provides webinars and resources to assist educators in teaching foundational reading skills using technology.	• *education.ufl.edu/ufli/virtual-teaching/main*
National Center for Improving Literacy	U.S. Department of Education	• Provides access to evidence-based approaches to screen, identify, and teach students with literacy-related disabilities.	• *improvingliteracy.org*
Intensive Intervention Practice Guides	National Center on Intensive Intervention	• Provides resources for implementing intensive academic or behavioral supports.	• *nclii.org/intensive-intervention-practice-guides*
International Dyslexia Association (IDA)	International Dyslexia Association	• Provides Knowledge and Practice Standards (KPS) for teachers.	• *dyslexiaida.org/wp-content/uploads/2015/01/DITC-Handbook.pdf*
Division for Learning Disabilities (DLD) Alerts	Division of Learning Disabilities, Council for Exceptional Children	• Provides explanations and research base for implementing evidence-based interventions.	• *teachingld.org/alerts*
Reading Rockets	U.S. Department of Education	• Provides modules to support preparation for the Knowledge and Practice Examination of Effective Reading Instruction (K-PEERI).	• *readingrockets.org/ teaching/reading101-course/ modules/course-modules*

TABLE 2.3. Examples of Explicit and Systematic Programs for Teaching Phonemic Awareness and Word Recognition

Author(s)	Program	Grades/ages	Recommended group size
Allor et al. (2018)	Friends on the Block	K–5	Individual, small group
Avrit et al. (2016)	Take Flight	Ages 7+	Individual, small group
Blachman et al. (2000)	Road to the Code	K–1	Individual, small group
Lindamood & Lindamood (1998)	Lindamood Phoneme Sequencing (LiPS)	K–3	Individual, small group
Mathes & Torgeson (2005)	Early Interventions in Reading	1–3	Small group
Simmons & Kame'enui (2002)	Project Early Reading Intervention (ERI)	K–1	Two to five students
Smith et al. (2016)	Enhanced Core Reading Instruction (ECRI)	K–2	Individual, small group
Lovett et al. (2000)	PHAST/Enpower ™	1–5	Small group
Vadasy et al. (1996)	Sounds Partners	K–2	Individual, small group
Vernon-Feagans et al. (2018)	Targeted Reading Intervention (TRI)	K–1	Individual, small group
Wilson (2002)	Fundations Wilson Language Training Wilson Reading System	K–3	Individual, small group

vulnerable low-socioeconomic backgrounds, who enter school with limited, or even culturally different, home language and literacy experiences. It may be challenging at times for teachers to determine whether students who are struggling to learn to read have (1) limited phonemic awareness and phonics, (2) limited print exposure, (3) linguistic differences, (4) speech or language delays, or (5) a combination of these factors. Some children may have English as a second language and may benefit from bilingual instruction. Researchers have shown that emerging bilinguals' ability to hear sounds in words or to decode words may be impacted by their knowledge of English vocabulary and also by the letter-sound or syllabic structure of their first language (August & Shannahan, 2006; Baker et al., 2014; Capin, Hall, & Vaughn, 2020; Cardenas-Hagan, 2011). Phonemic awareness and phonics are important regardless of the language. Phonemic awareness and the process of decoding and encoding also transfer from one language to another (e.g., Cardenas-Hagan, 2011).

Other children, including children from specific regions or cultures may have dialectal differences from standard academic English; the frequency of dialect production appears to be negatively related to reading and writing outcomes (e.g., Gatlin & Wanzek, 2015). Research indicates that if students have not yet learned to code shift, meaning to switch from their spoken dialect to standard English, they may benefit from dialect-informed instruction (e.g., Johnson & Gatlin-Nash, 2020; Terry, Gatlin, & Johnson, 2018). For example, if Ms. Ortiz noticed that Tim or other students in her class are speaking in their oral dialect, they may pronounce *ask* as *ax* or *cents* as *cent*. Other common features of dialectical differences may include some differential pronunciations of final consonants (with similar voicing of /b/, /d/, and /g/; deletion of final consonants; changes in order of blends, as in the prior example), as well as pronunciation of vowels, dipthongs, and *r*-controlled vowels. A helpful resource about variations across languages is found at *www.asha.org/practice/multicultural/phono*. Using dialect-informed instruction, Ms. Ortiz can value spoken dialect, and also help students learn to code shift to standard, or more formal, academic English when blending and segmenting, and decoding and spelling words. She might say, "Sometimes when speaking, we pronounce this word *cent* but the formal pronunciation of this word is plural. Listen again: 'I have 10 cents.' Say each sound with me in *cents*."

Reseachers have also noted that young children with speech or language impairments are slower to develop phonemic awareness, and those with language impairment, in particular, have elevated risk for reading problems in elementary school (e.g., Catts, Gillispie, Leonard, Kail, & Miller, 2002; Puranik, Petscher, Al Otaiba, Catts, & Lonigan, 2008). Teachers should also keep in mind that when students have received explicit and systematic instruction in phonemic awareness, the alphabetic principle, and phonics, but still have difficulty acquiring these skills or applying them while reading, this is a marker for risk for dyslexia and other specific learning disabilities.

RESEARCH ON INTERVENTIONS FOR PHONEMIC AWARENESS AND BASIC WORD RECOGNITION SKILLS

In this chapter, when we use the term *research*, we are referring to evidence from research studies (i.e., treatment-comparison experimental or single case designs) that demonstrates the magnitude, or size, of the effect of instruction or intervention, specifically for improving phonemic awareness and basic phonics skills (e.g., Cook & Odom, 2013; Institute of Education Sciences [IES], 2011). We also use *research* to refer to meta-analyses and syntheses of research studies that support instruction or intervention strategies (e.g., Foorman et al., 2016).

Intensive reading interventions are typically provided within the context of RTI, or multi-tiered systems of support (MTSS), when students like Maria or Tim have not made adequate progress within their core reading instruction, or Tier 1 instruction. Briefly, the tiers of reading intervention increase in intensity by decreasing the group size, increasing the dosage of intervention, and increasing the duration of intervention (e.g., IES RTI practice guide; Gersten et al., 2008). Tier 2 may include standardized intervention programs, such as those listed in Table 2.3. Some teachers may develop their own Tier 2 intervention plans. It is helpful to group children with similar needs for intervention time to provide explicit and systematic foundational skills of phonemic awareness, alphabetic awareness, basic phonics, and irregular word recognition. Tier 2 is less intensive than Tier 3, which is the most intensive and individualized tier.

Teachers, like Ms. Baker and Ms. Ortiz, monitor students' progress to plan to meet students' individual needs and to continue to adapt intervention to ensure that it accelerates skill acquisition and reading performance. Interventions may include multiple components, focusing not only on the foundational skills of phonemic awareness and word recognition that are our primary focus in this chapter but also on additional components, such as vocabulary, oral language, fluency, comprehension, spelling, or written expression. These additional components are the focus of other chapters.

Although our focus in this chapter is on elementary-grade students, it is still important for practitioners to know that the National Early Literacy Panel (NELP; 2008; e.g., Lonigan & Shanahan, 2009) reviewed 51 preschool studies examining the effect of direct training in phonological awareness and the alphabetic principle. This training had a large impact on young preschool children's phonological awareness (effect size [ES] = 0.82) in comparison to children who did not receive this training. The impact was even stronger for children who began the studies with the lowest alphabetic knowledge (ES = 0.99). Effect sizes provide an understanding of the magnitude of the effect of an intervention, and anything over 0.25 is considered meaningful and educationally important. Briefly, these large ESs help practitioners understand that, on average, students who received intervention outperformed students who did not receive the intervention by nearly 15 standard score points on a typical standardized reading test (i.e., with a mean score of 100 and a standard deviation of 15). In addition, practitioners should know that the NELP also reported that preschoolers' phonological awareness and alphabetic knowledge predicted future reading performance.

Ideally, if Maria and Tim had intervention in preschool, they may have entered school with relatively stronger skills. However, teachers like Ms. Baker and Ms. Ortiz want to know how and why the phonemic awareness and word-reading interventions they provide to their students are highly effective. Fortunately, converging evidence from several important meta-analyses supports that young students like Maria and older students like Tim will benefit from SL interventions that follow an explicit and systematic approach for teaching phonemic awareness and phonics (e.g., Foorman et al., 2016; NRP, 2000; Wanzek & Vaughn, 2008; Wanzek et al., 2016). For example, Wanzek and Vaughn (2008) conducted a meta-analysis to summarize findings from 18 studies examining the effects of intensive reading interventions, which were provided for a minimum of 100 sessions or more to students who were struggling readers in kindergarten through third grade. The average ESs ranged from 0.34 to 0.56 on measures of foundational reading skills (including phonological or phonemic awareness, phonics, and word reading). These effects are considered small to moderate, indicating that students who received intervention outperformed students who did not, by anywhere from a little over a third of a standard deviation, to more than half of a standard deviation. They reported that the ESs of interventions were larger when conducted in kindergarten and first grade, and when administered in very small groups. The interventions were all standardized intervention programs that followed a standard scope and sequence of lessons and materials. Some interventions allowed teachers to make modifications in response to student needs, and others allowed minimal modifications; both were similarly effective.

Teachers might also consider briefer, less intensive interventions, such as those described in a more recent meta-analysis conducted by Wanzek and colleagues (2016). They synthesized the findings of less intensive interventions that included between 15 and 99 sessions, again for students who were struggling readers in kindergarten through third grade. They reviewed a total of 72 studies, with an overall average effect of foundational skill interventions of 0.47 and an average effect for multicomponent interventions of 0.50 on standardized foundational reading skill measures. With the larger number of studies than in their prior meta-analysis, the authors were able to compare the size of effect based on more variables (including who implemented the intervention, in group size, and at what grade level). Encouragingly, the effects were similar regardless of whether research staff or teachers provided the intervention. This is important to Ms. Baker and Ms. Ortiz, because in many schools, classroom teachers most often provide Tier 2 interventions. The grouping size was not statistically different for 1:1 and small groups of two to three or four to five students—however, teachers should interpret this finding with caution because there were not enough interventions provided in groups larger than five to allow a comparison. The majority of studies focused on younger students like Maria, who were in kindergarten or first grade. Although the ESs for second and third grade were slightly smaller, they were not statistically different from the lower grades.

One limitation that Ms. Baker and Ms. Ortiz should be aware of is that in general, the studies did not describe the nature of Tier 1 core reading instruction. In other words, they cannot be sure whether Tier 1 was aligned with Tier 2 in terms of scope and sequence of instruction, instructional routines, and the degree of explicitness. One exception, conducted by Ryder, Tunmer, and Greaney (2008), found very large effects (1.90) when explicit instruction was provided to students in first grade who had been in whole-language programs. Upper elementary students, like Tim, may need interventions that are more targeted to their individual phonemic awareness and phonics skills because the core curriculum shifts from focusing on foundational skills for learning to read to a focus on reading to learn and comprehend (e.g., Wanzek et al., 2016).

Research on Assessing Phonemic Awareness and Basic Word Recognition Skills to Inform Instruction

To help students like Maria and Tim, teachers can use the research on data-based decision making. This research describes how assessment data informs what skills to target within phonemic awareness and basic phonics. Table 2.2 provides a link to resources teachers can use for data-based decision making. Most students in the elementary grades participate in universal screening at the beginning, middle, and end of the year to establish students' risk for reading difficulties. Some tests are computer administered (e.g., Northwest Evaluation Association—Measure of Academic Progress [NWEA-MAP]), and others may be delivered by teachers (e.g., Texas Primary Reading Inventory [TPRI]). One limitation, however, is that in third grade and beyond, this type of assessment may not provide much detail about which foundational skills Tim has mastered and which he needs to develop, because the focus of instruction shifts from learning how to read to learning from reading.

Teachers may be familiar with some of the following examples of widely used curriculum-based progress monitoring measures, including Acadience Reading K–6 (formerly DIBELS Next; Good et al., 2011), AIMSweb (Pearson Education, 2008), Formative Assessment System for Teachers (FAST; FastBridge Learning, 2015), and Dynamic Indicators of Basic Early Literacy Skills (DIBELS-8), and in Spanish, the Indicadores Dinámicos del Éxito en la Lectura (IDEL; Good, Baker, Knutson, & Watson, 2004). Some of these curriculum-based measures may also be used as universal screeners—if so, teachers may know and refer to these as benchmark assessments. These assessments are timed to provide information about how quickly or automatically students demonstrate these skills. Teachers may use brief (typically, 1 minute) curriculum-based progress monitoring measures to provide more detailed information about students' entry-level skills and data about their response to instruction and intervention. These data help teachers answer questions about whether students are making adequate growth in phonemic awareness, phonics, or word recognition, such as: How many correct letter sounds can a student name in a minute? How many correct phonemes can a student blend or segment correctly in a minute? How many words can a student read correctly in a list or within grade-level connected text? Which students are not making progress? How does a student's ability to read real words compare to his or her ability to read nonsense words? Kindergarten and first-grade teachers may appreciate that most curriculum-based measures (CBMs) focus on short vowels (CVC, VC patterns). However, by the end of first grade and into third grade, teachers of students like Tim may prefer to use a measure like the EasyCBM word-reading measure. This measure assesses most letters and phonics patterns, including some multisyllabic words, therefore providing additional data about the phonics skills of more advanced students.

There are also many diagnostic assessments that address foundational reading skills that can help Ms. Ortiz and Ms. Baker in their instructional decision making. For the purpose of this chapter, we do not address formal assessments that may require the expertise of a diagnostician, school psychologist, or other specialists. Formal and standardized assessments are often administered after a referral for dyslexia or special education services with the consent of parents. However, teachers may use untimed phonics inventories to sample student performance across the reading scope and sequence (e.g., beginning with letter sounds, to CVC words, CVC*e*). One example of this type of inventory is the Informal Decoding Inventory (IDI; McKenna, Walpole, & Jang, 2017). The IDI is a reliable and valid free inventory. Part 1 addresses single-syllable words that progress in difficulty from real words to pseudowords and includes short vowels, consonant blends and digraphs, *r*-controlled vowels, VC*e*, and vowel teams.

Another free tool is the CUBED Screening and Progress Monitoring, which is a set of brief assessments that are both criterion referenced and norm referenced for students in preschool through third grade (Language Dynamics Group, 2018), and is a criterion-referenced assessment for older students. Consistent with the simple view of reading, it measures specific skills within the domains of language and decoding, including phonemic awareness, word identification, decoding, fluency, listening comprehension, and reading comprehension. It has strong reliability and validity. There are multiple forms so it can be used for progress monitoring.

RESEARCH-BASED INSTRUCTION AND INTERVENTION ACTIVITIES FOR ACCELERATING PHONEMIC AWARENESS AND BASIC WORD RECOGNITION SKILLS

The Every Student Succeeds Act (ESSA; 2015) emphasizes that students should receive interventions and instructional strategies that meet the criteria for moderate to strong levels of evidence, meeting the rigor required by the What Works Clearinghouse standards (see *https://ies.ed.gov/ncee/wwc/multimedia/39*). Briefly, the level of evidence (strong, moderate, or minimal) for practice guides is determined by the number of studies with positive effects, whether the studies included a diverse range of students and school contexts, and whether the practices were experimentally tested against other practices (see *https://ies.ed.gov/ncee/wwc/multimedia/39* to learn more about how the panel determines the level of evidence). Numerous resources are available to support teachers in applying this research as they provide instruction to students like Maria and Tim (see Table 2.1).

One resource (see Table 2.2) that is readily available at no cost is the What Works Clearinghouse practice guide *Foundational Skills to Support Reading for Understanding in Kindergarten through 3rd Grade* (Foorman et al., 2016). Written by an expert panel, this practice guide summarizes key research in an easy-to-read format and provides practical, specific recommendations for practitioners. The panel made four key recommendations about the importance of academic language, phonemic awareness, decoding, and connected text. For ease of reference, we follow the numbering used in the practice guide (i.e., Recommendations 1–4). For this chapter, we focus mainly on the second and third recommendations: phonemic awareness and word recognition, respectively. These are the focus of this chapter and provide strong evidence, as we have already emphasized in our description of the research. Recommendation 2 is that teachers should focus instruction to help students develop an awareness of the segments of sound in speech and how they link to letters. They reported that all of the studies reviewed demonstrated positive impacts for this recommendation on students' knowledge of letter names and phonology. Foorman and colleagues provided three specific instructional strategies to teach this component: teaching students to recognize and manipulate the segments of sound in speech, teaching students letter–sound relations, and using word-building activities that link phonemic awareness with letters and sounds. Recommendation 3 is that teachers explicitly instruct students to decode words, analyze word parts, and write and recognize words. They provided several instructional strategies for teaching this component: teaching students to blend sounds and learn sound-spelling patterns, teaching common sound-spelling patterns, teaching students to recognize common word parts and read decodable words in lists and connected text, and teaching regular and irregular high-frequency words so they can be recognized efficiently.

Next we explain how Ms. Baker and Ms. Ortiz apply the second and third recommendations as they provide literacy intervention for Maria and Tim. For Maria, Ms. Baker focuses on addressing the development of the alphabetic principle and phonemic awareness. Although Maria knows the sounds for many letters, she is unable to make use of those letter sounds to read words because her phonemic awareness skills of blending and segmenting are very poor. She needs to practice blending and segmenting individual sounds in spoken words (see Figure 2.1 for examples). The practice guide provides detailed directions about how to explicitly teach to blend and segment with sound boxes. The student moves colored discs or letter tiles as they say each sound in a word (refer to p. 18 of the practice guide for a detailed example).

Ms. Baker recently attended a workshop where she learned how to pronounce sounds in isolation and occasionally asks the speech–language therapist at her school how best to demonstrate for students. In Figure 2.1, we provide an example of how to practice these skills as students play Bingo. In the game, the teacher says each individual sound in a word (e.g., /sss/ /uuu/ /nnn/), elongating sounds that can be stretched. The students say the whole word, *sun*, and put a marker on top of the picture of the sun. These are ideal activities for Maria, who would benefit from teacher modeling and

FIGURE 2.1. Sounds Bingo (phonemic awareness blending and segmenting). Reprinted with permission from Friends on the Block.

guided practice with feedback. Because she is already in first grade and because she knows so many letter sounds, she is also ready to begin linking the sounds to print, as described in the practice guide. We also provide an example of an activity in which sentences from books include a word to practice sounding out (see *had* and *sit* in Figure 2.2). While Maria is practicing these skills, she can also learn the rest of the most common sounds for individual letters and can practice high-frequency decodable and irregular words (Recommendation 3). Once Maria consistently decodes short vowel words, she will be ready to learn more advanced letter patterns that are described in Recommendation 3. Although not the focus of this chapter, Maria should also receive instruction related to academic language (Recommendation 1) and should begin reading very simple text (Recommendation 4).

Because Tim is already able to decode short vowel words consistently, he no longer needs this type of activity. Ms. Ortiz can be confident that Tim is ready for her to focus on more advanced letter patterns because he is even able to read short vowel nonsense words and spell words that follow the short vowel pattern. Ms. Ortiz should start by ensuring that Tim is familiar with a sounding-out strategy. This can be accomplished with a brief but explicit model, and practice saying each individual sound in a printed short vowel word and then saying the word. Even though Tim is able to read short vowel words, he needs to demonstrate an explicit understanding of the strategy of sounding out to ensure he is ready to apply this strategy with more complex letter patterns, such as a final silent-*e* (refer to p. 24 of the practice guide for a model). Sound boxes can also be used to teach the silent-*e* pattern. Once the silent-*e* pattern is mastered, Tim will be ready to learn more letter patterns and also to learn strategies for being flexible in decoding irregular words. To help him make meaningful connections to print, practicing words taken from text he is reading is an excellent way to practice this skill. We

FIGURE 2.2. I Got It (alphabetic principle and decoding). Reprinted with permission from Friends on the Block.

provide an example in Figure 2.2 with words that include the *-ay* spelling. As Tim's skill in reading single syllables improves, he can begin reading multisyllabic words made up of those patterns (e.g., *rabbit, insect*), as well as common prefixes and suffixes. Although there is no one exact sequence for teaching these various skills, research is clear that it is important to present skills in a systematic sequence and provide cumulative review.

Tim enjoys listening to audiobooks during independent time. Ms. Ortiz encourages Tim and another student with similar interests to listen to the same books and keep a short journal summarizing key events and describing characters. Ms. Ortiz also regularly conducts peer tutoring during which students take turns reading orally and providing feedback as the "coach." Ms. Ortiz knows she needs to identify books at the "just right" reading level and monitor that pair of students closely during peer tutoring (see Table 2.2, Project IRIS website for Peer-Assisted Learning Strategies; Fuchs, Fuchs, Mathes, & Simmons, 1997). She can encourage Tim and his partner to self-monitor; to identify when a word does not make sense within the context of a phrase, sentence, or paragraph; and to stop and read that word and section again, practicing flexible decoding strategies.

In addition to following these recommendations, Ms. Baker and Ms. Ortiz need to consider other factors as well, to intensify their instruction to ensure that Maria and Tim will be able to reach future benchmarks. Ms. Baker decides to provide teacher-led instruction to Maria in a small group of only three other students and to allocate time daily for her to meet with this group. She already uses peer tutoring regularly in her classroom, so she can be sure that Maria is practicing skills and reading books with her partner that reinforce what she is being taught in her small group. Ms. Baker will monitor Maria's response to this intensified instruction, as she knows that the research shows that intervening as early as possible is important.

Ms. Ortiz is concerned that Tim is far below expectations, so she has already decided to seek additional support. Tim is fortunate that there is an instructional specialist in his school with designated time to provide intervention for students like Tim, so he will receive small-group instruction from the specialist and Ms. Ortiz. The two teachers coordinate their instruction and plan for ongoing progress monitoring. Together they decide to refer Tim for further assessment to better understand his needs and determine whether he qualifies for special education or other services.

SUMMARY

The goal of this chapter is to provide practitioners with information they need to effectively and confidently provide explicit instruction in phonemic awareness and word recognition skills that will enable students like Maria and Tim to catch up to their peers on these foundational literacy skills. We began by describing the research on how these foundational skills typically develop to enable practitioners to identify how struggling students like Maria and Tim compare to typically developing readers. We synthesized the research on methods for effective instruction and intervention, as well as research on using assessments to inform instruction. We highlighted various resources, particularly the What Works Clearinghouse practice guide that addresses these foundational skills (Foorman et al., 2016), explaining how to apply this body of research to maximize early literacy outcomes for struggling students.

Application Activities

Activity 1

In the chapter, we discuss that it is important for students to avoid the habit of overreliance on context and looking at just a few letters and guessing a word during text reading. What were two or three of the strategies Ms. Baker and Ms. Ortiz were using to help Maria and Tim avoid overreliance on context and guessing?

POSSIBLE ANSWERS

Sound boxes; explicitly teaching the sounding-out strategy; practicing words that are taken directly from text being read.

Activity 2

Ms. Baker is pleased that Maria has been making excellent progress. The reading specialist asks Ms. Baker what she thinks has helped Maria the most. What are two or three things you think might be included in Ms. Baker's response?

POSSIBLE ANSWERS

1. *Modeling.* Maria already knew a lot of letter sounds but she was struggling to blend sounds together. After Ms. Baker demonstrated for Maria how to do this, particularly by elongating sounds that could be stretched, Maria was able to use all of her letter-sound knowledge to read many words. At this point she was able to figure out new words on her own (self-teaching hypothesis).
2. Using the sound boxes helped make sounding out more concrete for Maria.

Activity 3

Describe how Ms. Ortiz's instruction should help Tim to develop "orthographic maps" of words and how this contributes to his reading ability.

ANSWER

Ms. Ortiz is using techniques that require Tim to attend to each letter and letter pattern in words. When she uses the sound boxes, Tim matches the letter or letter patterns to words. For example, he says the three sounds in the word *play* and writes (or places) the corresponding letters in the boxes. Doing this helps him remember the complete spellings of words (i.e., orthographic map) and enables him to recognize these words more and more efficiently.

Activity 4

What are some of the benefits of peer tutoring as it is described in the chapter?

POSSIBLE ANSWERS

1. Peer tutoring increases the amount of practice. During the time that students are working with a partner, they are either reading (or participating in a reading activity) or following along as a coach. This provides more practice than many other instructional arrangements. Peer tutoring can also be very motivating and increase time on task.
2. During peer tutoring, it is likely that students will receive immediate corrective feedback when they make a mistake. Immediate feedback helps them avoid practicing an error.

ACKNOWLEDGMENTS

The research reported here was supported by the Institute of Education Sciences (IES), U.S. Department of Education, through Grant R324A160132 and Grant R324A200151 to Southern Methodist University. The opinions expressed are those of the authors and do not represent views of the Institute or the U.S. Department of Education. Stephanie Al Otaiba and Jill Allor are co-developers and co-own the Friends on the Block published curriculum (with Jennifer Cheatham). Development of the curriculum was funded by IES Grant R324A130102. Jill Allor and Stephanie Al Otaiba acknowledge a financial interest in the Friends on the Block books and curriculum. Any inquiries should be directed to the Office of Research Compliance at Southern Methodist University.

REFERENCES

Allor, J. H., Cheatham, J. P., & Al Otaiba, S. (2018). Friends on the Block. Richardson, TX: Friends on the Block. Retrieved from *www.friendsontheblock.com*

August, D. E., & Shanahan, T. E. (2006). *Developing literacy in second-language learners: Report of the National Literacy Panel on Language-Minority Children and Youth.* Mahwah, NJ: Erlbaum.

Avrit, K., Allen, C., Carlsen, K., Gross, M., Pierce, D., & Rumsey, M. (2006). *Take Flight: a comprehensive intervention for students with dyslexia.* Dallas: Texas Scottish Rite Hospital.

Baker, S., Lesaux, N., Jayanthi, M., Dimino, J., Proctor, C. P., Morris, J., et al. (2014). *Teaching academic content and literacy to English learners in elementary and middle school: IES practice guide* [NCEE 2014-4012]. Washington, DC: U.S. Department of Education.

Blachman, B. A., Ball, E. W., Black, R., & Tangel, D. M. (2000). *Road to the code: A phonological awareness program for young children.* Baltimore: Brookes.

Brady, S. (2020). Strategies used in education for resisting the evidence and implications of the science of reading. *Reading League Journal, 1*(1), 33–41.

Capin, P., Hall, C., & Vaughn, S. (2020). Evidence-based practices in the treatment of reading disabilities among English learners. *Perspectives on Language and Literacy, 46*(2), 26–32.

Cardenas-Hagan, E. (2011). Language and literacy development among English language learners. *Multisensory Teaching of Basic Language Skills*, 605–630.

Castles, A., Rastle, K., & Nation, K. (2018). Ending the reading wars: Reading acquisition from novice to expert. *Psychological Science in the Public Interest, 19*(1), 5–51.

Catts, H. W., Gillispie, M., Leonard, L. B., Kail, R. V., & Miller, C. A. (2002). The role of speed of processing, rapid naming, and phonological awareness in reading achievement. *Journal of Learning Disabilities, 35*(6), 510–525.

Cook, B. G., & Odom, S. L. (2013). Evidence-based practices and implementation science in special education. *Exceptional Children, 79*(2), 135–144.

Ehri, L. C. (2000). Learning to read and learning to spell: Two sides of a coin. *Topics in Language Disorders, 20*(3), 19–36.

Ehri, L. C. (2005). Learning to read words: Theory, findings, and issues. *Scientific Studies of Reading, 9*(2), 167–188.

Ehri, L. C. (2017). Orthographic mapping and literacy development revisited. *Theories of Reading Development*, 169–190.

Every Student Succeeds Act, Public Law No. 114-95 (2015).

FastBridge Learning. (2015). *Formative Assessment System for Teachers (FAST): Technical manual.* Minneapolis, MN: Author.

Foorman, B., Beyler, N., Borradaile, K., Coyne, M., Denton, C. A., Dimino, J., et al. (2016). Foundational skills to support reading for understanding in kindergarten through 3rd grade [NCEE 2016–4008]. Washington, DC: National Center for Education Evaluation and Regional Assistance, Institute of Education Sciences, U.S. Department of Education. Retrieved from *http://whatworks.ed.gov*

Fuchs, D., Fuchs, L. S., Mathes, P. G., & Simmons, D. C. (1997). Peer-assisted learning strategies: Making classrooms more responsive to diversity. *American Educational Research Journal, 34*(1), 174–206.

Gatlin, B., & Wanzek, J. (2015). Relations among children's use of dialect and literacy skills: A meta-analysis. *Journal of Speech, Language, and Hearing Research, 58*(4), 1306–1318.

Gersten, R., Compton, D., Connor, C. M., Dimino, J., Santoro, L., Linan-Thompson, S., et al. (2008). Assisting students struggling with reading: Response to intervention and multi-tier intervention for reading in the primary grades: A practice guide [NCEE 2009–4045]. Washington, DC: National Center for Education Evaluation and Regional Assistance, Institute of Education Sciences, U.S. Department of Education. Retrieved from *http://ies.ed.gov/ncee/wwc/publications/practiceguides*

Good, R. H., III, Baker, D. L., Knutson, M., & Watson, J. M. (2004). *IDEL: Indicadores Dinámicos del Éxito en la Lectura.* Eugene: University of Oregon.

Good, R. H., III, Kaminski, R. A., Cummings, K., Dufour-Martel, C., Petersen, K., Powell-Smith, K., et al. (2011). *Acadience Reading Assessment manual.* Eugene, OR: Dynamic Measurement Group.

Gough, P. B., & Tunmer, W. E. (1986). Decoding, reading, and reading disability. *Remedial and Special Education, 7*(1), 6–10.

Institute of Education Sciences. (2011). What Works Clearinghouse procedures and standards handbook (version 2.1). Retrieved from *http://ies.ed.gov/ncee/wwc/pdf/reference_resources/wwc_procedures_v2_1_standards_handbook.pdf*

Johnson, L., & Gatlin-Nash, B. (2020). Evidence-based practices in the assessment and intervention of language-based reading difficulties among African-American learners. *Perspectives on Language and Literacy, 46*(2), 19–25.

Kearns, D., Rogers, H. J., Koriakin, T., & Al Ghanem, R. (2016). Semantic and phonological ability to adjust decoding: A unique correlate of word reading skill? *Scientific Studies of Reading, 20*, 455–470.

Language Dynamics Group. (2018). CUBED. Retrieved from *www.languagedynamicsgroup.com/products/cubed2020*

Lindamood, P., & Lindamood, P. (1998). *The Lindamood phoneme sequencing program for reading, spelling, and speech: The LiPS program* [Multimedia Kit]. Austin, TX: Pro-Ed.

Lonigan, C. J., & Shanahan, T. (2009). *Developing early literacy: Report of the National Early Literacy Panel. Executive summary. A scientific synthesis of early literacy development and implications for intervention*. Washington, DC: National Institute for Literacy.

Lovett, M. W., Lacerenza, L., & Borden, S. L. (2000). Putting struggling readers on the PHAST track: A program to integrate phonological and strategy-based remedial reading instruction and maximise outcomes. *Journal of Learning Disabilities, 33*, 458–467.

Mathes, P., & Torgesen, J. K. (2005). *Early interventions in reading*. New York: McGraw-Hill.

McKenna, M. C., Walpole, S., & Jang, B. G. (2017). Validation of the Informal Decoding Inventory. *Assessment for Effective Intervention, 42*(2), 110–118.

National Early Literacy Panel. (2008). Executive Summary: Developing early literacy: Report of the National Early Literacy Panel. Washington, DC: National Institute for Literacy. Retrieved from *http://lincs.ed.gov/publications/pdf/NELPSummary.pdf*

National Reading Panel. (2000). *Teaching children to read: An evidence-based assessment of the scientific research literature on reading and its implications for reading instruction: Reports of the subgroups*. Washington, DC: National Institutes of Health.

Pearson Education. (2008). *AIMSweb*. San Antonio, TX: Author.

Perfetti, C. A. (1985). *Reading ability*. London: Oxford University Press.

Puranik, C. S., Petscher, Y., Al Otaiba, S., Catts, H. W., & Lonigan, C. J. (2008). Development of oral reading fluency in children with speech or language impairments: A growth curve analysis. *Journal of Learning Disabilities, 41*(6), 545–560.

Ryder, J. F., Tunmer, W. E., & Greaney, K. T. (2008). Explicit instruction in phonemic awareness and phonemically based decoding skills as an intervention strategy for struggling readers in whole language classrooms. *Reading and Writing: An Interdisciplinary Journal, 21*, 349–369.

Savage, R., Georgiou, G., Parrila, R., & Maiorino, K. (2018). Preventative reading interventions teaching direct mapping of graphemes in texts and set-for-variability aid at-risk learners. *Scientific Studies of Reading, 22*(3), 225–247.

Seidenberg, M. S. (2017). *Language at the speed of sight: How we read, why so many can't, and what can be done about it*. New York: Basic Books.

Share, D. L. (1995). Phonological recoding and self-teaching: Sine qua non of reading acquisition. *Cognition, 55*(2), 151–218.

Simmons, D. C., & Kame'enui, E. J. (2002). *Early reading intervention program*. Glenview, IL: Scott Foresman.

Smith, J. L. M., Nelson, N. J., Smolkowski, K., Baker, S. K., Fien, H., & Kosty, D. (2016). Examining the efficacy of a multitiered intervention for at-risk readers in grade 1. *Elementary School Journal, 116*(4), 549–573.

Snow, C. E., Burns, M. S., & Griffin, P. (1998). *Preventing reading difficulties in young children*. Washington, DC: National Academies Press.

Spear-Swerling, L., & Sternberg, R. J. (1996). Off track: *When poor readers become learning disabled*. Boulder, CO: Westview.

Steacy, L., Elleman, A. M., Lovett, M. W., & Compton, D. L. (2016). Exploring differential effects across two decoding treatments on item-level transfer in children with significant word reading difficulties. *Scientific Studies of Reading, 20*(4), 283–295.

Terry, N. P., Gatlin, B., & Johnson, L. (2018). Same or different. *Topics in Language Disorders, 38*(1), 50–65.

Tunmer, W. E., & Chapman, J. W. (2012). Does set for variability mediate the influence of vocabulary knowledge on the development of word recognition skills? *Scientific Studies of Reading, 16*(2), 122–140.

Vadasy, P. F., Wayne, S. K., O'Connor, R. E., Jenkins, J. R., Pool, K. W., Firebaugh, M., et al. (1996). *Sound partners: One-to-one tutoring instruction in early reading skills*. Seattle: Washington Research Institute.

Vernon-Feagans, L., Bratsch-Hines, M., Varghese, C., Cutrer, E. A., & Garwood, J. D. (2018). Improving struggling readers' early literacy skills through a tier 2 professional development program for rural classroom teachers: The targeted reading intervention. *Elementary School Journal, 118*(4), 525–548.

Wanzek, J., & Vaughn, S. (2008). Response to varying amounts of time in reading intervention for students with low response to intervention. *Journal of Learning Disabilities, 41*(2), 126–142.

Wanzek, J., Vaughn, S., Scammacca, N., Gatlin, B., Walker, M. A., & Capin, P. (2016). Meta-analyses of the effects of tier 2 type reading interventions in grades K–3. *Educational Psychology Review, 28*(3), 551–576.

Wilson, B. (2002). *The Wilson Reading System* (3rd ed.). Oxford, MA: Wilson Language Training Corporation.

CHAPTER 3

Structured Literacy Interventions for Reading Long Words

Devin M. Kearns
Cheryl P. Lyon
Shannon L. Kelley

This chapter concerns the needs of students with serious reading difficulty who have already learned how to read monosyllabic words. We begin with a case study that describes the common characteristics of these students.

> Jackson is currently a 12-year-old sixth grader just beginning middle school who was identified with dyslexia in third grade. Ms. Toussaint, his elementary special education teacher, provided Jackson with Structured Literacy (SL) intervention using high-impact strategies for building word recognition skills (see Al Otaiba, Allor, & Stewart, Chapter 2, this volume, on foundational SL intervention). Jackson responded well to the instruction in fourth and fifth grade. By the end of fifth grade, he was confident reading most monosyllabic words, including words with complex sound spellings, like *au* = /aw/, as in *gauzy*. However, Ms. Toussaint noticed that Jackson was struggling to read long words—with more than one syllable—more and more. He seemed frustrated when reading those words. Ms. Toussaint noted these difficulties when she sent his records to Ms. Chin, his sixth-grade special education teacher. Ms. Chin reviewed the information from Ms. Toussaint, and did assessments from the Essential Literacy Measurement System (see Figure 3.1).
>
> Ms. Chin also talked with Jackson's science teacher, Ms. Hemmings. She reported that Jackson was enjoying the concepts in their new geology unit but that he was finding reading the scientific names of new minerals (e.g., calcite) difficult and showed recent decreasing interest and motivation. Ms. Chin also asked Jackson how he felt about reading in science. He said, "I can't figure out the long words. I'll just say anything or skip it. I'm frustrated because I like

A.

ELMS

Essential Literacy Measurement System

Test of Reading Effectiveness and Efficiency

Item	Response	Score	Item	Response	Score
1. plains		1	2. gauzy		1
3. stretched		1	4. trounce		1
5. hammer	ham ... er s/c	1	6. razor	razz-or razzer?	0
7. wonderful	wonder (2x) ... ful? s/c	1	8. unreasonable	un-ree... IDK	0
9. location	lock-cat... IDK	0	10. various	vay-ar-sauce	0

B.

ELMS Decoding Inventory for Reading Test

Item	Score	Response
1. lemmit	1	let ... lem. sc
2. zatting	1	zing... zap... s/c
3. siler	0	sell.. sil... cellar
4. battum	0	bam... bottom
5. polide	0	polite
6. yirder	0	year... yerter

FIGURE 3.1. Data from the (A) ELMS Test of Reading Effectiveness and Efficiency and (B) Decoding Inventory for Reading Test. *Note.* ELMS is a made-up assessment designed to mimic common standardized tests.

learning about the different minerals but can't keep them straight because the names are hard to read." Here is a summary of assessment results that reveal the source of Jackson's difficulties:

1. He makes few mistakes even on words containing sound spellings that are less familiar to many readers—like the *au* in *gauzy* and *ou* in *trounce*. However, he read almost every word with more than one syllable incorrectly and did not appear to notice word endings that occur in many words (e.g., *-able* in *unreasonable*).
2. He reads nonsense words with more than one syllable generally incorrectly or without confidence. He sometimes substitutes real words for nonsense words even though the directions are clear that these are nonsense words.

3. The information about Jackson's participation in science from his teacher and from him directly show reading long words is limiting his science success and motivation.

These data indicate that Jackson does not need help reading monosyllabic words. He needs to learn how to read *polysyllabic* words (also called *multisyllabic* words).

WHY INTERVENTIONS FOR POLYSYLLABIC WORD READING ARE NECESSARY

Many older students with dyslexia and other reading difficulties are like Jackson. Polysyllabic words can be especially difficult for them, even if they are able to read shorter words easily. Students with reading problems often have challenges processing the sounds in words. This makes it hard to remember all the sounds when decoding unfamiliar words—a task that gets harder for longer words with more letters. In Jackson's case, this difficulty was apparent when he tried to decode *location*: He had to remember the pronunciation of *lo* as he tried to decode *ca*. By the time he got to *tion*, it was too much, and he gave up. Many students have this experience.

INTERVENTIONS FOR POLYSYLLABIC WORD READING ARE NECESSARY BECAUSE THEY CAN HELP

The good news is that we can help students read polysyllabic words more easily. Researchers have found that some strategies are especially useful for helping students read the long words—strategies that do not apply to monosyllabic words. In addition, English contains some patterns that make it easier, especially meaning patterns called *morphemes* that we describe further below. In this chapter, we review these strategies. We have divided the chapter into three parts. First, we describe strategies for reading polysyllabic words that involve using syllable information. Second, we describe strategies that use morphemes. Third, we explain how to teach students to be flexible when they use sound spellings. Throughout, we give examples of how these strategies can be applied to Jackson's experience.

SL INTERVENTIONS USING SYLLABLE INFORMATION

One fact about English is that every word has at least one syllable, defined as a word part containing a vowel sound. English readers use syllable information to help them read polysyllabic words quickly and correctly (Muncer & Knight, 2012). For example, a reader might divide *pumpkin* into *pump|kin* and *unbreakable* into *un|break|a|ble*.

Syllabification is valuable for reading polysyllabic words (Stanovich & Siegel, 1994), especially because it allows students to break words into smaller parts—but not all the way to the letter level. Figure 3.2 illustrates the difference between coming up with a pronunciation for each letter one at a time (Figure 3.2A) and pronouncing *kit* and *ten* (Figure 3.2B) before putting it together (Figure 3.2C). As a result, students who can read syllables more accurately and quickly in isolation (e.g., reading *mo* on its own) are better at reading polysyllabic words (Shefelbine, Lipscomb, & Hern, 1989).

Educators typically use one of two approaches for teaching syllabification: (1) rule-based syllabification using syllable types and syllable division rules, or (2) flexibly dividing words using vowel-based syllabification and knowledge of vowel pronunciation. Syllabification according to dictionary rules is the most well-known approach to teaching syllabification and is part of well-known intervention programs like Orton–Gillingham. However, some data indicate that the rule-based approaches (1) do not work very consistently (Kearns, 2020), (2) are too numerous and complex to be very helpful (Zuck, 1974), and (3) may tax students' working memory because they must remember the rules and the part of the word at the same time. There are also very few studies that have examined the effects of using syllable division rules specifically. Overall, the data do not strongly support teaching rule-based syllable division.

Educators and researchers have identified other ways of teaching syllabification that show evidence of improving students' reading skills: (1) teaching students to use vowels to identify syllables and decode and (2) teaching students to recognize patterns in polysyllabic words. Next, we describe how each strategy works.

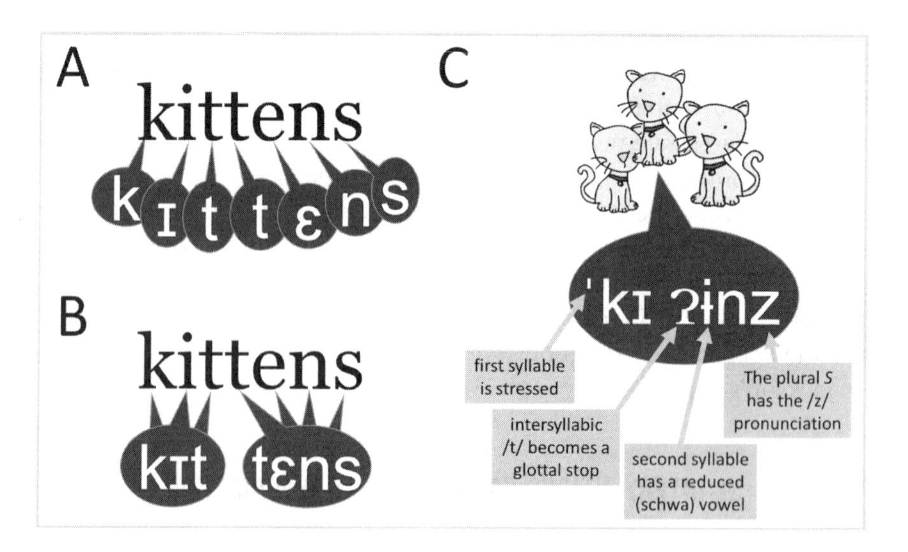

FIGURE 3.2. Comparison of the decoding of *kittens* with the pronunciation of *kittens*. *Note.* The International Phonetic Alphabet (IPA) is used to represent the phonemes. A glottal stop (/ʔ/ in IPA) often replaces /t/ when articulated between some syllables. Copyright © Devin M. Kearns (2020). Used with permission.

Syllabification Strategies to Teach

Syllabification Strategy 1: Teach Students to Use Vowels to Identify Syllables

Researchers have found that readers block words into parts using a vowel letter to identify each part (Chetail & Content, 2014). *Fantastic* is anchored by *a, a,* and *i.* O'Connor, Beach, Sanchez, Bocian, and Flynn (2015) used this fact to design their every syllable has at least one vowel (ESHALOV) strategy. Table 3.1 provides details about this strategy. ESHALOV evolved from two other strategies: discover, isolate, separate, say, examine, check, try (DISSECT; Lenz & Hughes, 1990) and break it apart, examine the base word, say each part, and try the whole word (BEST; O'Connor, Sanchez, Beach, & Bocian, 2015). Students require extensive practice using these strategies while reading words in isolation and in text. Students in O'Connor and colleagues' (2015; O'Connor, Sanchez, Beach, & Bocian, 2017) studies spent approximately 5–10 minutes a day practicing them, and those in Lenz and Hughes's study spent about 20 minutes a day for 6 weeks. O'Connor (2014) noted that it took students a week to fully process the method and 2 more weeks before they began applying the strategy on their own. Teachers should consider incorporating instruction in this method for 10–15 minutes daily for at least 4 weeks to ensure students have enough practice to internalize and apply the strategy on their own.

Syllabification Strategy 2: Teach Students to Recognize Patterns in Polysyllabic Words

One possible way to improve students' attention to all syllables in a word is to explicitly teach them to read and recognize letter-string patterns within longer words. Lovett, Lacerenza, and Borden (2000) designed an analogy-based syllabification strategy within a multicomponent reading intervention for younger children with learning disabilities: the *rhyming strategy*. The researchers taught students how to identify one-syllable key words within longer words by marking their spelling patterns ("the vowel and what comes after it"; Lovett, Lacerenza, De Palma, & Frijters, 2012, p. 164). Students then used these known key words to read unknown words with the same spelling patterns (see Figure 3.3A for an example dialogue).

Bhattacharya and Ehri (2004) designed a way to recognize patterns called *grapho-syllabic analysis*. Bhattacharya and Ehri's intervention is designed for older students who have larger oral vocabularies, so the researchers used word lists that had longer, more complex words that students could likely read independently the first time (they were corrected by the experimenter if they incorrectly read the word). In addition, the researchers emphasized that students should be flexible with where they split the syllables to reduce working memory load and increase the fluidity with which the students used the strategy (see Figure 3.3B for an example).

Over 50 years of research suggest that students use known letter-string patterns, often in the form of syllables, to decode and read unknown words (Kearns & Whaley,

TABLE 3.1. Overview of Syllabification Strategies

Strategy	Research	Looks like . . .	Best for students who . . .
1. Explicitly teach and practice two key rules: • Every syllable must have a vowel. • Syllables divide in predictable patterns.	DISSECT (Lenz & Hughes, 1990) BEST (O'Connor et al., 2015) ESHALOV (O'Connor et al., 2015, 2017)	Underline all the vowels (e.g., *mastermind*) Connect the vowel teams Separate the word into syllables (e.g., *mas* I *ter* I *mind*). Read each syllable Read the whole word	Can fluently read one-syllable words
2A. Teach students to read word parts by analogy	Cunningham (1979) Rhyming strategy (Lovett et al., 2000)	Checkmark the vowels (e.g., *upshot*) Underline the spelling patterns (the vowel and what comes after it; e.g., *upshot*) Identify/write the keyword (e.g., *up* = *cup*, *shot* = *pot*) Make the connection: "If I know *cup*, then I know *up*; if I know *pot*, then I know *shot*." The whole word is *upshot*.	Need additional practice generalizing syllable patterns
2B. Teach students to match the syllable spellings to pronunciations	Syllable-based word building (Shefelbine, 1990) Reading printed words by syllable and then the whole words (Archer, 1981; Archer, Gleason, & Vachon, 2000) Graphosyllabic analysis (Bhattacharya & Ehri, 2004)	Part I Teacher writes a multisyllabic word on the board syllable-by-syllable, pausing for students to read the syllables as teacher adds them. Have students read the whole word again (e.g., *de-fend-ing*, *defending*) Part II Teacher writes a multisyllabic word on the board and scoops under the syllables. Teacher points to each syllable and asks students to read them and then read the whole word. Part III Pronounce a written word. Divide the word into syllables orally. Match each spoken part to its written part (i.e., point and read syllables). Blend the parts and read the word.	Can consistently read two- and three-syllable words and needs additional practice

(A)

Ms. Chin teaches Jackson ESHALOV + look OK
Ms. Chin: **We're going to learn how to read multisyllabic words today. What kind of words?** Jackson: **Multisyllabic words.** Ms. Chin: **The first thing to learn about multisyllabic words is that every syllable must have a vowel. What must every syllable have?** Jackson: **A vowel.** Ms. Chin: **Let's look at an example** [*on the board*]. **This word is *buckwheat*. What word?** Jackson: ***Buckwheat.*** Ms. Chin: ***Buckwheat* has two syllables. I know this by marking the vowels and connecting the vowel teams.** [*Checkmarks the vowels and connects the vowel team.*] **How many syllables does *buckwheat* have? How do you know?** Jackson: **Two. It has one vowel, *u*, and one vowel team, *ea*.** Ms. Chin: **The second thing to know is that syllables divide in predictable patterns. How do they divide?** Jackson: **Into patterns.** Ms. Chin: **We can determine this by dividing them where they look like patterns we know and they look OK. Let's take a look at *buckwheat*. I'm going to divide it after the *k* and before the *w*. Do those patterns look OK? Now, I'll try reading the word by each syllable: *buck-wheat* and all together: *buckwheat*. You try it.** Jackson: ***Buck-wheat. Buckwheat.*** Ms. Chin: **Let's do some practice.** [*Writes* soundtrack, pattern, defend.] **What do we do?** Jackson: **Mark the vowels, join the teams, and divide the word where it looks OK.** Ms. Chin: [*For each word, she asks:*] **How many syllables does this word have? How do you know? Read the word in parts. Now read it as a whole.**

(B)

Ms. Chin teaches Jackson how to use "graphosyllabic analysis"		
Ms. Chin writes pedicure on the board, syllable by syllable. Ms. Chin: [*points*] **Read this.** Jackson: ***Ped*** Ms. Chin: [*points*] **Read this.** Jackson: ***i*** Ms. Chin: [*points*] **Read this.** Jackson: ***cure*** Ms. Chin: [*points*] **Read the whole word.** Jackson: ***Pedicure.*** *Ms. Chin continues this practice for a week in conjunction with the harder swooping practice.*	*Ms. Chin writes* astonished on the board with swoops connecting each syllable. Ms. Chin: [*points*] **Read this syllable.** Jackson: ***as*** Ms. Chin: [*points*] **This one.** Jackson: ***ton*** Ms. Chin: [*points*] **This one.** Jackson: ***ish*** Ms. Chin: [*points*] **This one.** Jackson: ***ed*** Ms. Chin: [*points*] **Read the whole word.** Jackson: ***Astonished.*** Ms. Chin: **What word?**	*Ms. Chin introduces true graphosyllabic analysis.* Ms. Chin: [*Writes* heartbroken on the board.] **Read this word.** Jackson: ***Heartbroken.*** Ms. Chin: **Divide the word into parts out loud.** Jackson: ***Heart. Broke. En.*** Ms. Chin: [*points*] **Read the first part.** Jackson: ***heart*** Ms. Chin: [*points*] **Read the second part.** Jackson: ***brok*** Ms. Chin: [*points*] **Read the last part.** Jackson: ***en*** Teacher: **Read the whole word.** Jackson: ***Heartbroken.***

(continued)

FIGURE 3.3. Syllable-based strategies for reading polysyllabic words.

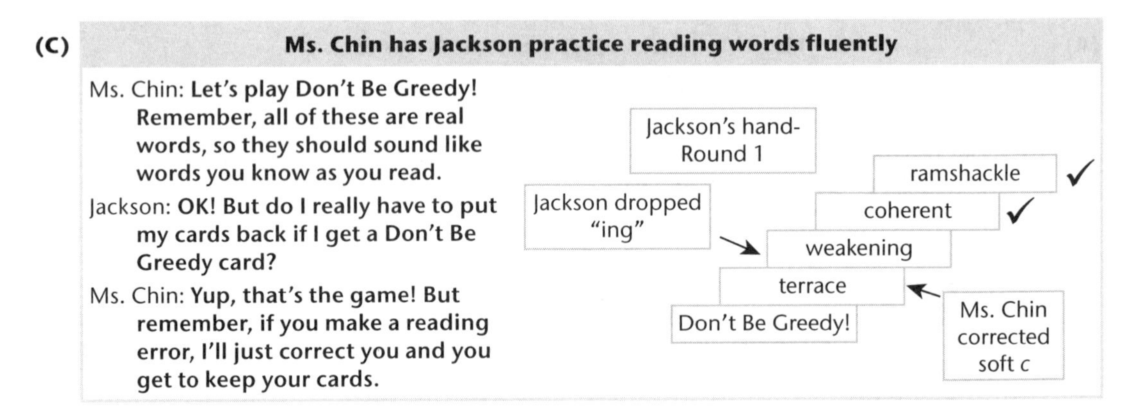

FIGURE 3.3. *(continued)*

2019; O'Connor, 2014; Shefelbine, 1990). Explicitly teaching students to analyze the letter strings in syllables promotes future automatic recognition of these patterns in unknown, polysyllabic words. Before choosing one of the strategies described above, teachers should consider the strength of their students' oral vocabularies and current reading levels to ensure students are tasked with practice that results in success. In addition, once students have had ample opportunity to practice applying these strategies to read words in isolation, they should be encouraged to actively apply the strategies to unknown words in texts they are reading.

Incorporating short games into daily lessons is a great way to ensure students are getting a substantial amount of varied practice to increase their fluency with syllable and word reading. In the game Don't Be Greedy! (Lab School of Washington, personal communication, June 20, 2017; Figure 3.3C), students read cards of syllables and/or polysyllabic words as quickly and correctly as possible. Teachers should ensure there are a variety of words and syllable types in the deck (i.e., *toenail, breakfast, undoing*), and encourage students to apply their syllable division strategies on challenging words. Other games you might consider incorporating for just 5 minutes a lesson include memory and word races.

SL INTERVENTIONS USING MORPHOLOGY-RELATED STRATEGIES

In addition to syllable division, strategies for morphological analysis are useful in helping students with reading disabilities read polysyllabic words. Data indicate that morphological knowledge and word reading skill are associated, and that students benefit from learning about morphemes (e.g., Carlisle & Stone, 2005). The association between morphology and reading is especially strong for polysyllabic words (Gilbert, Goodwin, Compton, & Kearns, 2013; Kearns, Steacy, et al., 2016). In struggling readers, morphological knowledge is related to reading and spelling skill—even when taking students' phonological awareness and oral language abilities into account (Siegel, 2008). In terms of learning, data show that instruction in morphology has beneficial effects on word-reading skill for students with reading disabilities and at risk for reading difficulty (e.g., Berninger et al., 2003; Bowers, Kirby, & Deacon, 2010; Elbro & Arnbak, 1996; Goodwin & Ahn, 2010, 2013; Kim et al., 2017). Researchers think that learning about morphology helps students because it helps provide a scaffold for students with phonological processing difficulties (Elbro & Arnbak, 1996; Reed, 2008). Because morphemes provide information about the meaning of words at the same time as their spelling and pronunciation, they help readers both decode *and* comprehend new polysyllabic polymorphemic words (O'Connor, 2014).

Long words are often the product of their morphemes: The meaning of *encampment* relies on the combination of the prefix *en-*, the base word *camp*, and the suffix *-ment*. In addition, many complex words are accessible through word families that contain the same base word (*help* to *helpful, helpfulness, unhelpfully*, etc.). Morphemes are helpful because they provide information for pronunciation of common word parts, like *tion*, and because they connect to meanings of the words (e.g., *sign* relates to *signature*; Wade-Woolley & Heggie, 2015). Words also generally have fewer morphemes than syllables, so this strategy is more efficient (Goodwin, Gilbert, & Cho, 2013; Kearns & Whaley, 2019) and does not require students to keep as much information in memory (Bhattacharya, 2020). Figure 3.4 shows that *unpresentable* has fewer morphemes than sound spellings or syllables. If the reader can identify the morphemes, there will be fewer parts to remember and less strain on students' phonological memory. Finally, it facilitates reading in instances when syllable division might result in confusing pronunciation, as in *reappear*. Without knowing about the morpheme *re-*, a reader could easily believe the word is pronounced "reep-pare" (Kuo & Anderson, 2006). This can even help students read words where a morpheme does not explain the whole word. Identifying *man* in *henchman* will help read that word, even if *hench* does not mean anything on its own (Taft & Kougious, 2004).

Morphology-Related Strategies to Teach

For students with reading difficulty, SL emphasizes the use of systematic, explicit strategy instruction (Fallon & Katz, 2020), with the goal of increasing generalization and

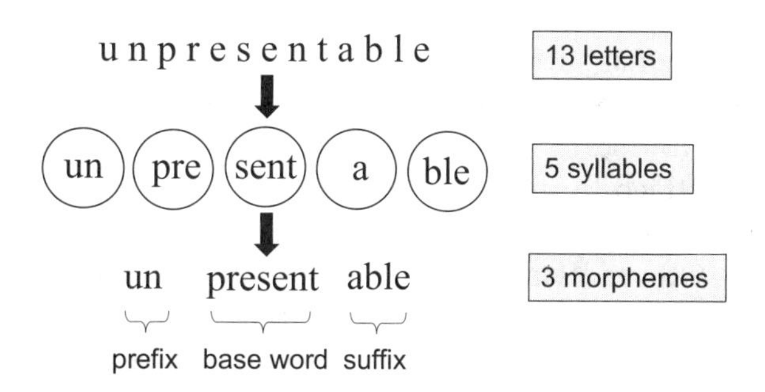

FIGURE 3.4. Comparison of the number of letters, syllables, and morphemes in *unpresentable*.

getting students to use the strategies, not just to be able to recite the steps (Archer, Gleason, & Vachon, 2003). Evidence supports the incorporation of more than one approach to morphological instruction for reading long words (Bhattacharya, 2020; Kearns & Whaley, 2019; Lovett et al., 2017), both for younger students (Goodwin & Ahn, 2013) and for adolescents (Archer et al., 2003; O'Connor, 2014). Here, we summarize strategies that have been shown to support word recognition and recommend the following morphology-based strategies for teaching students how to approach polysyllabic words: (1) teach the pronunciations and spellings of affixes (i.e., prefixes and suffixes), (2) teach bases by reading words in morphological families, and (3) teach students to locate affixes and bases, and then use them to decode words. Finally, students should practice extensively using the strategies described in this chapter to increase accuracy and automaticity. These strategies are described in Table 3.2.

Strategy 1: Teach the Pronunciations and Spellings of Affixes

Pronunciation of affixes is considered a "necessary preskill" (Archer et al., 2003, p. 91) for reading polysyllabic words. Targeted instruction in frequently occurring affixes can provide students with generalizable information for many other words (Baumann et al., 2002; Lovett et al., 2000). In fact, 97% of prefixed words contain just 20 prefixes, and just 10 suffixes account for 85% of suffixed words (White, Sowell, & Yanagihara, 1989). Affix knowledge is also important because some words contain spelling patterns that may or may not be an affix (e.g., *re-* in *reasonably* vs. *readmittance*; Berninger et al., 2003; O'Connor, 2014).

The focus of early elementary instruction in reading tends to be on inflectional morphology—plural forms (e.g., *cats, books, birds*), tense forms (e.g., *walk, walks, walked, walking*), and comparatives and superlatives (e.g., *big, bigger, biggest*; Kearns & Whaley, 2019). Affixes can be challenging, especially when they cause a phonological shift: In the plural examples given above, the *-s* is pronounced as /s/ in *books* and *cats*, but as /z/ in *birds*. The inflectional morpheme *-ed* can be pronounced three ways: /d/ as in *walked* and *jumped*, /t/ as in *stopped* and *marked*, or /'ɛd/ as in *graded*. Table 3.3 contains a list of the most frequently used inflectional affixes.

Derivational affixes are more numerous but appear less frequently, so they tend to be more difficult for students (Reed, 2008). Derivational prefixes like *un-* or *re-* affect meaning (as in *un* + *reliable*, the opposite of *reliable* and *re* + *apply*, which means to apply again), whereas derivational suffixes can either change part of speech (the noun *bombast* + *ic* becomes an adjective *bombastic*, and the adjective *normal* + *ize* becomes a verb: *normalize*), or meaning (the suffix *-less* turns *meaning* into its opposite: *meaningless*). Some derivational suffixes attach to free morphemes (*-ness, -er, -ize,* and *-ment*) and do not usually change the vowel pronunciation or the syllable stress; these are easier to learn (Tyler & Nagy, 1987). Others often attach to bound roots and affect both pronunciation and spelling (e.g., *-ify, -ive, -ous*: *gratify, pensive, porous*).

While rules exist for many spelling and pronunciation differences of affixes (e.g., final consonant doubling, changing *y* to *i*), teaching these rules is not one of the

TABLE 3.2. Overview of Morphology-Related Strategies

Strategy	Research	Looks like . . .	Best for . . .
Learn spellings and pronunciations of affixes	Peeling off (Lovett et al., 2000)	Teach one to two "beginnings" and "endings" a day, including multiple pronunciations (e.g., *-ed* can be pronounced /d/, /t/, or /'ɛd/). Add each to the appropriate side of the peeling-off tree. Practice all learned affixes daily.	Younger students
	Affix learning (Toste et al., 2017)	*Name it:* Teach up to three new affixes a day, including multiple pronunciations. Provide sample word and define it. Students generate sample words. *Write it:* Have students add new prefixes and suffixes to affix bank. *Review it:* Practice all learned affixes daily.	Adolescent students and students who would benefit from meaning instruction
Look for familiar word parts and use them to decode the word	I SPY (Lovett et al., 2000)	Look for small words or word parts in unknown words (e.g., "I spy *rain*. I'll put a box around *rain*. Now, I Spy *coat*. So the whole word is *raincoat*."	Dividing compound words
	Peeling off (Lovett et al., 2000)	Circle the prefixes and suffixes. Say the prefixes and suffixes. Say the root. Say the whole word: "I peel off ___________ at the beginning/end of the word. The root is ___________. The word is ___________."	Familiar base words and in combination with base word instruction
	Overt strategy (Archer et al., 2003)	Circle the word parts (prefixes) at the beginning of the word. Circle the word parts (suffixes) at the end of the word. Underline the letters representing vowel sounds in the rest of the word. Say the parts of the word. Say the parts fast. Make it a real word.	Students who are familiar with finding vowels through syllable division strategies
	Covert strategy (Archer et al., 2003)	Look for word parts at the beginning and end of the word, and vowel sounds in the rest of the word. Say the parts of the word. Say the parts fast. Make it a real word.	Students who are proficient with the more explicit steps of the overt strategy

TABLE 3.3. Lists of Frequent Affixes and Root Words

Prefixes	Suffixes	Base words
un-	*-s, -es*	*out*
re-	*-ed*	*up*
in-, im-, ir-, il- ("not")	*-ing*	*way*
dis-	*-ly*	*direct*
en-, em-	*-er, -or*	*in*
non-	*-ion, -tion, -ation, -ition*	*side*
in-, im- ("in or into")	*-ible, -able*	*line*
over- ("too much")	*-al, -ial*	*work*
mis-	*-y*	*act*
sub-	*-ness*	*light*
pre-	*-ity, -ty*	*land*
inter-	*-ment*	*time*
fore-	*-ic*	*use*
de-	*-ous, -eous, -ious*	*water*
trans-	*-en*	*hard*
super-	*-er* (comparative)	*day*
semi-	*-ive, -ative, -itive*	*air*
anti-	*-ful*	*draw*
mid-	*-ness*	*set*
under- ("too little")	*-est*	*place*

Note: Affix list is from White, Sowell, and Yanagihara (1989); root list is from Kearns and Whaley (2019).

recommended strategies for reading these words—rather, the goal is to build on implicit oral awareness of these pronunciation differences toward explicit awareness of their corresponding spelling patterns (Kearns, 2015). For example, while students may have no trouble shifting pronunciation from /d/ in *walked* to /t/ in *jumped* while speaking, or with generalizing implicit inflectional rules (think of young children who say *goed* for the past tense of *go*), they are likely unaware of how the words are spelled or would have difficulty reading the words in print. Rather than rule instruction, flexible approaches that build this awareness by focusing on identification of word parts, as well as vowel flexibility, are recommended for polysyllabic word reading (Kearns & Whaley, 2019).

WHAT IT LOOKS LIKE

For students to learn the spellings and pronunciations of affixes, and be able to recognize them in polysyllabic words, they must commit them to memory (Kearns & Whaley, 2019). In their 70-hour intervention for students with severe dyslexia, Lovett and colleagues (2000) included instruction of one to two affixes a day, up to 75 affixes in total. Teachers introduced new affixes explicitly, adding each one to either the "beginnings" or "endings" side of a bank of learned affixes (the "Peeling-Off Tree"; Lovett et al., 2000,

p. 471), and students practiced reading all affixes on the list daily. When an affix could be pronounced in more than one way, students practiced those multiple pronunciations each time they encountered the affix in isolation (i.e., each time they practiced the suffix *-ed*, they said all three pronunciations: /d/, /t/, *ed*). A sample lesson to introduce a new affix is shown in Figure 3.5A.

Strategy 2: Teach Bases by Reading Words in Word Families

Another strategy to support polysyllabic word reading is engaging students in reading base word families. This practice is most effective once students have mastered some affixes and can use them in conjunction with base words to decode unfamiliar words flexibly (Kearns & Whaley, 2019). Teachers can choose word families for students to read based on their readiness, and may decide to choose word families that coincide with a thematic curricular unit. See Table 3.3 for a sample of base words.

Several researchers have recommended instruction in bound bases (or *roots*; e.g., nonaffix morphemes that cannot stand alone as words, such as *vis*, *junct*, and *corp*) for polysyllabic word reading (e.g., Henry, 2019; O'Connor, 2014) because of the high percentage of words with Latin and Greek origins that comprise generally useful and content-specific academic words (Crosson, McKeown, Moore, & Ye, 2018; Goodwin, Lipsky, & Ahn, 2012). The bound base *geo* (referring to *earth* or *ground*) contributes meaning to the science-based words *geographic*, *geology*, *geothermal*, and *geophysics*, but would be a "false alarm" (Crosson & McKeown, 2016, p. 154), holding no meaningful value in the word *surgeon*. While correlational support for the relationship of morphological knowledge to literacy outcomes would appear to support bound root instruction for word reading, very few studies have focused on instruction solely in bound roots, and meta-analyses have not differentiated between bound and free base instruction and/or affix instruction (e.g., Goodwin & Ahn, 2010, 2013). It is difficult to determine whether instruction in bound roots *alone* would be beneficial for polysyllabic word reading, but in combination with other instruction and strategies, bound root instruction appears to improve students' ability to infer the meaning of unknown words (e.g., Bowers & Kirby, 2010; Crosson & McKeown, 2016) and, in some studies, to improve word recognition, although researchers were not specifically looking for recognition of polysyllabic words (Bowers et al., 2010; Reed, 2008). In short, there is currently not enough research to support explicit instruction in bound roots as a sole strategy to support polysyllabic word reading.

WHAT IT LOOKS LIKE

For practice and instruction in decoding polysyllabic words, explicit instruction in the meanings of affixes and bases is not one of the recommended strategies. Instruction in multiple strategies will target multiple outcomes (Goodwin & Ahn, 2013), so if the teacher's goal is to also target vocabulary knowledge, meaning instruction might provide some benefit—however, for students with dyslexia, it is more beneficial to discuss how affixes and base words affect meaning in context (Kearns & Whaley, 2019).

(A) Ms. Chin teaches Jackson frequently appearing affixes

By the end of fifth grade, it's apparent to Ms. Chin that many of Jackson's errors are morphological in nature. He can find the vowels and has some success with dividing long words through syllabification, but Ms. Chin notices that Jackson is not using information about the meaningful parts of the word when he tries to decode. He often mispronounces affixes, and he sometimes skips these parts entirely, like when he read the word purposefully as propose. Ms. Chin decides to introduce affixes, beginning with the most frequent prefixes and suffixes, to build Jackson's morphological awareness and ability to identify meaningful word parts in long words. She creates an affix bank where they'll add new affixes daily.

Ms. Chin displays a card with the new affix. **Our new beginning is *un*-. It says /ʌn /. What does it say?**

Jackson: **It says /ʌn/.**

Ms. Chin: **Would you find *un*- at the beginning or at the end of a word?**

Jackson: **At the beginning.**

Ms. Chin: **Yes, at the beginning. A word that begins with *un*- is *unable*. Can you think of a word that begins with *un*-?**

Jackson: ***Unhappy?***

Ms. Chin: **Yes! *Unhappy* begins with *un*-. Where should we put *un*- in our affix bank?** [*Ms. Chin asks Jackson to place it with prefixes or affixes.*]

Jackson: **With the beginnings.**

Ms. Chin: **Yes, *un*- goes with the beginnings. Let's review all the beginnings we've learned.** [*Jackson reads prefixes.*] **Let's review all the endings we've learned.** [*Jackson reads suffixes.*]

Ms. Chin introduces two new affixes a day using this script. Each day, Jackson also reads all of the affixes on the affix wall and practices peeling off familiar affixes with a set of 20 multisyllabic words, beginning with familiar base words (see Strategy 2 and Strategy 3 below).

(B) Jackson practices peeling off affixes and reading base words

Ms. Chin noticed other difficulties when Jackson tried to read long words. Jackson's receptive and expressive vocabulary was just under grade level, so even though he would probably have been familiar with both the sound spelling and the meaning of the base word, he did not use this information in a strategic way and sometimes guessed after looking at just the initial letter pattern of the word. Sometimes, Jackson's guessing came as the result of frustration that here was yet another long word he did not recognize, and he gave up before trying. Ms. Chin decides to teach Jackson the *peeling-off* strategy (Lovett, Lacerenza, & Borden, 2000) for approaching multisyllabic words.

Ms. Chin: **Look at this word.**

Jackson: **I peel off *sub* at the beginning of the word and /s/ /z/ at the end of the word. The root is *merge*. The word is *submerges*.**

Ms. Chin: **Great! The word is *submerges*. Now try this one.**

Jackson: **I peel off /*"re"*/ /*"ruh"*/ at the beginning of the word and /"ɪŋ"/ at the end of the word. The root is *form*. The word is *reforming*.**

Ms. Chin: **Yes, the word is *reforming*. Let's keep going!**

Jackson uses the peeling-off strategy to complete the set of practice words, then reads a short narrative that includes a number of multisyllabic words in connected text.

FIGURE 3.5. Examples of teaching frequent affixes and peeling-off practice.

For example, a teacher might decide to have students practice reading words from the base word family for *believe*: *believer, believed, believing, disbelieving, believable.* To discuss meaning—and help the student to access all of the words in this family—the teacher can use one of these words in a sentence and talk about what the word means in that context. The suffix *-able* means "capable of" and turns any base into an adjective (so *accept* becomes *acceptable* and *photograph* becomes *photographable*). Instead of having Jackson repeat "*able* means *capable of*" or "*believe* means *to have confidence in*," both abstract concepts that would be difficult for a struggling reader to understand or internalize, Ms. Chin might engage Jackson in a different way of understanding the word by saying:

> Let's look at this sentence: "Keisha's brother told her there were ghosts living in the basement, but Keisha didn't find that believable." When it says that Keisha didn't find ghosts to be *believable*, it means she didn't think ghosts were something she knew to be real or true. Can you use *believable* in a sentence?

Strategy 3: Teach Students to Locate Affixes and Bases and Use Them to Decode

One key to decoding polysyllabic words is being able to locate affixes and base words in order to segment long words into smaller parts. Students who recognize affixes can then isolate and decode the base word before reassembling the word parts to read the whole word. Whether teachers refer to prefixes and suffixes by their technical names, or as "beginnings" and "endings," does not matter, and several of the strategies recommended in this chapter use different terms. Lovett and colleagues' (2000) peeling-off strategy includes the memorization of affix spellings and pronunciations described earlier, followed by a systematic strategy for using their knowledge of those morphemes to deconstruct long words. Two other strategies, the *overt strategy* and the *covert strategy* (Archer et al., 2003), combine morphological identification with vowel flexibility strategies discussed earlier. The overt strategy is designed to be taught first because it is more explicit. The covert strategy, which students can use once they have sufficient practice with the overt strategy, does not involve physically circling affixes or underlining vowels. See Table 3.2 for a full description of each strategy.

A critical part of polysyllabic word instruction is for the student to connect the pronunciation of the blended word to a word the student knows. The ultimate goal of any word identification strategy is fluent reading for the purpose of comprehension. Being able to pronounce a polysyllabic word without making a lexical connection does not achieve the strategic purpose of instruction, so it is important for the teacher to make this link if the strategy does not do that explicitly. The final step of both the overt and covert strategies is to "make it a real word."

WHAT IT LOOKS LIKE

See Figure 3.5B for an example of Jackson using the peeling-off strategy (Lovett et al., 2000) to read the words *submerges* and *reforming*. Ms. Chin has made sure to instruct

Jackson to say both pronunciations for the suffix *-s* and the prefix *re-* during peeling off. This allows flexibility in determining which pronunciation will result in a word Jackson recognizes. When blending the parts together, Jackson chooses the appropriate pronunciation for the suffix.

If a student is not familiar with the meaning of the decoded word, the teacher can supply it. In one practice session with a group of fourth-grade students, a student struggled to decode the word *matador*. She easily located and correctly pronounced the spelling patterns she recognized (*mat* and *dor*), and used the vowel flexibility strategy she had learned (trying both the long and short sounds for *a*), but when she attempted to blend the word parts together, she did not recognize either pronunciation as a word she had ever heard before. In this case, the teacher gave her the correct pronunciation of the word along with a quick explanation of what the word meant.

SL INTERVENTION WITH SUPPORTING PRACTICES

Syllable-based and morpheme-based strategies are very powerful for teaching students to read unfamiliar words, and they are the focus of most SL instruction on reading polysyllabic words. These strategies should be complemented by the use of instructional principles and approaches that facilitate building word recognition skills.

Principle 1: Teach Flexibility

Why Should Teachers Provide Flexibility Instruction?

Syllable- and morpheme-based strategies are very valuable, but there is an implicit assumption in these strategies that is not quite correct: If you learn the parts of a word, you simply assemble them to pronounce the word. This is not really how you pronounce whole words from individual spoken sounds or syllables. Take the example of *kittens* in Figure 3.2. It seems straightforward to match the letters to the sounds or syllables, as Figures 3.2A and 3.2B show.

However, Figure 3.2C shows the differences between what is said in pronouncing each sound or syllable and what the pronunciation of the entire word sounds like. These differences are important because some students struggle to make these adjustments (Kearns, Rogers, Al Ghanem, & Koriakin, 2016).

These pronunciation differences are also frequent: They occur in almost all polysyllabic English words because the language frequently includes *reduced vowels, schwa* sounds that are very short forms of short *u* or short *i* represented by /ə/ or /ɨ/, and pronounced like the *a* in *about* and the second *e* in *enemy*. These shortened forms are convenient for speaking fluently, but they make it hard to read polysyllabic words even when each part of the word has been decoded correctly.

A critical principle that applies to reading words using syllable information or morpheme information is that students must learn to be *flexible*. Researchers have shown that good readers have the ability to adjust incorrect pronunciations and say the correct related word (Elbro, De Jong, Houter, & Nielsen, 2012; Kearns, Rogers, et al., 2016; Steacy et al., 2019; Tunmer & Chapman, 2012). For example, if *breakfast* is pronounced as "breek-fast," students are often able to figure out the correct word from the mispronunciation. The ability to make such corrections is critical for building word recognition skills.

How to Provide Flexibility Instruction

One prominent way to teach students to be flexible is to use the *vowel alert* strategy to prepare them to flex letter patterns with multiple pronunciations (Lovett et al., 2000). For vowel alert, students explicitly learn that certain letter patterns make multiple sounds (vowel letters like *a* or vowel teams like *ea*). The teacher provides an explanation why students need the strategy; explains that there are multiple pronunciations, and that they need to be flexible to say a real word; reviews the patterns; gives examples; and has students practice. Teachers should focus on the highest-frequency spellings. An analysis of words in grades 1–5 suggests that teachers should teach the different pronunciations for the five vowel letters: *y, i-e, ea, ow,* and *oo*. Figure 3.6A shows how Ms. Chin might teach Jackson to use the vowel alert strategy.

A second kind of flexibility is in the application of various strategies. Students need to be aware of the different strategies that are available to them and use them strategically. It is important that the flexible application of strategies does not take a lot of time and or much conscious cognitive processing. Sometimes students will need explicit teaching of how to combine strategies because it may not be intuitive to them to do so. Figure 3.6B shows how Ms. Chin taught Jackson to use his strategies flexibly.

Principle 2: Practice Extensively

All of the strategies mentioned in this chapter should be accompanied by many opportunities to practice to increase fluency (Archer et al., 2003; Kearns, 2015; Lovett et al., 2000). Archer and colleagues (2003, p. 96) used the example of a new driver: A new driver has not yet achieved automaticity and must pay attention to the mechanics of the car and consequently has fewer cognitive resources available to pay attention to the potential dangers of the road. In other words, until automaticity is achieved, the bulk of a reader's energy is focused on the laborious process of decoding individual words, with few resources left for seeing the big picture of the text itself.

This is why it is so important that students learn the simplest possible strategies that are usable while reading. The strategies already described were selected because they are simple. In addition, students must practice these strategies by reading as many words as possible in every lesson (Archer et al., 2003; Kearns, 2015). In their study, Archer and colleagues (2003) introduced up to 787 novel polysyllabic words and students continued practicing in connected secondary-level text containing many polysyllabic words. One simple way to decide whether students are getting enough practice is to count how many words they practice reading in a minute when using the strategies. The more words read, the better.

(A) **Ms. Chin Teaches Jackson to Combine Strategies Flexibly**

Jackson has learned multiple strategies, but Ms. Chin eventually decided to focus on two key strategies, the ESHALOV strategy and the peeling-off strategy. Jackson uses the peeling-off strategy consistently, but he does not always use ESHALOV. Ms. Chin thinks he would benefit from practice using both strategies together—knowing how to use them flexibly depending on the circumstances.

Ms. Chin: **Jackson, I have some long challenge words for you to read today. You have learned two strategies for reading long words, which are . . .**

Jackson: Peeling off by looking for prefixes, suffixes, and roots. And also that every syllable has at least one vowel and has to look OK when you break it apart.

Ms. Chin: **Great! You do a great job with both of these strategies, and you will need both of them for some words. I have some words where it will help you to combine the strategies. In these words, start with peeling off and then use the ESHALOV and "look OK" strategy if you need it to pronounce the root. Use the strategies you need to read the word—you might need both or just one. Tell me what you're doing as you read the word. Ms. Chin points to the word *reforming.***

Jackson: I peel off *R-E, ree,* at the beginning of the word and *I-N-G, ing,* at the end of the word. The root is *form*. The word is *reforming.*

Ms. Chin: **Yes, the word is *reforming*. You used peeling off but didn't need ESHALOV. Great! Try this word. She points to *disrespected.***

Jackson: I peel off *D-I-S, dis,* at the beginning of the word and *E-D, ed,* at the end. I can break the root into two parts with vowels that look OK. They say [*points to* re, *covering* pect *with the end of a pen*] *ress* and [*points to* pect] *pecked*. That's *ress . . . pecked, respect*. The root is *respect*. The word is *disrespected.*

Ms. Chin: **Excellent work combining the strategies to read that one. Let's try some more.**

Ms. Chin has Jackson read 10 other words this way.

(B) **Ms. Chin Teaches Jackson Vowel Alert**

Jackson has improved in his use of flexible syllabification strategy, but he still sometimes cannot remember the options for pronouncing single vowel letters. He also has trouble with vowel teams that have multiple pronunciations. Ms. Chin decides to teach Jackson vowel alert to help him adjust his pronunciations.

Ms. Chin: **It can be hard to know how to say some words because vowel letters have more than one sound. When you sound out a word, the parts may not sound the same as the real word because it has a different vowel. You're going to learn to watch out for vowels like this—a vowel alert. Our first vowel alert will be for the letter *i*. It has three different sounds, the long sound, /ī/, the short sound /ĭ/, and the "uh" sound called schwa. What are the sounds?**

Jackson: The long sound, short sound, and "uh," called schwa.

Ms. Chin: **Yes, when you see the letter *i* by itself in a word, like this word** [*shows* pilot], **it's a vowel alert. You have to try to read the word with the three sounds until you say a real word. What do you do when there's a vowel alert?**

Jackson: Try to read the word with the three sounds until it's a real word.

Ms. Chin: **Yes. Watch me. I see the *i* by itself. That's a vowel alert. I know the sounds are /ī/, /ĭ/, and /ə/. What are the sounds?**

Jackson: /ī/, /ĭ/, and /ə/

(continued)

FIGURE 3.6. Examples of using the (A) vowel alert strategy and (B) flexible strategy use.

Ms. Chin: **I'll try each one until I say a real word. I try /ī/. That's *pilot*. That's a real word! I got it. I would usually stop there, but I'll try the other ones for practice. I try /ĭ/, it's *pill-lot*. I try /ə/, it's *puhl-lot*. You try saying the sounds and the word all three ways.**

Jackson: /ī/, *pilot*, /ĭ/, *pill-lot*, and /ə/, puhl-lot

Ms. Chin: **Let's practice reading more words with the *i* vowel alert.**

Ms. Chin models and Jackson follows the model until he seems ready to do it on his own. Then she has him practice 10 other words.

Ms. Chin introduces the other vowel alert patterns. Each day, Jackson says the different pronunciations for each vowel alert and then practices reading words with them.

FIGURE 3.6. *(continued)*

When students make an error in word identification, it is important to prompt them to use the strategy at the moment they make a reading error; doing so greatly improves student autonomy and success at reading polysyllabic words (Archer et al., 2003).

Finally, it is important that teachers use words that are familiar to students phonologically—that is, they have heard them before even if they cannot read them. If teachers use rare words, students cannot engage in the important process of changing a mispronunciation into a correct word (Kearns, Steacy, et al., 2016). It is not necessary that students know a great deal about a given word. It just should not be so rare that it is actually a nonsense word for them. For example, one now-unused reading program included *hovel* as a "real" practice word. This rare word is very unlikely to be familiar to students. Words like this are not useful for teaching students to read polysyllabic words.

Less common words might still be used, however. Teachers could preview the words they will be reading at the beginning of the lesson by pronouncing them aloud and having students repeat them (making sure they are accurate). This would give students prior experience with the words that would help trigger the link to a familiar word during practice. In some cases, nonsense words might also be helpful—especially for students who tend to guess and need to use decoding skills more consistently. Notably, students who are learning English should probably not practice with nonsense words very much; they need as many opportunities to understand the English language as possible, and nonsense words will not help them. This caveat might also be extended to students with speech or language difficulties who need instruction to support vocabulary learning (in a limited way), in addition to word recognition skills.

SUMMARY

Polysyllabic words are difficult for students to read because they have many complexities that are not characteristic of monosyllabic words. There are multiple strategies that can be used to read these words, some focusing on the syllabic features of the words and some focusing on the morphological features of the words. The strategies that students learn should be the most efficient possible, such that students can use them efficiently when reading on their own. However, the strategies chosen must also meet the needs of individual students, so teachers always need to exercise careful judgment in selecting strategies and monitor student progress continuously to ensure they are profiting from learning the strategies. The goal is that we can help students like Jackson who have reached the late-elementary and middle school grades without reading success—and that we can prevent students with reading difficulties in lower grades from needing this help later on.

APPLICATION ACTIVITIES

Lian is a 10-year-old fifth grader who was identified with reading difficulty in the middle of fourth grade. She had done relatively well in reading through the end of second grade and began to fall behind in third grade. It was initially unclear to her teachers why she was falling behind. They examined her data carefully to decide what to do to help her (see the data presented in Figure 3.7).

A

Marshall Elementary
Sight Word Checklist (Grade 3) Lian Zhao (Student) 69/75 (Score)

only	know	come
me	where	around an...
most	because	another × and...
its	such	great answer?
over	even × ever	old
see	must	should
new	too	same × some
down	much	right
made	used	think
first	our	small
now	good	take
water	long	still
very × s/c ever every	day	off
also	before	find
did	go	place
make	came	help differing?
each	years × year	different × differ?"
way	work	away IDK
called	use	world
just	any	food
little	man	looked × Look
back	things	us
after	went	here
get	look	found
through	well	house

B

ELMS
Essential Literacy Measurement System
Test of Reading Effectiveness and Efficiency

1. plains Plain	0	2. gauzy goes?	0
3. stretched stretch	0	4. trounce trouble?	0
5. hammer	1	6. razor	1
7. wonderful wonder s/c	1	8. unreasonable un-reason?	0
9. location Lock? IDK	0	10. various versus? virus?	0

Total Score: 3

FIGURE 3.7. Lian's Sight Word Checklist and ELMS Test of Reading Effectiveness and Efficiency results. *Note.* IDK = "I don't know"; s/c = a self-correction of an error; X = an incorrect response; . . . = a pause; ? = use of a rising tone indicating a lack of confidence. Neither assessment is real, and the level of the words is not necessarily appropriate for third-grade students. It is given strictly as an example.

Current Data

Lian's third-grade teacher administered the school's sight-word checklist test (designed by the school, not designed for wide use) and found she did well. In fourth grade, her teacher also administered the ELMS Test of Reading Effectiveness and Efficiency (TREE). Her scores on both tests are below.

Activity Questions

1. Why might Lian perform better on the sight-word test than the TREE?

   ANSWER: Lian seems to be reading words mostly by sight. Most of her errors on the third-grade list involve substituting a more common word for the one on the test. The ELMS TREE test has less-common words, and she replaces these with more familiar ones.

2. What syllable-based strategy might help Lian?

   ANSWER: The teacher should begin with a flexible syllable-based strategy or reading parts by analogy. An advantage of a flexible division strategy is that it will give Lian a simple routine she can apply to all unfamiliar words. The teacher might also teach her both the long and short pronunciations of single-letter vowels. The advantage of an analogical strategy is that it allows Lian to analyze words carefully so she does not make errors associated with inattention to the pronunciations of the letters. Syllable division is not yet recommended. She does not have strength with syllable-based strategies, but it would be good to start with a less intensive strategy first.

3. What do Lian's errors on the words *different*, *years*, *looked*, *stretched*, and *unreasonable*—as well as her self-correction of *wonderful*—indicate about her difficulties?

   ANSWER: Lian is not consistently attending to all the morphemes in the words. In particular, she is not noticing the inflections (e.g., *-ed*) or derivational suffixes (e.g., *-ful*) in these words as parts she can use to read the words more easily.

4. What morpheme-based strategy might help Lian?

   ANSWER: Peeling off and affix learning could both work well. One advantage of peeling off is that Lian can find a known word at the core of the polymorphemic word. Finding a known word might be good for Lian because she already tends to focus on meanings. It will be a good complement to her syllable-based instruction. Advantages of affix learning are that it (a) involves teaching more affixes more quickly and (b) places more emphasis on the meaning of words containing the affixes. Both of these features can be beneficial for students in the upper-elementary and middle school grades who have greater capacity for learning affixes and need to learn word meanings. Overall, Lian might benefit from peeling off more because she makes many errors with simple affixes, and those errors involve inattention to the parts of the words rather than the meaning.

ACKNOWLEDGMENTS

Funding for Cheryl P. Lyon and Shannon L. Kelley was provided by the Office of Special Education Programs, Grant H325D170074. The authors have no conflicts of interest to report.

REFERENCES

Archer, A. L. (1981). *Decoding of multisyllabic words by skill deficient fourth and fifth grade students.* Unpublished doctoral dissertation, University of Washington, Seattle.

Archer, A. L., Gleason, M. M., & Vachon, V. L. (2000). *REWARDS: Reading excellence: Word attack and rate development strategies.* Longmont, CO: Sopris West.

Archer, A. L., Gleason, M. M., & Vachon, V. L. (2003). Decoding and fluency: Foundation skills for struggling older readers. *Learning Disability Quarterly, 26*(2), 89–101.

Baumann, J. F., Edwards, E. C., Font, G., Tereshinksi, C. A., Kame'enui, E. J., & Olejnik, S. (2002). Teaching morphemic and contextual analysis to fifth-grade students. *Reading Research Quarterly, 37*(2), 150–176.

Berninger, V., Nagy, W., Carlisle, J., Thomson, J., Hoffer, D., Abbott, S., et al. (2003). Effective treatment for children with dyslexia in grades 4–6: Behavioral and brain evidence. In B. R. Foorman (Ed.), *Preventing and remediating reading difficulties: Bringing science to scale* (pp. 381–417). Baltimore: York.

Bhattacharya, A. (2020). Syllabic versus morphemic analyses: Teaching multisyllabic word reading to older struggling readers. *Journal of Adolescent and Adult Literacy, 63*(5), 491–497.

Bhattacharya, A., & Ehri, L. C. (2004). Graphosyllabic analysis helps adolescent struggling readers read and spell words. *Journal of Learning Disabilities, 37*(4), 331–348.

Bowers, P. N., & Kirby, J. R. (2010). Effects of morphological instruction on vocabulary acquisition. *Reading and Writing: An Interdisciplinary Journal, 23*(5), 515–537.

Bowers, P. N., Kirby, J. R., & Deacon, S. H. (2010). The effects of morphological instruction on literacy skills: A systematic review of the literature. *Review of Educational Research, 80*(2), 144–179.

Carlisle, J. F., & Stone, C. A. (2005) Exploring the role of morphemes in word reading. *Reading Research Quarterly, 40*(4), 428–449.

Chetail, F., & Content, A. (2014). What is the difference between OASIS and OPERA? Roughly five pixels: Orthographic structure biases the perceived length of letter strings. *Psychological Science, 25*(1), 243–249.

Crosson, A. C., & McKeown, M. G. (2016). How effectively do middle school learners use roots to infer the meaning of unfamiliar words? *Cognition and Instruction, 34*(2), 148–171.

Crosson, A. C., McKeown, M. G., Moore, D. W., & Ye, F. (2018). Extending the bounds of morphology instruction: Teaching Latin roots facilitates academic word learning for English learner adolescents. *Reading and Writing, 32*(3), 689–727.

Cunningham, P. (1979). A compare/contrast theory of mediated word identification. *The Reading Teacher, 32*, 774–778.

Elbro, C., & Arnbak, E. (1996). The role of morpheme recognition and morphological awareness in dyslexia. *Annals of Dyslexia, 46*(1), 209–240.

Elbro, C., de Jong, P. F., Houter, D., & Nielsen, A.-M. (2012). From spelling pronunciation to lexical access: A second step in word decoding? *Scientific Studies of Reading, 16*, 341–359.

Fallon, K. A., & Katz, L. A. (2020). Structured literacy intervention for students with dyslexia: Focus on growing morphological skills. *Language, Speech, and Hearing Services in Schools, 51*(2), 336–344.

Gilbert, J. K., Goodwin, A. P., Compton, D. L., & Kearns, D. M. (2013). Multisyllabic word reading as a moderator of morphological awareness and reading comprehension. *Journal of Learning Disabilities, 47*(1), 34–43.

Goodwin, A., Lipsky, M., & Ahn, S. (2012). Word detectives: Using units of meaning to support literacy. *Reading Teacher Journal, 65*(7), 461–470.

Goodwin, A. P., & Ahn, S. (2010). A meta-analysis of morphological interventions: Effects on literacy achievement of children with literacy difficulties. *Annals of Dyslex*ia, *60*(2), 183–208.

Goodwin, A. P., & Ahn, S. (2013). A meta-analysis of morphological interventions in English: Effects on literacy outcomes for school-age children. *Scientific Studies of Reading, 17*(4), 257–285.

Goodwin, A. P., Gilbert, J. K., & Cho, S. J. (2013). Morphological contributions to adolescent word reading: An item response approach. *Reading Research Quarterly, 48*(1), 39–60.

Henry, M. K. (2019). Morphemes matter: A framework for instruction. *Perspectives on Language and Literacy, 45*(2), 23–26.

Kearns, D. M. (2015). How elementary age children read polysyllabic polymorphemic words. *Journal of Educational Psychology, 107*(2), 364–390.

Kearns, D. M. (2020). Does English have useful syllable division patterns? *Reading Research Quarterly, 55*(1), S145–S160.

Kearns, D. M., Rogers, H. J., Al Ghanem, R., & Koriakin, T. (2016). Semantic and phonological ability to adjust recoding: A unique correlate of word reading skill? *Scientific Studies of Reading, 20*, 455–470.

Kearns, D. M., Steacy, L. M., Compton, D. L., Gilbert, J. K., Goodwin, A. P., Cho, E., et al. (2016). Modeling polymorphemic word recognition: Exploring differences among children with early-emerging and late-emerging word reading difficulty. *Journal of Learning Disabilities, 49*(4), 368–394.

Kearns, D. M., & Whaley, V. M. (2019). Helping students with dyslexia read long words: Using syllables and morphemes. *Teaching Exceptional Children, 51*(3), 212–225.

Kim, J. S., Hemphill, L., Troyer, M., Thomson, J. M., Jones, S. M., LaRusso, M. D., et al. (2017). Engaging struggling adolescent readers to improve reading skills. *Reading Research Quarterly, 52*(3), 357–382.

Kuo, L., & Anderson, R. C. (2006) Morphological awareness and learning to read: A cross-language perspective. *Educational Psychologist, 41*(3), 161–180.

Lenz, B. K., & Hughes, C. A. (1990). A word identification strategy for adolescents with learning disabilities. *Journal of Learning Disabilities, 23*(3), 149–158.

Lovett, M. W., Frijters, J. C., Wolf, M., Steinbach, K. A., Sevcik, R. A., & Morris, R. D. (2017). Early intervention for children at risk for reading disabilities: The impact of grade at intervention and individual differences on intervention outcomes. *Journal of Educational Psychology, 109*(7), 889–914.

Lovett, M. W., Lacerenza, L., & Borden, S. L. (2000). Putting struggling readers on the PHAST track: A program to integrate phonological and strategy-based remedial reading instruction and maximize outcomes. *Journal of Learning Disabilities, 33*(5), 458–476.

Lovett, M. W., Lacerenza, L., De Palma, M., & Frijters, J. C. (2012). Evaluating the efficacy of remediation for struggling readers in high school. *Journal of Learning Disabilities, 45*(2), 151–169.

Lovett, M. W., Lacerenza, L., Steinbach, K. A., & De Palma, M. (2014). Development and evaluation of a research-based intervention program for children and adolescents with reading disabilities. *Perspectives on Language and Literacy, 40*(3), 21–31.

Muncer, S. J., & Knight, D. C. (2012). The bigram trough hypothesis and the syllable number effect in lexical decision. *Quarterly Journal of Experimental Psychology, 65*(11), 2221–2230.

O'Connor, R. E. (2014). *Teaching word recognition: Effective strategies for students with learning difficulties* (2nd ed.). New York: Guilford Press.

O'Connor, R. E., Beach, K. D., Sanchez, V. M., Bocian, K. M., & Flynn, L. J. (2015). Building BRIDGES: A design experiment to improve reading and United States history knowledge of poor readers in eighth grade. *Exceptional Children, 81*(4), 399–425.

O'Connor, R. E., Sanchez, V., Beach, K. D., & Bocian, K. M. (2017). Special education teachers integrating reading with eighth grade US history content. *Learning Disabilities Research and Practice, 32*(2), 99–111.

Reed, D. K. (2008). A synthesis of morphology interventions and effects on reading outcomes for students in grades K–12. *Learning Disabilities Research and Practice, 23*(1), 36–49.

Shefelbine, J. (1990). A syllabic-unit approach to teaching decoding of polysyllabic words to fourth- and sixth-grade disabled readers. In J. Zutell & S. McCormick (Eds.), *Literacy theory and research: Analysis from multiple paradigms* (pp. 223–230). Chicago: National Reading Conference.

Shefelbine, J., Lipscomb, L., & Hern, A. (1989). Variables associated with second, fourth, and sixth grade students' ability to identify polysyllabic words. In S. McCormick & J. Zutell (Eds.), *Cognitive and social perspectives for literacy research and instruction* (pp. 145–149). Chicago: National Reading Conference.

Siegel, L. S. (2008). Morphological awareness skills of English language learners and children with dyslexia. *Topics in Language Disorders, 28*(1), 15–27.

Stanovich, K. E., & Siegel, L. S. (1994). Phenotypic performance profile of children with reading disabilities: A regression-based test of the phonological-core variable-difference model. *Journal of Educational Psychology, 86*(1), 24–53.

Steacy, L. M., Wade-Woolley, L., Rueckl, J. G., Pugh, K. R., Elliott, J. D., & Compton, D. L. (2019). The role of set for variability in irregular word reading: Word and child predictors in typically developing readers and students at-risk for reading disabilities. *Scientific Studies of Reading, 23*(6), 523–532.

Taft, M., & Kougious, P. (2004). The processing of morpheme-like units in monomorphemic words. *Brain and Language, 90*(1–3), 9–16.

Toste, J. R., Williams, K. J., & Capin, P. (2017). Reading big words: Instructional practices to promote multisyllabic word reading fluency. *Intervention in school and clinic, 52*(5), 270–278.

Tunmer, W. E., & Chapman, J. W. (2012). Does set for variability mediate the influence of vocabulary knowledge on the development of word recognition skills? *Scientific Studies of Reading, 16*, 122–140.

Tyler, A., & Nagy, W. (1987). *The acquisition of English derivational morphology* [Technical Report No. 407]. Urbana: Illinois University, Urbana, Center for the Study of Reading.

Wade-Woolley, L., & Heggie, L. (2015). Implicit knowledge of word stress and derivational morphology guides skilled readers' decoding of multisyllabic words. *Scientific Studies of Reading, 19*(1), 21–30.

White, T. G., Sowell, J., & Yanagihara, A. (1989). Teaching elementary students to use word-part clues. *Reading Teacher, 42*(4), 302–308.

Zuck, L. V. (1974). Some questions about the teaching of syllabication rules. *Reading Teacher, 27*(6), 583–588.

CHAPTER 4

Structured Language Interventions for Spelling

Louisa C. Moats

LEARNING TO SPELL IS DIFFICULT!

Learning to spell is more difficult than learning to read. This is true for many typical learners, as well as students with dyslexia and language-learning disorders. Nevertheless, spelling is often treated as an afterthought in education, a skill that every student should be able to master because it seems "only" to involve memorizing a string of letters. Paradoxically, in spite of the number of students who struggle with spelling, language arts standards and curricula seldom treat spelling as a serious subject deserving of instructional time and expertise. Spelling practice may be limited to rote memorization of Monday's list of arbitrarily selected words followed by a spelling test on Friday. Failure to memorize the list may be interpreted as laziness or general inadequacy rather than a specific language-learning disability.

Spelling offers an opportunity to teach students about the structure of language. Reading and spelling are two sides of the same coin, each bolstered by awareness of the linguistic elements represented in print: phonemes, syllables, morphemes, and aspects of syntax. Learning to spell words supports accurate and fast recognition of those words during reading (Ouellette, Martin-Chang, & Rossi, 2017). Learning to spell, however, is harder than learning to read because spelling requires complete and accurate word memories. Reading words, in contrast, is possible even if word memories are not fully specified. That is why students with dyslexia may eventually learn to read many words they cannot spell.

The ability to spell is critical for expressing thoughts in writing (Graham, 1999; Graham et al., 2012). When students struggle with spelling, they often write fewer words, shorter sentences, and less complex ideas than they may be able to communicate orally. A poor speller's available attention during writing may be taxed simply by the effort of transcribing the words onto the page. Little attention is available for organizing thoughts, formulating sentences, or choosing precise words—especially if those words' spellings are unknown.

In this chapter, we explore why spelling can be so challenging and what can be done to help. On the way, we make as much sense of the English spelling system as we can, summarize the principles of intervention most likely to yield improvements, and explore some specific activities and teaching strategies consistent with a Structured Literacy (SL) approach.

PERSISTENT SPELLING DISABILITY: A CASE STUDY

In Table 4.1 are the spellings of a girl, JR, whom we followed in a private clinic between early second grade and mid-fifth grade. In spite of average intellectual ability (Full Scale IQ 97 on the Wechsler Intelligence Scales for Children—Revised [WISC-R; Wechsler, 1974]), this girl made very slow progress in both reading and spelling. On

TABLE 4.1. Spellings of a Girl with Reading and Spelling Disability on the WRAT Spelling Subtest over 3 Years

Given word	Test 1, grade 2.2	Test 2, grade 3.0	Test 3, grade 5.4
go	goo	go	go
cat	cat	cat	cat
in	in	on	in
boy	boy	boy	boy
and	ann	and	and
will	yel	wel	well
make	mac	make	mack
him	hme	hem	hem
say	ca	say	say
cut	cut	cut	cut
cook	coc	coc	cok
light	lot	lit	lite
must	must	must	nust
dress	jrs	bras	dres
reach	rek	reh	rech
order	ot	rnr	ordr
watch	yok	yoh	woch
enter	ntr	nt	netr
grown	gro	ron	gron
nature	nach	nar	nachr

Note. Accurate spellings are shaded.

each successive visit to the clinic, she took a lengthy series of tests, including the Wide Range Achievement Test (WRAT; Jastak, Jastak, & Bijou, 1965). Her spelling of the same words across time allowed us to observe slow growth in her spelling accuracy, as well as shifts in how she approached the task. Although she was about three grade levels behind by mid-fifth grade, we could observe gradual progress in how she thought about words. In addition, we made diagnostic inferences about the appropriate targets for instruction at each level. Her spelling attempts provide examples for our discussion of why, what, and how to teach spelling.

JR's very slow progress suggested that she experienced severe difficulties learning to spell words and learning the phoneme–grapheme correspondences and spelling patterns that are the foundation for orthographic learning. For example, even though she spelled *make* correctly in the second test, her third test showed she had not internalized that common long vowel spelling pattern. Her instruction was neither intensive enough nor focused on incremental development of the specific language skills necessary for spelling improvement to overcome these challenges. Her intervention program was focused on teaching reading but devoted very little time to spelling or writing instruction. Her case illustrates that reading remediation alone does not generalize to better spelling; JR needed explicit teaching, planned practice, and lots of review, in order to make better progress.

SPELLING: A WINDOW ON DEVELOPMENT OF UNDERLYING LANGUAGE SKILLS

Progression of Spelling Development

Spelling, the translation of words from speech to print, requires integrating information about several language systems and the way they are represented in English orthography: the phonemes and syllables in spoken words; the letters (graphemes) used to spell each phoneme; the conventions governing the spellings of sounds in specific positions in a syllable; other patterns or conventions of letter sequencing; morphology or the meaningful parts of words; and the grammatical role that a word plays in a sentence. Thus, learning to spell requires gradual consolidation of information about language systems that supports the formation of high-quality printed word memories (Adlof & Perfetti, 2014). Children's developing knowledge of these language layers can be observed from the very beginning of literacy development (Berninger, Abbott, Nagy, & Carlisle, 2010; Bourassa & Treiman, 2014; Treiman, 2017). Beyond learning the letters of the alphabet, how does that process work?

Phoneme Awareness

First, the learner must mentally analyze the sound sequence in a word and take the sounds of the word apart in order to represent each of them with a sequence of graphemes (letters or letter combinations that represent each sound). Our student, JR, in Test 1, did represent most of the phonemes in the one-syllable words, but she derived a spelling for /w/ from the letter name of *Y* and used the letter *K* to mark the final /ch/ in *watch* and *reach*. She spelled the sounds in *dress* logically, although her attempt does not look like standard spelling; the use of the letter *J* faithfully records an allophonic variation in the pronunciation of /d/ involving affrication or puckering of the mouth before /r/. The *-ess* rime in *dress* can be plausibly represented with the letter name *S*. Letter names were also the basis for spelling the long vowel sounds in *make, say,* and *reach*. At the first testing, JR demonstrated the ability to segment three phonemes in a spoken word but had not learned standard phoneme–grapheme correspondences for some consonants, some short vowels, or any long vowels. Words with more than one syllable were too challenging. Her strategy of deriving spellings from letter names was more typical of a 4- or 5-year-old than of a second grader.

Phoneme-Grapheme Correspondences

The next step for JR, after the first testing, would have been learning the most common graphemes for all of the consonant phonemes (including those spelled with digraphs—/th/, /sh/, /ch/, /wh/, /ng/), the short vowels, and the high-frequency long vowel patterns. However, she had made very little progress at the second evaluation, most likely from lack of appropriate instruction. She continued, for example, to use the letter name *H* to derive a spelling for /ch/ and did not know short *i,* short *e,* or standard ways of spelling long vowels. She had learned a few more words (*and, make, say*).

As words are read, practiced, and written, the brain increasingly recognizes many features of the print system, including redundant patterns or letter sequences, syllable structures, morphemes or meaningful parts, and which printed form belongs in a given context, such as *course* or *coarse, banned* or *band,* and *missed* or *mist*. JR's learning of those print patterns and when to use them was progressing very slowly.

Patterns and Generalizations in Letter Sequences and Letter Use

Words in English use certain graphemes to spell phonemes when they occur in the beginning or ending of a syllable or when they occur before or after other sounds and/or letters. For example, the letter *C* is used for /k/ before the letters *a, o,* and *u*; the letter *K* is used for /k/ before *e, i,* or *y*. The combination *CK* is used immediately after an accented short vowel. Good spellers may extract and internalize patterns like this with increasing exposure to written text. Poor spellers, however, usually do not, and must be taught them in a step-by-step, explicit manner.

At the third testing, JR had learned that *CK* comes after a vowel but had not learned what kind of vowel required that spelling for /k/. She had learned that a vowel–consonant–silent-*e* (VC*e*) pattern could possibly represent the long *i* in *light* but did not generalize that pattern to other long vowel words (*make, grown*). She did, for the first time, represent the second syllable in *order, enter,* and *nature* with a syllabic /r/, but did not apply the general principle in English that each written syllable requires a vowel letter. JR's reading was also about 2 years behind at this point, and lack of reading practice or print exposure, along with insufficient instruction, would have limited her brain's ability to recognize and extract some of these correspondence patterns.

Representation of Meaningful Parts of Words (Morphemes)

The words *grown* and *nature* each reflect the morphophonemic principle of English spelling: that it represents both sound and meaning. The words *grow* and *grown* are related in meaning, and that relationship distinguishes *grown* from *groan*. The word *nature* is related in meaning to other words that share the root *nat*, meaning to be born: *native, nativity, natural, nation*. The letters in *nature* do not directly represent the affricated /ch/ pronunciation of /t/ before /yu/. The word's spelling preserves the morpheme *nat* but does not reflect the word's pronunciation.

JR was still grappling with the base layers of representation in the writing system—sounds, sound–symbol correspondences, and position constraints governing when to use which grapheme—and was not yet using information about morphemes in her spelling attempts. She was struggling with every aspect of orthographic learning. In fifth grade, her instruction should have included explicit and intensive lessons in how to spell vowels, how the position constraints work, and how some common morphemes are written. Let's consider how such instruction should be carried out.

HOW AND WHAT TO TEACH: SPELLING IN SL

Designing Spelling Lessons

Older research on spelling instruction in the classroom established some basic parameters around effective teaching of this literacy component (Graham, 1999; Schlagal, 2002). Evidence supported the importance of organizing word lists by shared patterns that could be explained with reference to language structure. In addition, approximately 20 minutes, three times per week of teacher-led instruction was necessary for most students to progress. A pretest–study–posttest approach, in which students spent time learning the words they did not already know, got better results than a study-and-test approach in these reviews, because it helped both teachers and students focus on the words that needed more practice. Immediate feedback during practice sessions, especially when students participated in correcting their own writing, was helpful.

Research on teaching poorer spellers confirms that teachers' knowledge of language or familiarity with language structure is an important factor in how much the students will learn (McCutchen et al., 2002; Puliatte & Ehri, 2017). A knowledgeable teacher will have conceptualized a road map through the language system. He or she will teach concepts one element at a time in a cumulative fashion that follows a scope and sequence. The goal is to make sense of words by selectively referencing the factors that explain why a word is written the way it is. Then, a great deal of practice writing the target words in meaningful contexts is necessary for retention. Students cannot rely on spell-checkers in word processing until and unless their spelling is good enough to recognize a correct spelling alternative when it is presented.

A lesson or sequence of lessons should include the following steps. These steps are illustrated in greater detail in the chapter sections below.

1. Quick review of previously learned patterns or words, and pretest of the concept to be taught.
2. Oral language practice with phoneme, syllable, morpheme, and word identification; listening to spoken sounds, morphemes, or words; pronouncing the sounds and/or target words; and ensuring their meaning is understood.
3. Explanation of the spelling concept, correspondence, or pattern.
4. Guided practice analyzing words on a list and constructing them.
   a. Word building with manipulative grapheme tiles.
   b. Phoneme–grapheme mapping.
   c. Identifying correct and incorrect spellings of words being learned.
   d. Guided word sorting.
5. Practice, with immediate corrective feedback.
   a. Cloze passages—writing the words that will complete a passage.
   b. More word sorting.
   c. Constructing and writing sentences with words.
   d. Games—crossword, Magic Square, etc.
   e. Writing sentences or passages to dictation.
6. Test, provide corrective feedback, and reteach as necessary.

The Content of Lesson Components

Champion spellers know a lot about words, including their sounds, meanings, and (often) their language of origin. More challenged spellers will benefit from the same information, learned in smaller doses, in cumulative lessons, and with much more practice writing words singly and in sentences. Accordingly, the content of spelling instruction for both good and poor spellers should include (1) awareness of and identification of the consonant and vowel phonemes of English; (2) the most common phoneme–grapheme correspondences for spelling each of those sounds; (3) the most common position constraints governing phoneme–grapheme correspondences; (4) the concept of a morpheme, beginning with inflectional suffixes; (5) orthographic change rules for adding suffixes to words; (6) syllable spelling patterns and schwa; and (7) prefixes, roots, and derivational suffixes that mark a word's grammatical function. Of necessity, high-frequency, grammatical "glue" words must be taught as well, even though some have odd spellings.

Etymology, or the language from which a word came, often provides additional insight into why a word is spelled the way it is and should be referenced as appropriate. For example, *night* is from Old English, a Germanic language; *nocturnal* is from the word meaning "of the night" in Latin; and *astronomy* descends from Greek combining forms (*astro, nomy*), meaning the study of the stars.

Identification of Consonant and Vowel Phonemes

In printed word memory, graphemes are tethered to strings of phonemes. Phoneme sequences provide anchors for letters and letter groups that correspond to them.

Phoneme awareness includes not just segmentation of individual phonemes but differentiation of phonemes that share features or that are confusable because their place or manner of articulation is similar. Table 4.2 shows the consonant phonemes of English by place and manner of articulation, and Figure 4.1 lists the vowel phonemes in order of articulation (Moats, 2020; Moats & Tolman, 2019). Teachers can post and display this information on bulletin boards or their equivalent. In doing so, teachers help students conceptualize the inventory of speech sounds, model their pronunciation, and establish a point of reference for phoneme–grapheme correspondences.

Identifying a speech sound can include hearing it in isolation, saying it with attention to mouth formation or articulation, learning a key word that begins with that phoneme, and contrasting it with others with which it may be confused. For example, three pairs of stop consonants are distinguished by voicing /p/ and /b/, /t/ and /d/, and /k/ and /g/. Each voiceless stop is produced without vocal resonance and each has a voiced equivalent that is articulated the same way except that the vocal cords are engaged. Awareness of this difference is a prerequisite for distinguishing *back* from *bag* or *mob* from *mop*.

Phoneme segmentation and manipulation ability, or lack thereof, distinguishes good and poor spellers at all ages (Cassar, Treiman, Moats, Pollo, & Kessler, 2005;

TABLE 4.2. Consonant Phonemes of English by Place and Manner of Articulation

Place and manner	Lips together	Teeth on lower lip	Between the teeth	Tongue behind the teeth	Tongue against the palate	Tongue retracted, to velum	Glottal
				Stops			
Voiced	/b/			/d/		/g/	
Unvoiced	/p/			/t/		/k/	
				Nasals			
	/m/			/n/		/ng/	
				Fricatives			
Voiced		/v/	/th/	/z/	/zh/		
Unvoiced		/f/	/th/	/s/	/sh/		/h/
				Affricates			
Voiced					/j/		
Unvoiced					/ch/		
				Glides			
Voiced	/w/				/y/		
Unvoiced	/wh/						
				Liquids			
				/l/	/r/		

/ē/												
eagle	/ĭ/					[ə]					/ū/	/yū/
	itch	/ā/				*America*				/o͝o/	*ooze*	*use*
		ape	/ĕ/						/ō/	*book*		
			echo	/ă/				/aw/	*open*			
				apple	/ī/		/ŭ/	*audio*				
					idol	/ŏ/	*up*					
						octopus						
/oi/	/ou/								/er/	/ar/	/or/	
oyster	*ouch*								*earth*	*art*	*orca*	

FIGURE 4.1. Vowel phonemes of English, by place and manner of articulation, with example words. *Note:* Schwa (ə) is technically not a phoneme but an allophone or variation of other vowels when they are indistinct and unstressed. It is also called the neutral vowel or empty vowel.

Kilpatrick, 2015). Children may strengthen their phonemic awareness by placing a chip into a box for each speech sound in a word, saying each sound as the chip is moved, or stretching out a finger for each sound that is articulated. Once students can segment words with three phonemes successfully, they can start moving grapheme tiles into the boxes. Again, it is important to put *graphemes* that correspond to single phonemes, even though they may be more than one letter (i.e., *ng, ll, oy,* and *tch*), on these movable tiles.

Letter Names

As they are learning the phonemes, children should also learn the letter names if they do not already know them (Adams, 2013). Many letter names contain the phoneme that they usually represent. Others, such as *w, y,* and *h,* do not and are more difficult. Teaching the 26 letter forms, by linking each letter name, sound, and written form together in an association routine is important, but other phonemes that are represented by more than one letter should also be taught in the phoneme awareness portion of a lesson (/th/, /sh/, /ng/, /ch/, /oi/, /au/, etc.). Thus, teaching letter names, letter formation, *and* phonemes may be three parallel strands in beginners' lessons that will come together as soon as students can identify most letters and can segment and pronounce single or beginning phonemes.

Phoneme–Grapheme Correspondences

Explicit phoneme–grapheme mapping (Ehri, 2014; Grace, 2007; Moats & Tolman, 2019) requires the learner to match the letters or letter combinations in a word to the speech sounds they represent. (See Moats, 2020, for specific phoneme–grapheme correspondences in English.) Again, in the English orthographic code, letters and letter groups can represent each speech sound or phoneme in the word.

The learner must pay attention to the internal details of both speech and print in order to map phoneme–grapheme relationships. A grapheme, which is any letter or letter combination that represents a single phoneme, has value only as it functions in correspondence with speech. Thus, the letter *u* represents the central vowels in *put* and *pun,* but it represents /w/ in *quick* and marks the separation of *g* and *e* in *guest.*

One approach to building awareness of print to speech mapping is to use a simple grid, wherein each box of the grid represents a phoneme. Using a list of words that contain the correspondence or pattern being taught, students explicitly segment each word, grapheme-by-grapheme. The teacher says the word, and then the students repeat it, segment the sounds, and write the grapheme for each phoneme in sequence. For example, *throne* spells the long *o* with the separated two-letter grapheme *o_e,* and begins with a consonant blend containing a digraph. Note that a consonant blend is two phonemes, not one, and a consonant digraph is two letters representing one phoneme. Four boxes are needed to map *throne*. The silent-*e* does not get a box.

To map the word grove, the student would use four boxes because there are four phonemes: /g/ /r/ /o/ /v/. Two boxes are needed for the *gr* blend and one box for the vowel *o_e*. The final *-ve* goes in one box. The job of *e* is not only to mark the vowel but also to prevent the word from ending in *v*.

Phoneme–grapheme mapping is fundamental at any grade level but is especially helpful with second- and third-grade students who have gaps in learning the basic code. It should be a teacher-led activity (not an independent activity) because its value is in consciously analyzing how print is representing speech in a teacher-directed dialogue. Figure 4.2 illustrates a lesson on phoneme–grapheme mapping with the silent-*e* vowel pattern (see Form 4.1 at the end of the chapter for a blank template of this activity).

Orthographic Patterns and Position Constraints

English orthography has a number of conventions governing the way letters can be sequenced and used. For example, only some letters can be doubled: *k, h,* and *i,* for example, cannot. Words never end in the letters *j* or *v*. The letter *c* spells /k/ before *o, a,* and *u,* and introduces initial blends, as in *clean* and *crown*. The combination *-ck* occurs right after a stressed short vowel. This and other position-based spellings can be found in Table 4.3.

Good spellers may intuit these and other patterns after seeing many examples in print, but most students—especially those with spelling difficulties—benefit from

This activity should be preceded by explanation and modeling of the silent-*e* vowel pattern, changing *hat* to *hate, tub* to *tube, quit* to *quite, rod* to *rode, bit* to *bite,* and *plan* to *plane.* Long vowels and short vowels should be identified on the vowel sound chart in Figure 4.1.

Read the pattern words in the left column. Say the vowel sound in each word. Say the final sound in each word. Underline the letter(s) that represents the vowel sound in each word. Then, map each word's spelling to its sounds, using the grid. Segment the sounds in each word to decide how many boxes you need for each word. Remember, one box is for one phoneme or speech sound. The first two words have been done for you.

rode	r	o	d(e)	
bite	b	i	t(e)	
tape	t	a	p(e)	
tube	t	u	b(e)	
Pete	P	e	t(e)	
quite	q	u	i	t(e)
globe	g	l	o	b(e)
snake	s	n	a	k(e)
flute	f	l	u	t(e)
these	th	e	s(e)	

This activity is followed by many other activities that involve analyzing the words, writing the words in sentences, and identifying the vowel sound in long and short vowel words.

FIGURE 4.2. Phoneme–grapheme mapping with the silent-*e* (VCe) vowel patterns.

explicit instruction paired with guided word sorting. For example, instead of telling students how the letters *k* and *c* and *ck* are used to represent /k/, give them a list of words with those three graphemes. See whether students can discover the pattern. Usually, this process must be directed closely by teacher questions, such as "What letter comes immediately before (or after) the spelling for /k/?" Consciously processing and describing the patterns at work helps students establish higher-quality mental images for the words. An example of a word sort is in Figure 4.3 (see Form 4.2 at the end of the chapter for a blank template of this activity).

Inflectional Suffixes

Inflections (*-ed, -s, -es, -ing, -er, -est,* which are also called grammatical suffixes) are morphemes that change the number, person, or tense of the word to which they are added, and thus its meaning, but they do not change its part of speech. Inflections should be introduced early because they are so essential for writing basic sentences, but they must be practiced year after year for students to internalize the awareness necessary for spelling.

The spelling errors in intermediate students' writings frequently involve inflections, especially *-ed* and plural *-s* and *-es* (Moats, Foorman, & Taylor, 2006). These "simple" endings "hide" at the ends of spoken words. If students speak a nonmainstream dialect, they may also be omitting these endings altogether in their speech, so learning to spell them is doubly challenging (Gatlin-Nash, Johnson, & Lee-James, 2020). In the case of both the past tense and plural, pronunciation does not match the written form and pronunciation varies according to the last sound of the word to which each ending

TABLE 4.3. Examples of Position-Based Spelling Patterns

Phonemes	Graphemes	Position-based spelling principle or generalization
/f/ /l/ /s/ /z/ at the ends of one-syllable words	*ff, ll, ss, zz*	The "floss" rule: When a one-syllable word ends in /f/, /l/, /s/, and sometimes /z/, double the *f, l, s,* or *z*. Examples: *shell, fluff, mass, buzz*
/ch/	*ch, -tch*	When /ch/ comes right after a stressed short vowel, use *-tch*. Examples: *batch, blotch, fetch, Dutch, pitch* Exceptions: *which, such, much, rich, sandwich*
/j/	*j, -ge, -dge*	The letter *J* never ends a word. When /j/ comes right after a stressed short vowel, use *-dge*. Examples: *badge, dodge, wedge, ridge, fudge* Use *-ge* if the vowel is unstressed, as in *village, college,* and *stoppage*.
/ng/	*ng, n*	When /ng/ ends a word, use *ng*. When /ng/ immediately precedes /k/ or /g/, use the letter *N*. Examples: *rang, song, hung; clank, honk, chunk, language, sinkable*
/k/	*c, k, -ck, q(u)*	Use the letter *C* before *o, a,* and *u*. Use the letter *K* before *e, i,* or *y*. Use *-ck* right after a stressed short vowel. Use *qu-* if the word begins with /k/ /w/. Examples: *cat, coat, cut; kite, keg, Kyle; stack, deck, pluck, frock, wick; quite, quack, question, queen*
/ā/	*ai, ay*	*Ai* is used for long *a* in the middle of a word. *Ay* is used at the ends of words. Examples: *bait, bay; gait, gain, gay; paid, pain, pay; afraid, refrain, fray; maid, main, may; jail, jay* Oddity: *said, say*
/oi/	*oi, oy*	*Oi* is used for the diphthong /oi/ in the middle of a word, and *oy* is used at the ends of words. Examples: *toil, toy; boil, boy; avoid, ahoy, join, joy*

Read the words. Underline the letter(s) that represent /k/ in each word. Then, sort the words by the spelling for /k/. When you have finished the sort, answer the questions.

candy	speak	black	kitchen	kite	case	clean	deck	oak
flick	kettle	copper	milk	crown	ketch	coat	stock	jerk
truck	Kyle	spunk	cute	cup	cloak	speck	Kym	

Beginning *c*	Beginning *k*	Ending *ck*	Ending *k*
candy	*kitchen*	*black*	*speak*
case	*kite*	*deck*	*oak*
copper	*kettle*	*flick*	*milk*
coat	*ketch*	*stock*	*jerk*
cute	*Kyle*	*truck*	*spunk*
cup	*Kym*	*speck*	*cloak*
clean			
crown			

When *c* spells /k/ in the beginning of a word, what letters come after *c*? (Answer: *o, a, u,* or another consonant.)

When *k* spells /k/ in the beginning of word, what letters come after *k*? (Answer: *e, i,* or *y*.)

When *-ck* spells /k/ at the end of a word, what kind of vowel sounds precede (come before) it? (Answer: A stressed short vowel spelled with a single vowel letter.)

When *k* spells /k/ at the end of a word, what sounds come before it? (Answer: A consonant or a vowel spelled with a vowel team.)

Can you add a word to each column?

FIGURE 4.3. Word sort activity, spellings for /k/.

is added. Without phonemic and morphemic awareness, students will miss the important changes of meaning that inflections signify.

Consider the details that must be explained and understood for students to become consciously aware of these morphemes. The suffix *-ed* has three pronunciations: /d/ as in *hummed,* /t/ as in *puffed,* and /id/ as in *wanted.* Only the last form is a syllable that matches the spelling. The other two are voiced (/d/) and voiceless (/t/) single consonants in speech that in turn are added to words ending in voiced sounds (*pinned, paved*) or voiceless sounds (*kissed, puffed*).

A step-by-step approach that constantly pairs spoken words with print is necessary to shed light on this complexity. An example of a word sort designed to teach the past tense is in Figure 4.4 (see Form 4.3 at the end of the chapter for a blank template of this activity).

Orthographic Change Rules

There are three suffix addition rules in English orthography that never fail to challenge all spellers, and especially poor spellers. We double certain final consonants when vowel suffixes are added to words (*running, hopped*), we drop silent *e* at the ends of words when we add suffixes beginning with vowels (*hoping, smiled*), and we change *y* to *i* when any suffix is added to a word except one that begins with the letter *i* (*studies, merrily*). These rules must be tackled because they are so commonly used. If possible,

To show the past tense, we add *-ed* to regular verbs. The past tense *-ed* has three pronunciations: /t/ as in *kissed,* /d/ as in *pulled,* and /id/ as in *wanted.* Read the pattern words. Write the base word or main part of the word in the first column in the table. Write the word with the past tense added in the second column. Write the sound of *-ed* in the right hand or third column. Let's do them together.

drifted smelled planted clenched scratched crunched

thrilled ended cracked planned flubbed quacked

Main or base word	Word with past tense	/t/, /d/, or /id/
drift	drifted	/id/
smell	smelled	/d/
plant	planted	/id/
clench	clenched	/t/
scratch	scratched	/t/
crunch	crunched	/t/
thrill	thrilled	/d/
end	ended	/id/
crack	cracked	/t/
plan	planned	/d/
flub	flubbed	/d/
quack	quacked	/t/

FIGURE 4.4. Introducing the past tense *-ed*. This activity is adapted from Hooper and Moats (2011), *Primary Spelling by Pattern,* Level 2, pages 38–39.

familiarize students with inflected forms that do not change the base word (*mended, punted, huffed, misses, killer, bringing*) before introducing the change rules one at a time. Start by decomposing familiar words with inflections by taking off the ending and finding the base word: *hoping* = *hope* + ing, *studious* = *study* + ous, *committed* = *commit* + ed. Then start combining base words and endings. (For more details about these rules and how to teach them, see Carreker, 2018; Moats, 2020; Moats & Tolman, 2019.)

Table 4.4 summarizes the rules for adding suffixes to base words.

Multisyllable Words and Schwa

Knowledge of the six basic written syllable types (for a listing, see Carreker, 2018; Moats, 2020) can support spelling, although learning these patterns should be a stepping-stone toward the understanding and use of morphology. Familiarity with the open, closed, and consonant–*le* written syllable types enables spellers to know when and why double consonants occur in words that end with a consonant–*le* syllable. When an open syllable is combined with a consonant–*le* syllable—as in *noble, title,* and *maple*—there is no doubled consonant. In contrast, when a closed syllable is combined with a consonant–*le* syllable—as in *dabble, little,* and *topple*—a double consonant results. Note that this is purely a convention of writing, not a transcription of speech. We do not pronounce two separate /p/ consonants in the middle of words like *apple.*

TABLE 4.4. Orthographic Change Rules for Adding Endings

Name of rule	Word examples	Features of the rule
Consonant doubling rule	*spinning, wettest, sparring, humming, topper*	When a one-syllable word with one vowel letter ends in one consonant, double the final consonant before adding a suffix that begins with a vowel (such as *est, er, ing, ish*). Do not double if the suffix begins with a consonant (*ment, less, ful, ness,* etc.).
Drop silent-*e* rule	*confining, smoking, yoked, faker*	When a root or base ends in silent-*e,* drop the *e* when adding a suffix that begins with a vowel. Do not drop the *e* when adding a suffix beginning with a consonant.
Change *y* to *i* rule	*study, studied, studying; bounty, bountiful; prettier, prettiest; monkeying*	When a word ends in -*y* preceded by a consonant, change the *y* to *i* before any suffix, except suffixes that begin with *i.* Do not change -*y* if it is part of a vowel team (*ey, ay, oy*).
Advanced doubling	*conferring, excelled, compelled; opening, worshiper*	When a word has more than one syllable, double the final consonant when adding a suffix beginning with a vowel if the final syllable is accented or stressed, and is spelled with one vowel and one final consonant.

TABLE 4.5. Words to Introduce Schwa

Final syllables	Initial syllables
wag + on	*at + tend*
cir + cus	*of + fend*
trum + pet	*re + duce*
king + dom	*sup + pose*
cap + tain	*ef + fect*

Multisyllable words bring up the unavoidable problem of schwa (/ə/), the unaccented vowel sound that has been emptied of its identity and can be described as a lazy vowel. Teach children that some vowel sounds have the stuffing taken out of them when they are unstressed. After students spell a word, such as *prob-lem, a-dept,* or *com-mit,* they can say the word naturally and mark the syllable that has a schwa. Instruction about schwa helps students understand why some words do not sound the way they are spelled—and reminds teachers not to rely exclusively on "spell it by sounding it out," because that strategy is limited with multisyllable words. Examples of words that can be used to introduce schwa are in Table 4.5.

A helpful activity for students who do not identify separate syllables in longer words reliably is to dictate a word slowly and ask the student to write one syllable at a time on a mason board, sticky note, or flash card. Then, the word can be synthesized and written as a whole. Note that syllable boundaries and morpheme boundaries often differ, and when syllables are the focus, students may not simultaneously recognize morphemes (e.g., *trans-port-a-(t)ion*). Be clear about the level of language analysis that is expected in the activity. Figure 4.5 illustrates dictation of multisyllabic words (see Form 4.4 at the end of the chapter for a blank template of this activity).

Using index cards, sticky notes, or Masonite boards, the student writes dictated syllables one at a time. The teacher supports as necessary, helping the student remember the correct letters in each syllable. In this type of activity, morpheme boundaries (*pro-duc-tive* vs. *pro-duct-ive*) may not be relevant because they are not obvious in speech. Ask the student to say the word syllable-by-syllable and then as a whole word before writing it again.

1	2	3	4	Word
noc	tur	nal		nocturnal
fan	tas	tic		fantastic
in	ter	nal	ize	internalize
pro	duc	tive		productive

FIGURE 4.5. Dictation of multisyllable words, one syllable at a time.

Latin-Based and Greek-Based Prefixes, Suffixes, and Roots

Having already learned the common inflectional endings, students should be ready to move on to Anglo Saxon and Latin prefixes (i.e., *pre-, sub-, re-, mis-,* and *un-*) and suffixes (i.e., *-en, -ly, -y, -ful, -less,* and *-ness*; Henry, 2018). Prefixes and suffixes have stable spellings and meanings. Derivational suffixes—such as *-ly, -al, -ment,* and *-ous*—also signify the part of speech of the word to which they are added. The stability of morpheme spellings assists with their recognition and recall, even though the meaning of a word may not simply be the sum of its parts (e.g., *apartment* and *matchless*).

Knowledge of morphemes facilitates spelling, reading, vocabulary acquisition, and general reading comprehension (Carlisle & Goodwin, 2014). Researchers have analyzed academic English to catalogue the most common morphemes that, if taught explicitly, are most likely to benefit literacy acquisition in general (Lane, Gutlohn, & van Dijk, 2019). Instruction should begin with the most transparent and consistently spelled prefixes, roots, and suffixes. See Table 4.6 for the types of morphemes derived from each base language of English: Anglo Saxon, Latin, and Greek.

If words sharing derivation from specific root morphemes are taught together, students can learn to think of the meanings of words as they are spelling them and use knowledge of a base or other related form to figure out how a word is probably spelled. For example, *part* and *partial, magic* and *magician,* and *confuse* and *confusion* retain the spelling of the base word even though the pronunciation of the last syllable obscures that relationship. Ambiguous vowels can be recovered in groups of meaning-related words, such as *compete, competition, competitive; confide, confidence, confidential; resign, resignation;* and *express, expression, expressivity.* Commonly misspelled words, such as *different* and *family,* can be taught in relation to *differ* and *familial,* where the often-omitted, unaccented second syllable becomes audible.

An abbreviated spelling scope and sequence for regular correspondences, position-based patterns, syllable types, and basic morphemes can be found in Table 4.7. It can be used to estimate the relative difficulty of specific concepts, to select instructional goals for students, and to judge what to expect of students at a given grade or skill level.

TABLE 4.6. Historical Layers of Language in English and Common Morpheme Types Associated with Each

Anglo Saxon	Compounds (*yellowtail, blackbird*)
	Inflectional suffixes (*-ed, -s, -ing, -er, -est*)
	Suffixes (*-hood, -ward, -en*)
Latin	Prefixes (*ad-, re-, in-, sub-, pre-*)
	Roots (*dict, ject, vers, fer, port*)
	Derivational suffixes (*-ion, -ive, -ity, -ous, -ful*)
	Latin plurals (*datum, data; alumni, alumnae*)
Greek	Combining forms (*tele, bio, phone, graph, (o)logy*)
	Plurals (*parenthesis, parentheses*)

TABLE 4.7. Abbreviated Scope and Sequence for Spelling Instruction

Grade level	1	2	3	4	5	6
Beginning consonants	*b, c, d, f, g, h, j, k, l, m, n, p, r, s, t, v, w, y, z*	*qu*	Soft *c* and *g* (*cent, gent*)			
Ending consonants	*b, d, g, m, n, p, t*	*x, ng; ff, ll, ss, zz; -ck*				
Beginning blends		*bl, cl, fl, gl, pl, sl; br, cr, dr, fr, gr, pr, tr; sc, sk, sm, sn, sp, st, sw*	*scr, spr, spl, str, squ*		*sch, sph*	
Ending blends		*mp, nd, ft, lt, nt, lf, st, nk*				
Digraphs		*ch, sh, th, ng, wh*	*ph, ch/tch*	Greek *ch* (*chorus*)		
Silent letters			*wr, kn, gn*			
Short and long vowels	Short *i, e, a, o, u*	VC*e* *a-e, o-e, i-e, u-e, e-e*	Jobs of *y* *y* as in *cry*, *y* as in *baby*		*y* for short *i* in Greek-based words	
Vowel teams		*ai, ay, ee, oa, ea, oi, ou*	*eigh, ough*; au, aw, oo, ew	*ie* and *ei*		
Vowel-*r*		*er, ar, or, ir, ur*	*air, are, ear, eer*	Homophones *for/fore/four; our/hour; pare/pear*; etc.		
Open/closed syllables		Concept of closed- and open-syllable types	Schwa in two-syllable words			
Other syllable juncture		Compound words; syllable identification	Divide and combine closed, open, and *cle* syllables	Divide and combine VCCV and VCV words		
Prefixes		*un, re, in*	*pre, dis, mis, ex, in, trans, non*	*con, per, com, a, ad, tri, bi, quad*	*inter, semi, super, sub, multi*	*bi, mal, bene, circum, ultra, auto; in/il/ir/im*
Inflectional suffixes	*ing, s, -es, ed* with no change in base	*ed, er, est*, with the doubling rule and the drop silent-*e* rule	All ending rules, including change *y* to *i*	Irregular plurals and past tense		Advanced doubling rule for stressed/unstressed final syllables
Latin/Greek roots			*port, form, struct*	*duc/duc; spec/spect; rupt, graph*	*nat, script, dict, ject, photo*	*aqua, anni, nym, phon, derm*
Derivational suffixes		*-ly, -y, ish, en, -ful*	*-ness, less, -ment, er/or*	*-ion, -age, -ive, -ic*	*-ous, -ian, able, -ible, -al, -ism, -ology*	*-ence, -ance, -ent, -ture*
Contractions		*I'm, he's, she's, it's*	*we'll, aren't, I've*	*they're, we're you're*		

High-Frequency Words with Less Predictable or Odd Spellings

Because they are often very old words from Anglo Saxon whose pronunciation—but not spelling—has changed, high-frequency words may have more odd or irregular correspondences than lower-frequency content words with a Latin or other romance-language base. Often called "sight words," these words (*of, said, your, do, does,* etc.) are not, in fact, learned by sight or by a rote visual memory process. Evidence for this fact is simply that shorter words, such as *of,* are misspelled more often than some regularly spelled, longer words in the written work of students with dyslexia (Moats, 1996), and if word learning simply involved memory for strings of letters, then shorter words should be easier. Memory for all words is mediated through the phonological and orthographic systems, wired into the language centers of the brain, and when speech and print do not match up as expected, remembering involves extra mental work. The student must recall associations that are unusual or nonconforming to general patterns in the language, so there are fewer mental "hooks" to hang the word on.

Although it may seem counterintuitive, the foundational skills of phoneme awareness and phoneme–grapheme matching also facilitate learning the less common or odd words (Kilpatrick, 2015; Treiman, 2017)—that is, students who are good spellers of predictable words are also better at spelling less predictable words. Irregular words are learned most easily by students who already know common phoneme–grapheme correspondences and who can explicitly analyze the speech-to-print mapping system. This is because irregular words have some regular correspondences, and also because a good speller makes mental comparisons between what a spelling ought to be and what it is (*of* sounds like it should be *uv*) to form a detailed mental image of the word. Awareness of phoneme–grapheme correspondences, regular and irregular, is the "glue that holds the word in memory" (Ehri, 2004, p. 155). The close correlation between the ability to spell regular and so-called irregular words led to a major publisher abandoning two separate word lists from the Test of Written Spelling (Larsen, Hammill, & Moats, 2013) and combining them into one.

Some suggested methods for teaching words with less common patterns or correspondences include (1) grouping words with some memorable similarity (*two, twice, twenty, twilight, twin; one, only, once; their, heir; where, here, there*), (2) calling attention to the odd part of a word (*friend, any*), (3) pronouncing the word the way it looks (*was* sounds like /w/ /ă/ /s/, not /w/ /ŭ/ /z/), (4) using mnemonics (there is *a rat* in *separate*; the *principal* is my *pal*), and (5) asking the learner to pay very close attention to the letter sequence by visualizing it and building it backward and forward with letter tiles before saying and writing it.

Homophones

Homophones are words that have the same sound but different spellings and meanings. Some of the most commonly misspelled are *your, you're; their, they're, there; to, too, two;* and *its, it's*. Examples of other words that sound the same but differ in meaning include *course* and *coarse, knight* and *night,* and *prophet* and *profit*. Poor spellers may practice these for months before remembering which is which, and even then, homophone confusion is one of the most common spelling problems exhibited by students with dyslexia and other language-based learning disabilities. Therefore, a kind and understanding teacher will select and practice only those few homophone pairs that are essential for a student to remember and encourage use of a spell-checker to complement explicit instruction.

Strategies that may be helpful include learning each spelling of a homophone in the context of a phrase or sentence, embedding spellings in pictures that convey their meaning, or, when appropriate, having the student concoct a strategy for remembering each spelling. It's important to tackle these one or two at a time and to practice them repeatedly in short, distributed, recall activities.

Avoid These Practices

Finally, avoid telling students that English is just crazy. Do not have them mindlessly write each word 10 times in a list. Do not make students take spelling tests unless you know they will succeed.

SUMMARY

Teaching spelling according to the principles of SL means teaching words with reference to the structure of language at all levels, including phonology, phoneme–grapheme correspondences, orthographic patterns and constraints, and meaningful parts of words (morphemes) and their grammatical roles. Students remember best what they have thought about and understand, so the goal is to make sense of print and how it represents speech (King, 2000). This done, all of the other SL components and practices together can rescue struggling students and help them to become competent readers and writers.

APPLICATION ACTIVITIES

Activity 1

This 12-year-old girl has scored in the superior range of verbal comprehension ability on earlier testing. She was slow to learn to read but, after private tutoring, is now at grade level in reading comprehension. Her school district determined that she is not eligible for special services. Figure 4.6 is an excerpt from an uncorrected writing assignment, modified to guard the individual's identity.

1. Would you say that the student is representing most of the sounds in words? What does that observation suggest about her phoneme awareness?

   ANSWER: The student does represent most of the speech sounds in words. Phoneme awareness does not need to be a major focus of her lessons.

What happend out there askt my older bother. I relly don't Know I said. Ovcours I did Know. I have had those imaoges for a cople months now. It achully started on my B-day. I don't want to worry my family so I don't tell them. Well whatever happends we might have to tack a few more lessons says my mom who pops up from the computer. Why is it the day she actuly whatch me I do terabule.

FIGURE 4.6. Writing sample, Activity 1.

2. With what level of morphology is the student having difficulty?

   ANSWER: The student has not yet internalized recognition and spelling of inflectional suffixes. She is spelling the past tense (*happened, asked*) phonetically. She omits the tense marker *-es* on *watches.*

3. How would you design spelling lessons to address these gaps in her processing of language?

   ANSWER: Focus on identifying, listening for, understanding, and writing inflectional suffixes in dictated sentences; rehearse spelling of high-frequency words, such as *of course*; begin inflectional morphology instruction so that she learns to think of words such as *actually* as related to *act* and *actual,* and words such as *terrible* as related to *terror.*

Activity 2

This 8-year-old student had been recently enrolled in a day school program specializing in treatment of dyslexia when he produced this writing sample (see Figure 4.7).

1. Which inflectional suffix does the student need to learn to spell?

   ANSWER: The *-ing* marker on the present tense.

2. Which short vowel sound does the student seem to have mastered?

   ANSWER: Short *a* words are accurately spelled, and a few other short vowels are also correct.

3. Which high-frequency words would you prioritize next for dictation practice?

   ANSWER: *One, was, and,* and *of,* because they are among the most often used words in writing.

4. Which letters is this student having trouble forming? What additional instruction does he need with letter formation?

   ANSWER: Lower-case letters *b, d, p, l, t,* and others. Using upper-case seems to be a strategy to avoid possible confusion of *d* and *b.*

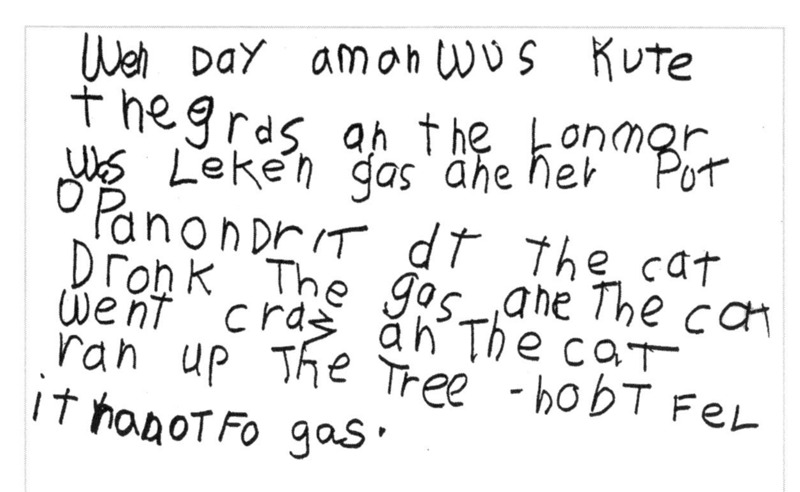

Translation: One day a man was cutting the grass and the lawn mower was leaking gas and he put a pan under it but the cat drank the gas and the cat went crazy and the cat ran up the tree—but fell it ran out of gas.

FIGURE 4.7. Writing sample, Activity 2.

5. Where in a spelling scope and sequence do you believe this student should be working?

   ANSWER: Continued practice with short vowel, single-syllable words with single consonants, consonant digraphs, and consonant blends.

Activity 3

This girl had been in first grade only a few weeks. She scored in the "somewhat at-risk" range on the district's early screening and was then given a spelling inventory to help determine where her instruction should focus (see Figure 4.8).

1. Which of the speech sounds in words can the student represent reliably?

   ANSWER: In general, the initial consonant and some final consonants.

2. Why would the student write so many extra letters that do not correspond to sounds?

   ANSWER: She realizes that words are generally of a certain length. She is aware of some features of written language, such as the doubling of *t*, as she supplies "filler" letters.

3. Does the student need to improve her letter formation? In what way?

   ANSWER: She needs explicit instruction in upper- and lower-case letters, as well as when to use each.

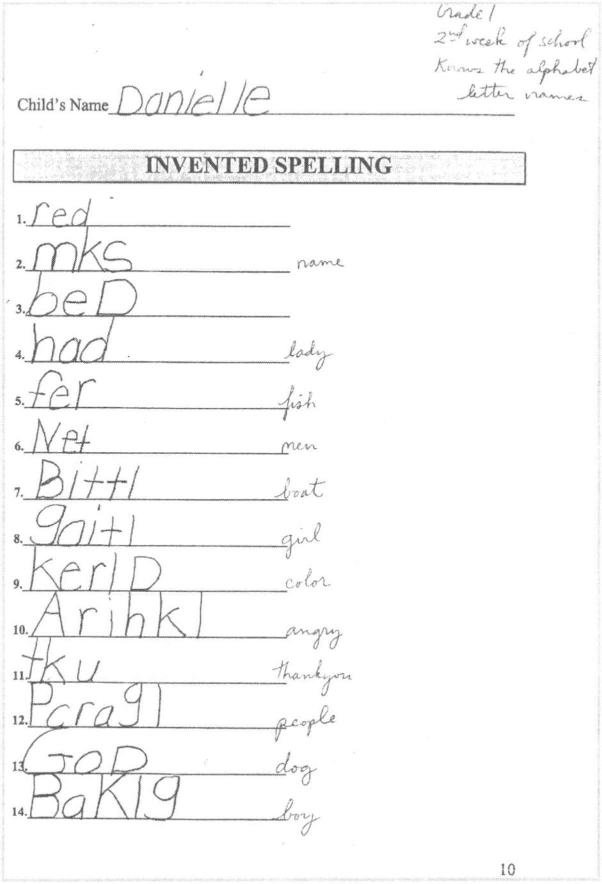

Grade 1
2nd week of school
Knows the alphabet
letter names

Child's Name Danielle

INVENTED SPELLING

1. red
2. mks name
3. beD
4. had lady
5. fer fish
6. Net men
7. Bittl boat
8. 9ait l girl
9. KerlD color
10. Arihkl angry
11. tKu thankyou
12. Pcra9l people
13. GOD dog
14. BaKl9 boy

10

FIGURE 4.8. Spelling inventory, Activity 3.

4. What would be the next targets for spelling instruction?

   ANSWER: Segmentation, identification, and correct sequencing of all phonemes in three-phoneme words; spelling of one-syllable words with short vowels; and spelling of consonant digraphs *sh, th,* and *ch* in one-syllable words.

5. Describe at least one kind of appropriate practice activity for this student.

   ANSWER: Using sound boxes and grapheme tiles, have the student construct dictated short vowel words sound-by-sound, and then write them. Write simple, dictated sentences using a few of the pattern words and learned high-frequency words.

REFERENCES

Adams, M. J. (2013). *ABC foundations for young children: A classroom curriculum*. Baltimore: Brookes.

Adlof, S. M., & Perfetti, C. A. (2014). Individual differences in word learning and reading ability.

In C. A. Stone, E. R. Silliman, B. J. Ehren, & G. P. Wallach (Eds.), *Handbook of language and literacy: Development and disorders* (2nd ed., pp. 246–264). New York: Guilford Press.

Berninger, V., Abbott, R., Nagy, W., & Carlisle, J. (2010). Growth in phonological, orthographic, and morphological awareness in grades 1 to 6. *Journal of Psycholinguistic Research, 39,* 141–163.

Bourassa, D. C., & Treiman, R. (2014). Spelling development and disability in English. In C. A. Stone, E. R. Silliman, B. J. Ehren, & G. P. Wallach (Eds.), *Handbook of language and literacy: Development and disorders* (2nd ed., pp. 569–583). New York: Guilford Press.

Carlisle, J. F., & Goodwin, A. P. (2014). Morphemes matter: How morphological knowledge contributes to reading and writing. In C. A. Stone, E. R. Silliman, B. J. Ehren, & G. P. Wallach (Eds.), *Handbook of language and literacy: Development and disorders* (2nd ed., pp. 265–282). New York: Guilford Press.

Carreker, S. (2018). Teaching spelling. In J. Birsh & S. Carreker (Eds.), *Multisensory teaching of basic language skills* (4th ed., pp. 389–430). Baltimore: Brookes.

Cassar, M., Treiman, R., Moats, L., Pollo, T. C., & Kessler, B. (2005). How do the spellings of children with dyslexia compare with those of nondyslexic children? *Reading and Writing, 18,* 27–49.

Ehri, L. C. (2004). Teaching phonemic awareness and phonics: An explanation of the National Reading Panel meta-analysis. In P. McCardle & V. Chhabra (Eds.), *The voice of evidence in reading research* (pp. 153–186). Baltimore: Brookes.

Ehri, L. C. (2014). Orthographic mapping in the acquisition of sight word reading, spelling memory, and vocabulary learning. *Scientific Studies of Reading, 18,* 5–21.

Gatlin-Nash, B., Johnson, L., & Lee-James, R. (2020, summer). Linguistic differences and learning to read for nonmainstream dialect speakers. *Perspectives on Language and Literacy,* 28–35.

Grace, K. (2007). *Phonics and spelling through phoneme–grapheme mapping.* Longmont, CO: Cambium Learning Sopris.

Graham, S. (1999). Handwriting and spelling instruction for students with learning disabilities: A review. *Learning Disability Quarterly, 22,* 78–98.

Graham, S., Bollinger, A., Booth Olson, C., D'Aoust, C., MacArthur, C., McCutchen, D., et al. (2012). Teaching elementary school students to be effective writers: A practice guide [NCEE 2012-4058]. Washington, DC: National Center for Education Evaluation and Regional Assistance, Institute of Education Sciences, U.S. Department of Education. Retrieved from *http://ies.ed.gov/ncee/wwc/publications_reviews.aspx#pubsearch*

Henry, M. (2018). The history and structure of written English. In J. Birsh & S. Carreker (Eds.), *Multisensory teaching of basic language skills* (4th ed., pp. 540–555). Baltimore: Brookes.

Hooper, B., & Moats, L. C. (2011). *Primary spelling by pattern, level 2.* Dallas: Cambium Learning Sopris.

Jastak, J. F., Jastak, S. R., & Bijou, S. W. (1965). *Wide Range Achievement Test, Revised.* Wilmington, DE: Guidance Associates.

Kilpatrick, D. A. (2015). *Essentials of assessing, preventing, and overcoming reading difficulties.* Hoboken, NJ: Wiley.

King, D. (2000). *English isn't crazy: The elements of our language and how to teach them.* Austin, TX: Pro-Ed.

Lane, H. B., Gutlohn, L., & van Dijk, W. (2019). Morpheme frequency in academic words: Identifying high-utility morphemes for instruction. *Literacy Research and Instruction, 58*(3), 184–209.

Larsen, S. C., Hammill, D. D., & Moats, L. C. (2013). *Test of Written Spelling* (5th ed.). Austin, TX: Pro-Ed.

McCutchen, D., Abbott, R. D., Green, L. B., Beretvas, S. N., Cox, S., Potter, N. S., et al. (2002).

Beginning literacy: Links among teacher knowledge, teacher practice, and student learning. *Journal of Learning Disabilities, 35*(1), 69–86.

Moats, L. C. (1996). Phonological errors in the spelling of dyslexic adolescents. *Reading and Writing: An Interdisciplinary Journal, 8*(1), 105–119.

Moats, L. C. (2020). *Speech to print: Language essentials for teachers* (3rd ed.). Baltimore: Brookes.

Moats, L. C., Foorman, B. R., & Taylor, P. (2006). How quality of writing instruction impacts high-risk fourth graders' writing. *Reading and Writing: An Interdisciplinary Journal, 19,* 363–391.

Moats, L. C., & Tolman, C. (2019). *LETRS: Language essentials for teachers of reading and spelling* (3rd ed.). Dallas, TX: Voyager Sopris Learning.

Ouellette, G., Martin-Chang, S., & Rossi, M. (2017). Learning from our mistakes: Improvements in spelling lead to gains in reading speed. *Scientific Studies of Reading, 21,* 350–357.

Puliatte, A., & Ehri, L. (2017). Do 2nd and 3rd grade teachers' linguistic knowledge and instructional practices predict spelling gains in weaker spellers? *Reading and Writing: An Interdisciplinary Journal, 31*(2), 239–266.

Schlagal, B. (2002). Classroom spelling instruction: History, research and practice. *Reading Research and Instruction, 42*(1), 44–57.

Treiman, R. (2017). Learning to spell words: Findings, theories, and issues. *Scientific Studies of Reading, 21,* 265–276.

Wechsler, D. (1974). *Manual for the Wechsler Intelligence Scale for Children—Revised.* New York: Psychological Corporation.

FORM 4.1. Phoneme–Grapheme Mapping with the Silent-*e* (VC*e*) Vowel Patterns

This activity should be preceded by explanation and modeling of the silent-*e* vowel pattern, changing *hat* to *hate, tub* to *tube, quit* to *quite, rod* to *rode, bit* to *bite,* and *plan* to *plane*. Long vowels and short vowels should be identified on the vowel sound chart in Figure 4.1.

Read the pattern words in the left column. Say the vowel sound in each word. Say the final sound in each word. Underline the letter(s) that represents the vowel sound in each word. Then, map each word's spelling to its sounds, using the grid. Segment the sounds in each word to decide how many boxes you need for each word. Remember, one box is for one phoneme or speech sound. The first two words have been done for you.

rode	r	o	d(e)	
bite	b	i	t(e)	
tape				
tube				
Pete				
quite				
globe				
snake				
flute				
these				

FORM 4.2. Word Sort Exercise, Spellings for /k/

Read the words. Underline the letter(s) that represent /k/ in each word. Then, sort the words by the spelling for /k/. The first four words have been done for you. When you have finished the sort, answer the questions.

candy	speak	black	kitchen	kite	case	clean	deck	oak
flick	kettle	copper	milk	crown	ketch	coat	stock	jerk
truck	Kyle	spunk	cute	cup	cloak	speck	Kym	

Beginning *c*	Beginning *k*	Ending *ck*	Ending *k*
candy	*kitchen*	*black*	*speak*

When *c* spells /k/ in the beginning of a word, what letters come after *c*? ____________________

When *k* spells /k/ in the beginning of word, what letters come after *k*? ____________________

When -*ck* spells /k/ at the end of a word, what kind of vowel sounds precede (come before) it?

____

When *k* spells /k/ at the end of a word, what sounds come before it? ____________________

Can you add a word to each column?

FORM 4.3. Introducing the Past Tense *-ed*

To show the past tense, we add *-ed* to regular verbs. The past tense *-ed* has three pronunciations: /t/ as in *kissed,* /d/ as in *pulled,* and /id/ as in *wanted.* Read the pattern words. Write the base word or main part of the word in the first column in the table. Write the word with the past tense added in the second column. Write the sound of *-ed* in the right hand or third column. The first two words have been done for you. Let's do them together.

drifted smelled planted clenched scratched crunched

thrilled ended cracked planned flubbed quacked

Main or base word	Word with past tense	/t/, /d/, or /id/
drift	*drifted*	/id/
smell	*smelled*	/d/

This activity is adapted from Hooper and Moats (2011), *Primary Spelling by Pattern,* Level 2, pages 38–39.

FORM 4.4. Dictation of Multisyllable Words, One Syllable at a Time

Using index cards, sticky notes, or Masonite boards, the student writes dictated syllables one at a time. The teacher supports as necessary, helping the student remember the correct letters in each syllable. In this type of activity, morpheme boundaries (*pro-duc-tive* vs. *pro-duct-ive*) may not be relevant because they are not obvious in speech. Ask the student to say the word syllable-by-syllable and then as a whole word before writing it again.

1	2	3	4	Word

CHAPTER 5

Structured Literacy Interventions for Reading Fluency

Roxanne F. Hudson
Erin Munce Anderson
Melissa McGraw
Rebecca Ray
Alison Wilhelm

With a quick shuffle and a tap of her papers on the reading table, Ms. Kay ponders her students' most recent scores on the district-required oral reading fluency (ORF) tests. Most of her students did well and several even surpassed her expectations. However, she cannot stop thinking about Celia and Josh. Both students demonstrated a low reading rate and accuracy on the test, but show very different levels of skill in everyday classroom instruction. Ms. Kay asks herself, "How can they be so different, yet score the same?"

Josh's score was quite a surprise! "But he seems completely on track, loves books, and knows so much about space," she thought. "Maybe this score is a fluke?" Ms. Kay looked back at her records, and to her chagrin, Josh's scores have just skirted the benchmark on the last two screening administrations. Reflecting back, Ms. Kay recalls that Josh often selects nonfiction books in his topics of interest, like science, and when he approaches difficult vocabulary, he uses his content knowledge to guess unknown words. His frequent guessing, misreading, and repeating cause him to stall or stutter, but eventually, he builds phrases that "work" with the text. His phrasing is choppy and uneven, and he rarely pauses for punctuation. He doesn't seem to be thinking about meaning while he is reading and just says each word. His love of picture books and science vocabulary had disguised his struggle with fluency.

On the other hand, Celia's score aligned with Ms. Kay's observations in the classroom. During one-to-one reading, Celia's reading is slow and laborious.

She can read accurately, but it takes her a long time to sound out each word. Ms. Kay decided to do some more assessment to determine just where the issue seemed to be. While Celia knew all of the letter sounds, she was slow, scoring only 40 correct sounds per minute, well below the 60 needed for quick decoding in text. Celia was accurate when reading nonsense words, but very slow there, too. Ms. Kay knows that Celia treasures their time at the reading table and is eager to make progress in reading. She is determined to figure out a strategy that helps Celia improve her automaticity, but is unsure of what to do next.

Ms. Kay has taught second grade for 3 years, and she has already exhausted all of her knowledge of effective practices for teaching reading. She knows her students need more intensive instruction, but differentiating at such extreme levels seems insurmountable. Second grade is drawing to a close, and she knows that without intervention, Josh and Celia will be left behind in the upper grades. Setting herself to task, she thinks, "Clearly, my Tier One instruction isn't working for Josh and Celia. What should I do now?"

ELEMENTS OF READING FLUENCY

Teaching students to become proficient readers may be one of the most important instructional tasks for teachers like Ms. Kay (Mayer, 2004). One of the critical components of proficient reading is developing fluency in one's reading (Adams, 1990; Fuchs, Fuchs, Hosp, & Jenkins, 2001). Reading fluency is complex and multifaceted and involves a student's ability to translate text into spoken language in an effortless manner (Fuchs et al., 2001; Hudson, Torgesen, Lane, & Turner, 2012). It involves a plethora of applied skills, including reading words "by sight" while simultaneously constructing meaning from the text (Samuels, 2006). Fluency is often measured by the number of words read correctly in 1 minute (Shinn, Knutson, Good, Tilly, & Collins, 1992). Fluent readers are able to accurately decode text automatically and for long periods of time, even after periods of no practice, and are able to generalize skills across a variety of texts, unlike Josh from above. While difficulties with fluent reading may come from problems with comprehension, this chapter primarily focuses on children whose fluency problems are based at least partly in word reading. It does not address children who have highly accurate and automatic decoding skills but who read slowly only because they are struggling to comprehend.

Reading fluency consists of three key elements: *accurate* reading of connected text at a conversational *rate* with appropriate *prosody* or expression (National Reading Panel, 2000; see Figure 5.1).

Accuracy

Accuracy is one of the key elements in reading words fluently and includes a student's ability to recognize and decode words correctly. A fluent reader possesses a solid grasp

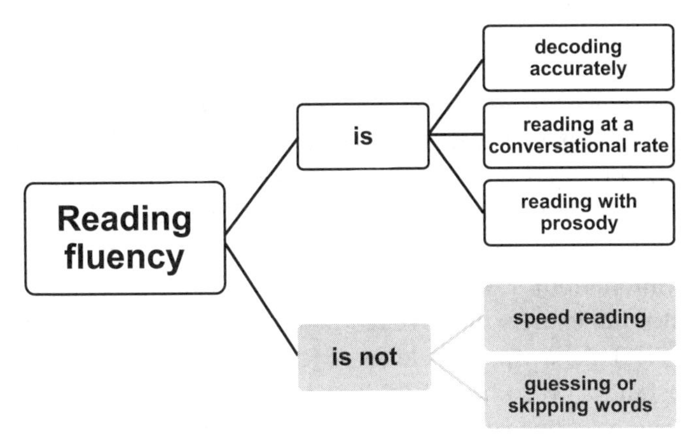

FIGURE 5.1. Elements of reading fluency.

of the alphabetic principle, knows a large number of high-frequency words, and demonstrates the ability to blend sounds together (Ehri & McCormick, 1998). When readers follow a common strategy of guessing or skipping challenging and unfamiliar words, it impacts their word-reading accuracy, leading to their inability to understand the author's purpose and/or to interpret the text. Accurate word recognition is an important element of fluency—however, it is not the only element necessary for fluent reading (National Reading Panel, 2000).

Automaticity

Automaticity is another key element in fluent reading and includes a student's ability to read a great number of words automatically and without conscious effort (Kuhn, Schwanenflugel, & Meisinger, 2010; La Berge & Samuels, 1974). When students are able to automatically read text without consciously having to think about decoding, it opens up their ability to focus on the meaning of the text (Adams, 1990; Kuhn et al., 2010).

When further investigating automaticity at the letter level, students should be able to quickly and effortlessly identify letter sounds. Slow access to identifying letter sounds leads to disrupted decoding accuracy and fluency (Hudson et al., 2012). However, automaticity at the letter level is insufficient. Students must also become automatic at the word level. At this level, students are able to quickly and effortlessly identify words "by sight" (Ehri & McCormick, 1998), reducing their cognitive load and allowing additional resources to be devoted to comprehension (La Berge & Samuels, 1974). The final level is automaticity at the text level. Here, a student is able to read connected text at a fluid pace with expression and good phrasing. They reflect some of the meaning of the text in their voice as they read. Often when students have reached this level of automaticity, their rate of reading is measured in words read correctly per minute (WCPM), which is an important measure of reading proficiency (Fuchs & Fuchs, 1992; Fuchs et al., 2001).

Prosody

The third and final key element of reading fluency is *prosody*, which is a linguistic term for the sounds of speech that convey meaning across multiple words, such as a rising tone at the end of a question or indicating sarcasm through one's tone when saying, "This is fun" (Miller & Schwanenflugel, 2008; Schwanenflugel, Hamilton, Kuhn, Wisenbaker, & Stahl, 2004). The prosodic features of reading fluency include the rise and fall of pitch (intonation), stress patterns (syllable prominence), and duration (length of time) that contribute to an expressive reading of a text (Dowhower, 1991; Kuhn et al., 2010; Schreiber, 1991). As a student's level of reading fluency increases, they begin to demonstrate substantial prosodic variability and are able to make prosodic distinctions to match the meaning of the text (Schwanenflugel & Benjamin, 2016). In other words, as fluency skills increase, a student's pauses in sentences become fewer in number as well as shorter and less variable (Benjamin & Schwanenflugel, 2010; Kuhn et al., 2010; Miller & Schwanenflugel, 2008).

Students' prosody sounds like their speaking voices—if they speak with little prosody, then one would expect them to read with a flat tone. If they speak English with an accent due to where and when they learned it, then one would expect them to read with one. Overall, prosodic reading provides evidence that the reader understands what is being read. Reading prosody and reading comprehension seem to have a reciprocal relationship where they affect each other (Breznitz, 2006). Though research continues to develop in this area, we do know that measurements of prosody from simple texts do not seem to contribute much to reading comprehension (Schwanenflugel et al., 2004)—however, prosody within more complex texts predicts reading comprehension skills (e.g., Benjamin & Schwanenflugel, 2010). It appears that having a proficient level of reading prosody is independently related to good reading comprehension and might thus be an important area of focus for fluency instruction for some students. Attention to prosody might also be helpful in combination with intervention in other areas, including accuracy of text reading or comprehension development, depending on individual students' needs.

It is important for teachers to consider the whole picture when assessing their students and to use diagnostic assessments to determine their strengths and areas for growth. In reading fluency, this means that all three aspects of reading are important to assess: accuracy, rate (automaticity), and prosody. In order for Ms. Kay to effectively plan for Josh's and Celia's reading fluency interventions, she needs to determine the most appropriate next steps by assessing their reading fluency in each element.

ASSESSMENT FOR INTERVENTION IN READING FLUENCY

Assessment of reading fluency provides a good overall estimate of students' reading proficiency, especially in the elementary grades, and is a strong predictor of reading comprehension success (Fuchs & Fuchs, 1992). ORF assessment gives teachers the information necessary to make appropriate decisions regarding a student's instructional text level, monitor their responsiveness to instruction, and identify those who may require additional interventions (Fuchs et al., 2001). Effective fluency assessments provide teachers like Ms. Kay with information about a student's current performance and helps guide them in choosing appropriate and impactful interventions.

Assessing Accuracy

Measurement of students' word-reading accuracy can take numerous forms. Simply listening to oral reading and counting the number of errors per 100 words can provide invaluable information for the selection of appropriate text for various instructional purposes for an individual or group of students. Through careful examination of error patterns during a student's oral text reading, a teacher can determine which strategies the student is using and which strategies the student is failing to use. For example, observation of a student's attempts to figure out an unknown word might yield evidence of which letter sounds the student knows, how well they can blend them together, and what the student does when they make a mistake (i.e., try to self-correct or keep reading). These observations can provide information about decoding skills needing further instruction designed to improve word-reading accuracy.

Assessing Rate

The most frequent measure of reading rate is ORF, which is a part of curriculum-based measurement (CBM) and measures a reader's rate and accuracy in connected text (Deno, Marston, Shinn, & Tindal, 1983; Fuch & Fuchs, 1992). To conduct ORF CBM, the teacher listens to a student read aloud from an unpracticed, grade-level or instructional-level passage. The teacher notes any errors the student makes. At the end of 1 minute, the number of errors is subtracted from the total number of words read. The score is expressed as WCPM. The WCPM can be compared to a normed table (Hasbrouck & Tindal, 2017) and be used to create goals and establish an appropriate instructional level. Using a table like that of Hasbrouck and Tindal is important because expectations for rate vary by grade level. For example, a first grader reading 41 WCPM in text written at the middle of a first-grade level meets and even exceeds expectations for rate, while a third grader reading at that rate would be well below grade expectations. Accuracy of reading should also be considered. Teachers should aim for 91–95% accuracy at the instructional level and 96% or above accuracy at the independent level. In addition, it is important to note that factors such as a reader's background knowledge about text content may affect rate and overall fluency of reading in a specific passage.

If students do not demonstrate ORF at the appropriate level, then additional assessment is needed to determine where the issues lie. Like other screeners, such as body temperature or blood pressure, a low ORF score indicates only that there is potentially a problem, not where the problem lies or whether there indeed is an issue. Additional assessment of students' automaticity in high-frequency words, in decoding nonsense words, and in letter sounds is needed to determine where the breakdown is occurring and where intervention will be most effective. If a student has difficulty with isolated letter sounds, then practice in reading connected text will not address the underlying problem and can lead to frustration and lack of progress. In addition to ORF, prosody is also important to assess.

Assessing Prosody

Assessing prosody requires teachers to listen to the pitch, stress, and duration with which students read a connected text. Determining these specific features of speech can be challenging to assess in reliable and efficient ways (Dowhower, 1991). However, it is still important that teachers assess their students' prosody of reading. One method that teachers have used to reliably measure their students' reading prosody is a rating scale or rubric. General ideas of what to listen for can be found in Table 5.1. A more descriptive scale can be found in the CORE *Teaching Reading Sourcebook* (Honig, Diamond, & Gutlohn, 2018, p. 334).

RESEARCH ON EFFECTIVE READING FLUENCY INTERVENTIONS

Elementary-Age Students and Effective Reading Fluency Interventions

Most of the research on reading fluency instruction and intervention has been done with elementary-age children, although research on effective interventions for secondary students is increasing (e.g., Powell & Gadke, 2018). Repeated reading is the method for improving reading fluency that has the best evidence to support it (Samuels, 1979; Strickland, Boon, & Spencer, 2013).

Meta-analyses are methods used to analyze a body of research to determine the relative effectiveness or strength of individual elements of an instructional method or intervention. They yield effect sizes (ES), which are estimates of the type of improvement one might expect from the intervention. Anything above 0.8 is considered large and anything below 0.2 is considered small. There have been several meta-analyses of

TABLE 5.1. Informal Assessment of Phrasing Prosody

Level 1 (beginner)	Phrasing is slow and choppy. Excessive pauses after each word or at unnatural places. No variation in punctuation cues and does not stop at the end of each sentence. (more than 10 errors)
Level 2 (novice)	Student follows end of sentence cues with varying success. Attempting phrases within sentences with some success. Expression is not evident or minimal. (5–10 errors)
Level 3 (intermediate)	Student correctly pauses at the end of sentences, but struggles with within-sentence phrasing. Sometimes odd or awkward in length. Some attention to punctuation differences and reads with some expression. (fewer than five errors)
Level 4 (mastery)	Reads naturally on unmarked texts with minimal errors. Sentence-level phrasing is accurate and demonstrates fluid prosody. Expression appropriately guided by context of the text. (fewer than three small errors)

reading fluency intervention in elementary school (Chard, Vaughn, & Tyler, 2002; Lee & Yoon, 2017; Morgan & Sideridis, 2006; National Reading Panel, 2000; Therrien, 2004). Some of these meta-analyses included research with students with learning disabilities and some did not. We try to clarify these distinctions when reporting results.

Looking at just repeated reading across these meta-analyses, it had a larger effect on the transfer of reading fluency among students with learning disabilities (ES = 0.79) than for students without disabilities (ES = 0.59) across elementary and secondary grades (Therrien, 2004), and had a large effect on the reading rate and accuracy of elementary students with reading disabilities (ES = 1.63; Lee & Yoon, 2017). As well, Lee and Yoon found that among elementary and secondary students with reading disabilities, listening to a preview of the text (ES = 1.95) was more effective than no listening preview. Among all types of readers, repeated reading with modeling from a recording is more effective than no preview at all, but not as effective as modeling from an adult (Chard et al., 2002; Shany & Biemiller, 1995), although Lee and Yoon did not find a significant difference between the two types of previews.

Across several studies focused on interventions with students with learning disabilities, providing corrective feedback after each reading was found to be particularly effective (Therrien, 2004), whereas Morgan and Sideridis (2006) found that goal setting and feedback were more effective than previewing, listening, and repeated reading across 30 single-case research studies focused on students at risk or with learning disabilities. Therrien (2004) found that when interventionists had students with and without learning disabilities read a passage until they reached a rate and accuracy criterion, it was much more effective in increasing reading fluency (ES = 1.70) than simply reading for a set number of times (ES = 1.38)—this is the type of repeated reading we focus on in this chapter.

Research with English Learners in Reading Fluency Instruction

The number of school-age students in the United States who are considered English learners (ELs) has grown significantly over the past decade (National Center for Education Statistics [NCES], 2017). Given this ever-growing population of students, it is likely that teachers like Ms. Kay will have students acquiring English in their classrooms at some point in their teaching careers. Though there is a considerable body of literature on effective instructional reading fluency practices for monolingual English-speaking students, there is less available research on this topic when focused on EL students. A review completed on approaches to reading instruction for EL students (August, McCardle, & Shanahan, 2014) found various instructional procedures were effective in developing their ORF. One study focusing on guided repeated oral readings found it to be an effective practice for EL students (VanWagenen, Williams, & McLaughlin, 1994). In addition, six studies found positive fluency results for EL students that were taught in small groups or one-on-one settings (Denton, Wexler, Vaughn, & Bryan, 2008; Gunn, Smolkowski, Biglan, & Black, 2002; Gunn, Smolkowski, Biglan, Black, & Blair, 2005; Kamps et al., 2007; VanWagenen et al., 1994). A great deal more research is needed on effective methods to develop reading fluency among those who are acquiring English.

In the meantime, a focus on vocabulary and exposure to print, along with repeated reading, is recommended (Francis, Kieffer, Lesaux, Rivera, & Rivera, 2006).

SL INSTRUCTION IN READING FLUENCY

Because reading fluency is a complex and multifaceted construct (Hudson, Pullen, Lane, & Torgesen, 2009; Hudson et al., 2012), instruction and intervention are also multifaceted. Careful diagnostic assessment helps teachers uncover the underlying aspects of reading leading to dysfluent reading: some focus on accuracy, some on automaticity, and others on prosody. This section discusses methods for addressing all three areas, as well as one popular method that is not effective in developing reading fluency.

Round Robin Reading

Before we begin to discuss instruction that can facilitate the development of fluent reading, we turn our attention to a common practice that has been found ineffective and should therefore be avoided. Round robin reading (RRR) continues to be a commonly used practice despite substantial evidence that it is ineffective. Ash, Kuh, and Walpole (2009) describe RRR as an approach to reading "in which students are called on in a predetermined order, usually following their current seating arrangement" (p. 88). This includes a family of practices with similar characteristics. For example, popcorn reading has students take turns reading aloud in a random order, while popsicle reading consists of teachers drawing students' names written on popsicle sticks to determine the next student to read aloud. Combat reading is a similar practice in which a student calls on the next reader, with the goal of identifying a peer who has been off task. All are variations of having students take turns reading small portions of material aloud in order to collectively read a text.

Why is this a problem? RRR limits students' reading practice due to limited opportunities to respond because the majority of the instructional time is spent listening to peers (Allington, 1980). In addition, RRR interferes with students' opportunities to independently solve challenging words because peers and teachers are likely to provide words for students before they are able to decode such words themselves (Allington, 1980). It also tends to ignore the need for corrective feedback. Finally, as demonstrated by reader reports and stories of trauma heard by all of the authors, as well as in research, this practice is often damaging to students' social/emotional well-being, with some students feeling reluctant to read aloud; other students feeling anxious, embarrassed, or unmotivated to read; and still others becoming disengaged because RRR moves along too slowly for their reading skill level (Sanden, 2018).

Interventions Focused on Accuracy

In general, the best candidates for fluency interventions are students with slow, accurate reading. Teachers with students who are not accurate and need decoding instruction must start there before other types of fluency intervention. Automaticity develops from repeated accurate practice. In order to accurately decode words, students need to be able to (1) identify letter sounds; (2) blend these sounds together to read words; (3) read phonograms (common patterns across words); and (4) use letter-sound and meaning cues to accurately determine the correct pronunciation and meaning of the word being used in the text, such as knowing how to correctly pronounce *bow* in a particular context. I stood on the *bow* of the ship versus my dog has a *bow* in its hair. See Al Otaiba, Allor, and Stewart, Chapter 2, and Kearns, Lyon, and Kelley, Chapter 3, this volume, for effective methods to teach decoding.

Intervention Focused on Automaticity: Timed Repeated Reading

As Ms. Kay reflects on Josh's and Celia's reading performance, she thinks that one possible intervention that could benefit both of them is timed repeated reading (TRR). TRR is an intervention designed to support the development of fluent reading with a focus on automaticity for slow, but accurate readers. TRR can be used to support fluency in reading letter sounds, words, or connected text, depending on the students' needs.

Similar to the use of ORF to assess a reader's rate and accuracy, TRR involves the use of a timer. However, it is different in several important ways. First, TRR is not intended as an assessment. Rather, the goal is to *improve* a student's ORF. Second, TRR is designed for use with students who have difficulty reading with fluency specifically, making it an inappropriate practice for many readers, but not all. Finally, students participating in TRR should be engaged with connected text at their instructional or independent reading levels and not grade-level text. It is particularly important that TRR not be used with readers who are already fluent. While it is very motivating to readers who are dysfluent, it can take the fun out of reading for those who are already automatic.

To provide sufficient practice with enough continuity, TRR should take place at least three times a week. It is important to provide students with practice on carefully selected materials at either the letter, word, or text level. Session lengths will vary depending on how many timings are done. Generally, sessions last between 5 and 15 minutes of sustained practice.

Materials

LETTER SOUNDS AND WORDS

If students are not automatic at naming letter sounds, meaning that they cannot name at least 60 correct letter sounds per minute with two or fewer mistakes, then automaticity building at the letter level is warranted. If teachers work on automaticity at this level, it is important that they also build automaticity at the word level by reading words with those letter sounds. An example of these materials can be found at *https://education.uw.edu/faculty-and-research/hudson/teaching-materials*. In addition, many students benefit from building automaticity in reading high-frequency words. It is not uncommon for a student to do three TRRs per session: one focused on letter sounds, one focused on words with those sounds, and one in connected text.

TEXT LENGTH, GENRE, AND CONTENT

Connected text for fluency practice can come from a wide range of sources as long as it is at the correct difficulty level (at least 90% accuracy) and is age appropriate for the student. A general guideline is to use passages between 50 and 200 words in length. Use shorter passages with beginning, slower readers. Include a variety of genres: short stories, articles, biographies, informational text, songs, or poetry. It is helpful to select text that is all on one page (not spread out throughout a book). Many teachers type the passage out in a document for the student to read and use a second copy with word counts for recording errors and time.

Many struggling readers do not want to read an entire passage once, let alone multiple times. Choosing the right passage can be the key to motivation, especially when establishing a routine. Teachers should consider whether the topic can hold the student's interest. Additionally, passages that contain overlapping words support transfer of fluent reading (Rashotte & Torgesen, 1985). Therefore, teachers may want to include texts with common themes whenever possible. For example, students reading a series of passages about habitats may encounter *environment, species, features, conditions,* and *organisms* across the texts.

Procedures

While they may seem complex at first, the steps of TRR recur during each session and students and teachers quickly learn the routine. The cycle of instruction can be found in Figure 5.2 with fuller explanations, and teacher and student activities in Table 5.2.

Logistics/Practical Solutions

TRR is most effective when the student reads directly with the teacher. However, we acknowledge that this may not always be realistic! Here are a few suggestions for how to make this intervention work given all the constraints of classrooms:

- Invite and train parent volunteers to serve the teacher role.
- Plan to rotate which days you work with specific students so each student gets a session three times a week, but you are not working with the entire class at once.
- In small groups, have students practice reading with one another, and rotate a targeted learner each day.
- Have a reading fluency center with a paraprofessional or co-teacher that students can rotate through for their timings.
- Select reading materials for several weeks at a time and create a themed "packet" of passages.

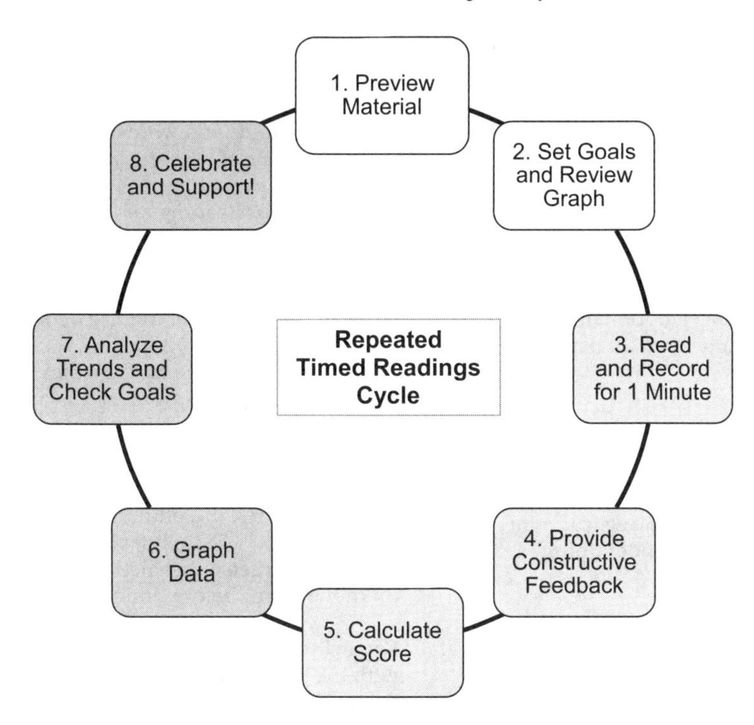

FIGURE 5.2. Procedures for timed repeated reading.

All of us successfully used TRR as special education teachers and found that this targeted practice was particularly helpful to students with disabilities. The power of this intervention lies in its use of careful assessment and task difficulty, repeated readings, goal setting, feedback, and the use of a rate/accuracy criterion that gradually increases over time.

Intervention Focused on Prosody: Phrase-Cued Texts

Ms. Kay recognizes that Josh could also benefit from targeted practice with prosody. One of the characteristics of a fluent reader is the ability to read with appropriate phrasing–chunking words together into meaningful units. Dysfluent readers may read word-by-word, fail to adhere to punctuation markers, or combine phrases in a way that interferes with comprehension. Keeping in mind the reciprocal relationship between prosody and comprehension, phrase-cued texts may be useful for students who have difficulty with comprehension, as well as those with word-reading difficulties who are not integrating meaning into their oral reading.

A phrase-cued text is a passage in which phrase boundaries are explicitly marked, or cued, for the reader. Research supports the marking of phrase boundaries in printed text. For example, O'Shea and Sindelar (1983) found that when first- through third-grade

TABLE 5.2. Teaching Timed Repeated Readings

Materials needed	Resources for reading material
• Letter-sound timings • Word timings • Reading passages, 100–250 words at the student's instructional or independent reading level • Reading passages with word count (teacher) • Student graph • Plastic cover sheet (optional) • Dry-erase marker, pen, or pencil • Timer	• Letter sounds and words (see, e.g., *https://education.uw.edu/faculty-and-research/hudson/teaching-materials*) • Great Leaps Reading for letter sounds, words, and text (*greatleaps.com*) • Jamestown Timed Reading (*mheducation.com*) • QuickReads Fluency Library (*textproject.org*) • Primary Phonics Decodable Books (*eps.schoolspeciality.com*) • Children's nonfiction magazines • Released passages from state achievement tests
Students will . . .	Teacher will . . .
Step 1. Preview material. Practice reading the passage from start to finish at least once, under untimed conditions.	Model correct pronunciations of words or sounds that are difficult for the student to read independently. Use this step as an opportunity to provide targeted instruction and help with unknown items before timing.
Step 2. Set goals and review graph. Review the graph from previous sessions and set a progress goal for the current session (e.g., "I will read five more words in 1 minute").	Review student graph from the previous session with the learner to encourage and motivate. Positively restate student goals (e.g., "You are working very hard to improve your WCPM score!").
Step 3. Read and record for 1 minute. Read the timed reading passage aloud.	Tell the student to begin reading and start a countdown timer for 1 minute, out of view of the student. As the student reads, mark all errors on the instructor's copy. Provide correct pronunciations after 3 seconds of pausing to avoid student stalling their momentum.
Step 4. Provide constructive feedback. Evaluate their own effort and performance. Reread to correct errors with teacher support.	Provide positive and specific feedback. Supply correct pronunciations for errors and provide an opportunity for the student to practice corrections.
Step 5. Calculate score. Identify the last complete line and count forward to the last word to identify the total words read.	Count the number of errors and subtract from the total words read to calculate WCPM. Errors include incorrect words, omissions, insertions, and misread proper nouns (counted as one error per passage). *Note:* Repeated words are not counted as errors.
Step 6. Graph the data. Help teacher fill out the graph. Graph independently once able.	Record the number of WCPM and student errors. Mark values you want to increase with dots and values you hope to decrease with an *X*. Document the correct date with a line to separate new phases of data—new reading probes, vacations, illness, new instruction. Only connect data points within the same reading probe and phase.

(continued)

TABLE 5.2. *(continued)*

Students will . . .	Teacher will . . .
Step 7. Analyze trends and check goals. Reflect on their graph and data. State any noticeable differences. Draw aim lines to stair-step interim goals with teacher support.	Detect trends—3 data points define a trend. Check goals for rate and accuracy—both aims must be met before moving to a new passage. Students repeat each probe until meeting mastery. If trends are not progressing favorably, consider alternative methods of instruction to meet student needs.
Step 8. Celebrate and support. Celebrate their own progress and congratulate themselves for working hard. Create future goals (e.g., "I had a hard time with silent-*e* words. I will practice them at home for next time").	Celebrate students meeting or approaching their goals. State specific accomplishments. Support students who are struggling by attributing success to hard work and practice. Discuss strategies and additional practice that might help students make progress.
Repeat steps for next timing practice (sounds, words, or text).	

students read phrase-cued text, their reading comprehension increased. The effect was especially pronounced for slow, accurate readers. Additionally, a review of research by Rasinski (1990) showed that marking phrase boundaries can improve the reading comprehension of a range of readers, from college-age students to elementary students defined as good and poor readers. None of the students in Rasinksi's review appeared to have identified reading disabilities.

Materials and Procedures

Like TRR, text for phrase cues can come from a wide range of sources, as long as the student is at least 95% accurate and the topic is interesting to the student. Poems and songs or other text with a rhythm and pattern particularly lend themselves to work on prosody. At the beginning, each text needs to be annotated with the phrase-cued marks as outlined in Table 5.3. As students improve, teachers can transition to texts without cues.

The steps for phrase-cued texts are outlined with full explanations and teacher and student activities in Table 5.4.

TABLE 5.3. Visual Legend for Phrase-Cued Texts

/ = short pause	, = short pause	. = lower voice and pause
// = longer pause	? = raise your voice	! = excitement or strong emotion

Do you know what makes a good reader? When good readers read, they chunk words and phrases together. Remember to read like you speak and pause when you reach the end of a sentence. You can do it!

TABLE 5.4. Teaching Phrase-Cued Texts

Materials needed	Resources for reading material
• Annotated text passages • Unmarked text passages • Visual legend for annotation marks • Teacher sample passage (Step 1)	• Same passages as TRR • Photocopies from texts or trade books • Increasing fluency with high-frequency word phrases (*timrasinski.com*)

Students will . . .	Teacher will . . .
Step 1. Introduce phrasing. Listen closely as the teacher reads. Consider and explain how the first and second readings of the sample passage differed.	Explain the purpose of phrasing. Note that fluent readers read sentences in meaningful chunks and use expression in their voices. Demonstrate incorrect phrasing with a few sentences from a sample passage, then reread with correct phrasing.
Step 2. Explain annotation and preview text. Follow along and find examples as the teacher reviews annotation marks. Restate what each symbol indicates.	Using a visual legend (see Table 5.3), review the meanings of each phrase-cued mark and the common features of punctuation. Check for student understanding.
Step 3. State the purpose and model phrasing. State why phrasing is important in their own words. Read silently with the teacher and pay close attention to phrases in the text.	Mark text with cues right on the passage that will be read. Remind students that using natural phrasing helps readers understand the meaning of the passage better. Read the passage with appropriate phrasing and expression as a model. Ask students to analyze prosody.
Step 4. Practice, practice, practice with phrase-cued text. Practice reading the phrase-cued passage. Follow directions for each chosen practice type.	Using annotated texts, have students practice in the format most appropriate: *Guided whole group:* Teacher and students chorally read. *Student choral reads:* Students chorally read in small groups. *Partner reads:* Students read paragraph-by-paragraph. Student 1 reads aloud, while student 2 listens. Student 2 provides feedback and roles switch. *Individual:* Create an audio or video recording of student's independent reading. Praise students for hard work and state specific observations on performance. Provide corrective feedback and modeling as needed.
Step 5. Practice, practice, practice with unmarked text. Practice reading passages with correct phrasing and expression. Follow directions for each chosen practice modality.	Plan for generalization of the skill to new texts. Have students practice with unmarked texts as above. Praise students for hard work and state specific observations on performance. Provide corrective feedback and modeling as needed.

SUMMARY

As this chapter comes to a close, it is essential to remember that fluency is a combination of many elements that allow students to effortlessly translate text into spoken words. Students whose fluency difficulties are based in word reading experience difficulties with comprehension due to the level of sustained effort needed to decode and process individual words. Reading fluency is determined by three key elements: accuracy, automaticity (or rate), and prosody. For readers who are struggling, intervention in accuracy and automaticity support fluent reading, and developing prosody may bolster comprehension.

When considering options for intervention, SL practices with explicit instruction and progress monitoring practices will yield the largest gains for students. TRRs and phrase-cued texts are easy-to-implement SL practices that can be used for classroom intervention. In addition to these interventions, frequent assessment and progress monitoring are invaluable tools to gauge the success of interventions. Remember that all parts—accuracy, automaticity, and phrasing—work together to build fluency. Focusing on automaticity and focusing on meaning are not mutually exclusive. In fact, teaching students that reading is only about speed misses the point of teaching fluency, which is to enable students to have sufficient attention to reach a deep understanding of the text they read.

APPLICATION ACTIVITIES

Activity 1

Mario is a fourth grader who is bilingual in Spanish and English and has received instruction in both languages since first enrolling at his current dual-language school in kindergarten. Mario has a diagnosis of learning disability in reading and receives specially designed instruction in reading. Based on ORF, Mario's oral reading rate and accuracy are within the end of the third-grade-level benchmark range in Spanish and within the second-grade range in English. Mario's difficulties are evident in his oral reading prosody in both languages. He has difficulty applying appropriate stress and intonation to reflect appropriate expression. He often skips over punctuation marks and does not stop at the end of sentences. He attempts phrases within sentences, but often pauses inappropriately in the middle of them, and occasionally skips lines of text with no indication that he has noticed. Mario often groups words in phrases in ways that differ from his oral language. If you were Mario's teacher, what specific skills would you want to target? What interventions could you adapt to improve his progress?

ANSWER

Because Mario's ORF is below what one might expect, he likely needs continued intervention in decoding words, as well as timed repeated oral reading in text at his instructional level (e.g., 92–95% accuracy). Because of his issues with prosody, Mario would likely benefit from extensive modeling of phrased, fluent reading and immediate corrective feedback during practice. You may also consider adapting the interventions to include checks for understanding, as Mario's difficulty with prosody is interfering with his ability to comprehend the text adequately.

Activity 2

Sean is a second grader who has been receiving extra help three times a week from a paraprofessional in class to support his difficulties with decoding. He has been receiving this extra support since first grade. He has made good progress with his ability to accurately decode one- and two-syllable words—however, he continues to read in a slow and choppy manner. His most recent ORF score indicated that he was performing around the beginning of the first-grade benchmark. When reading more challenging multisyllabic words, Sean often skips the words completely or spends so much time attempting to decode them correctly that it greatly impacts his ability to recall what he was reading. When he selects books to read during independent reading time in class, he often chooses graphic novels that are of high interest to himself and his peers but much too challenging for him to read independently. Which specific skills does Sean need to work on next?

ANSWER

Sean would benefit from interventions for multisyllabic word reading (see Kearns, Lyon, & Kelley, Chapter 3, this volume). In addition, given that his accuracy in decoding words has improved, he would also benefit from timed repeated oral readings. This will increase his automaticity in reading connected text. Given that Sean's preferred text to read is above his current reading level, it is important that appropriate connected text is used and that he is provided opportunities to read daily with adult feedback.

Activity 3

Bella is a third grader with Down syndrome. Bella spends the majority of her day in the general education setting with various supports from co-teachers and paraeducators. She currently receives services under a primary eligibility of other health impairments, with a secondary eligibility of intellectual disability. Math may not be her favorite subject, but she loves to read! She most looks forward to her instructional time in her inclusive, co-taught classes for reading and language arts. During her most recent district assessment, she placed in the 24th percentile of her grade-level peers for timed oral readings. However, she earned the lowest possible score (1 of 5) in her postreading screen for comprehension. Bella is an accurate and rapid reader, but her word reading is often robotic and she often reads each word as if it is in a list, with no attention to meaning. She rarely attends to punctuation or reads with expression. Based on your assessment, what is the most appropriate intervention and at what level? Would you consider any adaptations or modifications to this intervention? What adaptations and why?

ANSWER

Bella would benefit from targeted intervention using phrase-cued texts on an early third-grade level due to her ORF score that shows that she is just a bit below the norms for her grade level. In consideration of Bella's needs, she may need more intensive direct instruction in identifying cues in marked and unmarked texts. Specifically, it may be necessary to engage in some explicit teaching for reading single sentences with expression based on punctuation before transitioning to longer passages. Due to Bella's secondary disability, it may be necessary to use a task-analysis approach to teaching discrete skills and build to more complex interventions, like phrase-cued texts. Intervention in prosody will support Bella's comprehension of texts on her reading level.

REFERENCES

Adams, M. J. (1990). *Beginning to read: Thinking and learning about print*. Cambridge, MA: MIT Press.

Allington, R. L. (1980). *Poor readers don't get to read much*. East Lansing, MI: Institute for Research on Teaching.

Ash, G. E., Kuhn, M. R., & Walpole, S. (2009). Analyzing "inconsistencies" in practice: Teachers' continued use of round robin reading. *Reading and Writing Quarterly, 25*, 87–103.

August, D., McCardle, P., & Shanahan, T. (2014). Developing literacy in English language learners: Findings from a review of the experimental research. *School Psychology Review, 43*(4), 490–498.

Benjamin, R. G., & Schwanenflugel, P. J. (2010). Text complexity and oral reading prosody in young readers. *Reading Research Quarterly, 45*, 388–404.

Breznitz, Z. (2006). *Fluency in reading: Synchronization of processes*. Mahwah, NJ: Erlbaum.

Chard, D. J., Vaughn, S., & Tyler, B. J. (2002). A synthesis of research on effective interventions for building reading fluency with elementary students with learning disabilities. *Journal of Learning Disabilities, 35*, 386–406.

Deno, S. L., Marston, D., Shinn, M., & Tindal, G. (1983). Oral reading fluency: A simple datum for scaling reading disability. *Topics in Learning and Learning Disabilities, 2*(4), 53–59.

Denton, C. A., Wexler, J., Vaughn, S., & Bryan, D. (2008). Intervention provided to linguistically divest middle school students with severe reading difficulties. *Learning Disabilities Research and Practice, 23*, 79–89.

Dowhower, S. L. (1991). Speaking of prosody: Fluency's unattended bedfellow. *Theory into Practice*, 165–175.

Ehri, L. C., & McCormick, S. (1998). Phases of word learning: Implications for instruction with delayed and disabled readers. *Reading and Writing Quarterly: Overcoming Learning Difficulties, 14*, 135–163.

Francis, D. J., Kieffer, M., Lesaux, N., Rivera, H., & Rivera, M. (2006). *Practical guidelines for the education of English language learners: Research-based recommendations for instruction and academic interventions*. Houston, TX: RMC Research Corporation, Center on Instruction.

Fuchs, L. S., & Fuchs, D. (1992). Identifying a measure for monitoring student reading progress. *School Psychology Review, 21*, 45–58.

Fuchs, L. S., Fuchs, D., Hosp, M. K., & Jenkins, J. (2001). Oral reading fluency as an indicator of reading competence: A theoretical, empirical, and historical analysis. *Scientific Studies of Reading, 5*, 239–256.

Gunn, B., Smolkowski, K., Biglan, A., & Black, C. (2002). Supplemental instruction in decoding skills for Hispanic and non-Hispanic students in early elementary school: A follow-up. *Journal of Special Education, 36*, 69–79.

Gunn, B., Smolkowski, K., Biglan, A., Black, C., & Blair, J. (2005). Fostering the development of reading skill through supplemental instruction: Results for Hispanic and non-Hispanic students. *Journal of Special Education, 39*, 66–85.

Hasbrouck, J., & Tindal, G. (2017). *An update to compiled ORF norms* [Technical Report No. 1702]. Eugene: Behavioral Research and Teaching, University of Oregon.

Honig, B., Diamond, L., & Gutlohn, L. (2018). *Teaching reading sourcebook* (3rd ed.). Novato, CA: Arena Press.

Hosp, M. K., & Fuchs, L. S. (2005). Using CBM as an indicator of decoding, word reading, and comprehension: Do the relations change with grade? *School Psychology Review, 34*, 9–26.

Hudson, R. F., Pullen, P. C., Lane, H. B., & Torgesen, J. K. (2009). The complex nature of reading fluency: A multidimensional view. *Reading and Writing Quarterly, 25*(1), 4–32.

Hudson, R. F., Torgesen, J. K., Lane, H. B., & Turner, S. J. (2012). Relations among reading skills and sub-skills and text-level reading proficiency in developing readers. *Reading and Writing: An Interdisciplinary Journal, 25*, 483–507.

Kamps, D., Abbott, M., Greenwood, C., Arreaga-Mayer, C., Wills, H., Lonstaff, J., et al. (2007). Use of evidence-based, small-group reading instruction for English language learners in elementary grades: Secondary-tier intervention. *Learning Disability Quarterly, 30*, 153–168.

Kuhn, R. M., Schwanenflugel, P. J., & Meisinger, E. B. (2010). Aligning theory and assessment fluency: Automaticity, prosody and definitions of fluency. *Reading Research Quarterly, 45*, 230–251.

La Berge, D., & Samuels, S. J. (1974). Toward a theory of automatic information processing in reading. *Cognitive Psychology, 6*, 293–323.

Lee, J., & Yoon, S. Y. (2017). The effects of repeated reading on reading fluency for students with reading disabilities. *Journal of Learning Disabilities, 50*, 213–224.

Mayer, R. E. (2004). Teaching of subject matter. *Annual Review of Psychology, 55*, 715–744.

Miller, J., & Schwanenflugel, P. J. (2008). A longitudinal study of the development of reading prosody as a dimension of oral reading fluency in early elementary school children. *Reading Research Quarterly, 43*, 336–354.

Morgan, P. L., & Sideridis, G. D. (2006). Contrasting the effectiveness of fluency interventions for students with or at risk for learning disabilities: A multilevel random coefficient modeling meta-analysis. *Learning Disabilities: Research and Practice, 21*, 191–210.

National Center for Education Statistics. (2017). The condition of education. Retrieved from *https://nces-ed-gov.offcampus.lib.washington.edu/programs/coe/indicator_cgf.asp*

National Reading Panel. (2000). *Report of the National Reading Panel. Teaching children to read: An evidence-based assessment of the scientific research literature on reading and its implications for reading instruction: Reports of the subgroups* (NIH Publication No. 00–4769). Washington, DC: U.S. Department of Health and Human Services, National Institute of Child Health and Human Development.

O'Shea, L. J., & Sindelar, P. T. (1983). The effects of segmenting written discourse on the reading comprehension of low- and high-performance readers. *Reading Research Quarterly*, 458–465.

Powell, M. B., & Gadke, D. L. (2018). Improving oral reading fluency in middle-school students: A comparison of repeated reading and listening passage preview. *Psychology in the Schools, 55*, 1274–1286.

Rashotte, C. A., & Torgesen, J. K. (1985). Repeated reading and reading fluency in learning disabled children. *Reading Research Quarterly*, 180–188.

Rasinski, T. V. (1990). Investigating measures of reading fluency. *Educational Research Quarterly, 14*, 37–44.

Samuels, S. J. (1979). The method of repeated readings. *Reading Teacher, 32*, 403–408.

Samuels, S. J. (2006). Toward a model of reading fluency. In S. J. Samuels & A. E. Farstrup (Eds.), *What research has to say about fluency instruction* (pp. 24–46). Newark, DE: International Reading Association.

Sanden, S. (2018). Round-robin reading: Learning from the research and from the stories of readers. *Illinois Reading Council Journal, 46*, 32–42.

Schreiber, P. A. (1991). Understanding prosody's role in reading acquisition. *Theory into Practice, 30*, 158–164.

Schwanenflugel, P. J., & Benjamin, R. G. (2016). The development of reading prosody and its assessment. In J. Thomson & L. Jarmulowicz (Eds.), *Linguistic rhythm and literacy* (pp. 187–213). Amsterdam: John Benjamins.

Schwanenflugel, P. J., Hamilton, A. M., Kuhn, M. R., Wisenbaker, J. M., & Stahl, S. A. (2004). Becoming a fluent reader: Reading skill and prosodic features in the oral reading of young readers. *Journal of Educational Psychology, 96*(1), 119–129.

Shany, M. T., & Biemiller, A. (1995). Assisted reading practice: Effects on performance for poor readers in grades 3 and 4. *Reading Research Quarterly, 30*(3), 382–395.

Shinn, M. R., Knutson, N., Good, R. H., III, Tilly, W. D., III, & Collins, V. L. (1992). Curriculum-based measurement of oral reading fluency: A confirmatory analysis of its relation to reading. *School Psychology Review, 21*, 459–479.

Strickland, W. D., Boon, R. T., & Spencer, V. G. (2013). The effects of repeated reading on the fluency and comprehension skills of elementary-age students with learning disabilities (LD), 2001–2011: A review of research and practice. *Learning Disabilities: A Contemporary Journal, 11*, 1–33.

Therrien, W. J. (2004). Fluency and comprehension gains as a result of repeated reading: A meta-analysis. *Remedial and Special Education, 25*, 252–261.

VanWagenen, M. A., Williams, R. L., & McLaughlin, T. F. (1994). Use of assisted reading to improve reading rate, word accuracy, and comprehension with ESL Spanish-speaking students. *Perceptual and Motor Skills, 79*, 227–230.

CHAPTER 6

Structured Literacy Interventions for Vocabulary

Michael D. Coyne
Susan M. Loftus-Rattan

Violet Walker is enjoying her class of 21 kindergarten students even more than usual this year. Granted, they are a handful, but seeing the world anew each year through the eyes of a different group of kindergarteners never gets old. And this year's class has delighted her over and over again with their surprising insights and unique perspectives on the world.

The conversations that Violet has had with her students this fall has gotten her thinking about the importance of language and the power of words to describe our experiences and engage with learning. Although all of her students want to participate in discussions with their teachers and peers, and all have important contributions to share, some just have greater facility with words and language that allows them to more fully engage in these conversations and interactions.

Violet knows that one of her most important roles as a teacher is to help all of her students develop deep and flexible knowledge of words and language that will enable them to access content, communicate their thoughts and opinions, and actively participate in the work of school. She also knows that rich vocabulary knowledge is essential to ensure that her students are able to comprehend text as they become readers over the course of the next 2 years. Violet thinks that it is especially important to help this year's class develop their vocabulary knowledge.

The core reading and language arts program that her school has adopted provides good read-aloud selections and includes strategies for engaging students in discussions about the content of the texts and how they relate to their own experiences. The program also identifies a few key vocabulary words to preview before each read-aloud selection. However, Violet is not sure that this is enough to ensure that all of her students learn these important academic vocabulary words. She hears some of her students continuing to use these words after the read-aloud, but for many of her students, it seems like this brief exposure provides only a fleeting introduction that is insufficient to develop a deep and lasting understanding of these words.

Violet believes strongly in the evidence supporting Structured Literacy (SL) approaches for teaching beginning reading skills, like alphabet knowledge, phonemic awareness, and word-reading strategies. She wonders whether she can use an SL approach for supplementing the vocabulary instruction in her core reading program, enhancing its effectiveness, and supporting her students' vocabulary and language development.

RESEARCH ON VOCABULARY INSTRUCTION

A large body of research evidence supports the importance of vocabulary knowledge to reading success. There is a strong positive relationship between vocabulary knowledge and reading comprehension (e.g., Elleman, Lindo, Morphy, & Compton, 2009; Ouellette, 2006). Across studies, vocabulary is consistently one of the strongest predictors of reading comprehension (Sénéchal, Ouellette, & Rodney, 2006; Snow, Burns, & Griffin, 1998). In a seminal study, Cunningham and Stanovich (1997) found that vocabulary knowledge in the elementary grades was not only associated with students' current reading comprehension but continued to predict reading comprehension in high school and beyond.

There are a number of theoretical explanations for the powerful relationship between vocabulary knowledge and overall reading ability (Anderson & Freebody, 1981), but perhaps the most straightforward is the instrumentalist hypothesis (Spencer, Quinn, & Wagner, 2017; Stahl, 1991). The instrumentalist hypothesis suggests that to comprehend text, students need to know what the individual words in that text mean. For example, to understand the sentence "Sophia was ecstatic about the science assignment," a student would need to know that ecstatic means "very happy and full of excitement." Moreover, the deeper a student's understanding of an individual word, the more full and rich that student's comprehension of that text will be. Again, if a student knows that the word *ecstatic* means more than just glad or pleased, but *very* happy and excited, they will have a fuller and more nuanced understanding of the sentence.

Research evidence also supports the effectiveness of vocabulary instruction and intervention for accelerating students' vocabulary knowledge and improving comprehension. For example, there is extensive evidence that instruction and intervention are effective in helping students in the elementary grades learn new vocabulary (Foorman et al., 2016; Marulis & Neuman, 2013). Research-supported vocabulary instruction directly and explicitly teaches students the meanings of words they do not know and provides carefully planned interactive activities that maximize opportunities for students to hear and use new vocabulary in supportive and varied contexts (Beck, McKeown, & Kucan, 2002; Stahl, 1986).

Research also shows that vocabulary instruction can improve students' comprehension, particularly comprehension of text that includes vocabulary that has been taught directly (Coyne et al., 2021; Elleman et al., 2009). In the example above, if the word *ecstatic* is taught using effective instruction, students will not only learn the meaning of ecstatic, they will also better understand sentences and texts that include the word.

TEACHING VOCABULARY THROUGH ORAL LANGUAGE ACTIVITIES

Vocabulary instruction is often incorporated into reading and writing instruction. Teachers select vocabulary words from texts that students are reading and students are supported in using new vocabulary in their writing. However, there is also an important role for supporting vocabulary development through oral language activities—for example, teaching vocabulary from texts that are read aloud to students and encouraging students to use new vocabulary in their speaking. Although teaching vocabulary through oral language activities may seem less connected to students' reading development, it is of central importance for ensuring that all students develop deep and flexible vocabulary knowledge (Coyne, Neugebauer, Ware, McCoach, & Madura, 2015).

The Simple View of Reading (Gough & Tunmer, 1986; Nation, 2019), an influential and widely accepted model of reading comprehension, suggests that successful reading is influenced by two distinct dimensions: students' ability to read or decode words and sentences, and students' ability to understand the words and sentences that they read. The Simple View of Reading suggests that once students use their decoding and word identification skills to read text, they leverage their oral language abilities to understand what they are reading. These oral language abilities include vocabulary knowledge, listening comprehension, and background knowledge. In other words, when students read, they translate written text into language, and then use the same language comprehension processes they use when understanding speech to comprehend what they read.

According to the Simple View of Reading, understanding oral language is a primary contributor to successful reading comprehension, and young students' oral vocabulary knowledge should directly influence later reading comprehension. Therefore, teaching vocabulary through oral language activities should be a primary focus for teachers in the early grades because these skills serve as a necessary precondition for successful comprehension. Supporting vocabulary through oral language is also particularly important for students in grades K–6 who are experiencing reading difficulties, like dyslexia, and may not yet be proficient readers because their access to vocabulary through what they are reading is limited by the relatively simple texts that they can read and decode. However, because these students' language abilities are often much more highly developed than their reading abilities, they are well positioned to learn more sophisticated content and vocabulary through oral language activities. Therefore, a central way for students in grades K–6 to learn important academic vocabulary is through intentionally planned oral language activities, like explicit vocabulary instruction.

TEACHING VOCABULARY THROUGH STRUCTURED LITERACY

A large and growing body of research supports the effectiveness of direct and extended vocabulary instruction that is aligned with an SL approach for increasing the oral vocabulary knowledge of students in the elementary grades (Beck et al., 2013; Coyne et al., 2021; Foorman et al., 2016; Marulis & Neuman, 2013).

Features of direct and extended vocabulary instruction (see Figure 6.1) include (1) focusing on teaching academic vocabulary that reflects the decontextualized language common in books and across content areas (Foorman et al., 2016), (2) giving students clear and understandable definitions of words targeted for instruction, (3) introducing vocabulary in supportive and meaningful contexts, (4) teaching vocabulary using explicit instruction, (5) providing extended instruction that maximizes opportunities for students to discuss words in interactive activities that promote deep processing, (6) giving students immediate feedback that specifically reinforces the correct use of target vocabulary and corrects errors, and (7) incorporating review of taught vocabulary by ensuring that students encounter words over time in different meaningful contexts. Teaching vocabulary in small groups is also a way to intensify instruction and optimize students' engagement and interactions with new vocabulary. The next sections of this chapter expand on each of these features of effective vocabulary instruction.

Providing Small-Group Intervention

Small-group vocabulary instruction is an effective way to support vocabulary growth for all students and is particularly important for students who are at risk for reading difficulties or not responding adequately to whole-class instruction. Small-group instruction does not replace core classroom instruction but instead supplements it to increase dosage or overall instructional time. Small-group supplemental instruction supports students at risk by reviewing, or previewing, content that is taught in whole-class settings. Additional exposure to the content, however, is not the only benefit of small-group instruction. Small groups provide opportunities to intensify instruction. For

- Focus on teaching academic vocabulary.
- Give students clear and understandable definitions.
- Introduce vocabulary in supportive and meaningful contexts.
- Teach vocabulary using explicit instruction.
- Provide extended interactive instruction that promotes deep processing.
- Give students immediate feedback that reinforces correct use of vocabulary and corrects errors.
- Incorporate review of taught vocabulary over time in different meaningful contexts.

FIGURE 6.1. Features of direct and extended vocabulary instruction.

example, smaller groups afford students more opportunities to use extended language, respond to questions, and engage in interactive activities with content, the instructor, and with one another. Additionally, this format allows teachers to more easily provide immediate corrective feedback to individual student responses. Experts recommend providing supplemental small-group instruction between three and five times a week for 20–40 minutes each time (Gersten et al., 2009).

Violet's Experience

Violet decided that she wanted to provide additional, small-group vocabulary intervention for some of her students in addition to the vocabulary instruction included in the core program. She identified four students who she considered to be at risk for language and literacy difficulties based on beginning-of-the-year early literacy assessments. She identified two additional students who were not determined to be at risk based on assessments but who appeared not to be responding adequately to core vocabulary instruction. She noticed that they seemed lost during the whole-class instruction and did not participate in class discussions of new vocabulary. Violet planned to meet with this group of six students four times per week for 30 minutes during a shared intervention period. She decided that during small-group instruction she would explicitly teach key vocabulary before these words were introduced in core instruction. She thought that previewing target words would provide these students with a stronger foundation of initial word knowledge that would allow them to better take advantage of the core vocabulary instruction.

Choosing Words to Teach

Deciding what vocabulary to teach can seem like an overwhelming task. There are many words that are good candidates for instruction, so how do you select the words that will be most beneficial for your students? Fortunately, there is some guidance from experts in the field that can help make this decision-making process less daunting. First, it is important to select academic vocabulary to teach directly. Academic vocabulary includes relatively sophisticated words that are common in books and in the language of school (Foorman et al., 2016). It also includes words that frequently appear across subject areas and in instructions for assignments and activities (e.g., *contrast, evidence, locate, definition, investigate*). Although students learn much language and vocabulary naturally through communications outside of school, academic vocabulary is less likely to be a part of these everyday conversations with friends and family, and therefore needs to be taught explicitly.

Second, there are a number of strategies and resources that can help teachers identify academic vocabulary. One strategy is to look at the frequency of words in print and select words, or word families, that students are likely to encounter in their reading. For example, the Academic Word List (Coxhead, 2000) and the Academic Vocabulary List (Gardner & Davies, 2014) identify high-utility academic vocabulary ranked by frequency along with related word forms. Figure 6.2 includes some example words

relate	*relates, related, relationship, relation, relational, unrelated, interrelated*
structure	*structures, structured, restructure, restructuring, structural, structurally, unstructured*
contribute	*contributes, contributed, contributing, contribution, contributions, contributor*
distinct	*distinction, distinctions, distinctive, distinctively, distinctly, indistinct, indistinctly*
secure	*secures, secured, securely, securing, securities, security, insecure, insecurity, insecurities*
distribute	*distributes, distributed, distributing, distribution, distributor, redistribute, redistributed, redistributing, redistribution*
system	*systems, systematic, systematically, unsystematic, subsystem*
interpret	*interprets, interpreted, interpreting, interpretation, interpretive, misinterpret, reinterpret, reinterpretation*

FIGURE 6.2. Examples of high-frequency academic vocabulary with associated word families.

from these lists and related word families. Another approach for selecting academic vocabulary to teach is to examine words that students with well-developed vocabularies tend to know in specific grades. Information about what words students know at what grades can help teachers identify important commonly known academic vocabulary words that can be targeted for instruction, especially for students who may have less developed vocabularies and may be at risk for reading and language difficulties. One resource that has compiled grade-specific vocabulary is a word list that contains 5,000 root words that are likely to be known by students in kindergarten through sixth grade (Biemiller, 2009). Hiebert, Goodwin, and Cervetti (2018) also suggest focusing on morphological families that are found frequently in texts.

Finally, you can use a process that helps to determine the overall utility of words by sorting them into different tiers. Beck and colleagues (2013) developed this three-tier approach to help identify words that are important for students to know and can be described in ways that are easy for students to understand. This three-tier system is not to be confused with the tiers of intervention in a response-to-intervention or multi-tiered system of support framework. In the Beck and colleagues model, Tier One contains words that are basic and that most students will know before entering school (e.g., *cup, dog, car*). Tier Three contains words that are narrow and often highly specific to particular areas of study and are better suited to be taught in content-area instruction, such as science, social studies, or geography (e.g., *isotope, fascism, longitude*). Tier Two contains academic vocabulary words that are unlikely to be known by students but represent known concepts, are able to be described in simple terms, and will likely be useful for students to know (i.e., they may see these words in their reading, hear them in conversation, or use them expressively in conversation). These Tier Two words (e.g., *peculiar, gigantic, drenched*) are a good fit for general vocabulary instruction. It is also important to teach any word meanings that are important for understanding content that students are learning, whether that is during a science lesson or a class read-aloud.

Violet's Experience

Violet looked through the list of words covered in her core reading program. She thought about Beck and colleagues' (2013) categories for classifying vocabulary and determined that most of the words introduced in the core program would be considered Tier Two academic vocabulary words with a smaller number of Tier Three words that were important for understanding the content of specific read-aloud selections. Violet felt comfortable with the word list and decided that these were the right words to teach her students. She also thought that explicitly teaching the meanings of these words to her students in the intervention group before they were introduced during whole-group literacy instruction would provide them with an important foundation for better responding to the core instruction and for comprehending the read-aloud selections.

Developing Student-Friendly Definitions

The next step after selecting words to teach directly is developing meaningful definitions for students. This may seem like a simple task since all word definitions can be found in a dictionary. Unfortunately, however, dictionary definitions are often complex and difficult to understand for students who are learning word meanings for the first time, particularly students in the earlier grades. Instead, providing simple, student-friendly definitions that are easy to understand can help to facilitate initial word learning (Beck et al., 2013). Learners' dictionaries can be a useful tool when thinking about student-friendly definitions (e.g., online learners' dictionaries from Collins, Oxford, and Merriam–Webster), but even these definitions may need to be adjusted so that they are clear and simple. Sometimes just thinking about the basic meaning with consideration of your students' level of understanding can help you to come up with a meaning that will work best in that situation. When students are first learning a new word, it is fine to provide a definition that does not capture all of the nuances of the word but rather provides a general meaning that is easy to understand. As the students come across

Target word	Correct but complex definition	Student-friendly definition
apex	The uppermost or culminating point	The place at the very top of something
peculiar	Eccentric, odd, or unusual	Strange
plummet	To drop sharply and abruptly	To fall very fast

FIGURE 6.3. Examples of complex and student-friendly definitions.

that word again in the future, they will be able to refine that initial understanding to appreciate those nuances. Figure 6.3 shows examples of complex and student-friendly definitions for students in the early grades.

Violet's Experience

Violet read through the definitions of the vocabulary words that were provided in the core literacy program. Although she liked the vocabulary words, she thought that some of the definitions were complex and might not be helpful for many of her students. She decided to rewrite the definitions by consulting a learners' dictionary and thinking about simple wording that would be meaningful for her students. After she settled on new definitions for the vocabulary words, she decided to use the new definitions for whole-class instruction, as well as for her intervention group. She thought that all of her students could benefit from the student-friendly definitions she created.

One of the vocabulary words that was a part of the curriculum was *flexible*. Violet decided to use the definition "bends easily" to teach this new word to her students because this was how the word was used in the read-aloud selection. She believed that the definition would make sense to her students and she planned to use demonstrations and pictures to ensure that every student had a clear understanding of the new word's meaning. She did not introduce the additional meaning that involves being able to adapt to changing situations. She knew that introducing both definitions to her young students at the same time would likely confuse them and result in not learning either meaning well, but she planned to introduce this second related meaning later in the year after students had established deep knowledge of this primary meaning.

Providing Both Definitions and Context

If a teacher only provides a new word and the word's definition, students are likely to rely solely on memorizing the definition without developing a deeper understanding of the word. Additionally, they may not truly understand the meaning of the new word if they are not exposed to examples of how the word is used in different authentic contexts. Introducing a word within a meaningful context provides students with a concrete example of how the word is used in practice. A natural place to find useful contexts is in books. Selecting words for instruction that students will encounter while reading or listening to a text provides an excellent opportunity to teach new word meanings and show an example of that word being used in a context that is meaningful and easy for the students to understand (Wasik, Hindman, & Snell, 2016). When providing instruction on vocabulary words during a read-aloud, it can be beneficial to take a few minutes before reading the book to prepare a simple lesson. Thinking about the words, their meanings, and examples that you want to share can help the lesson run smoothly. Using a lesson plan, such as the example in Figure 6.4, can help prepare for instruction (see Form 6.1 at the end of the chapter for a blank template of this lesson plan). Another option is to create one or more sentences that contain the new vocabulary word and provide supportive contextual information that will help students understand the

Step 1. Select three to five words from a book you are going to read aloud to your class.
Sauntering Drenched Timid
Step 2. Create student-friendly definitions for each of the chosen target words.
Sauntering—walking Drenched—really wet Timid—a little scared or shy
Step 3. Introduce the target words to your class prior to reading the book.
"When I read this story, I want you to listen for these magic words. Repeat after me: 'sauntering' [*repeat*], 'drenched' [*repeat*], and 'timid' [*repeat*]. When you hear these words in the story, raise your hand."
Step 4. Teach the word meanings when you encounter them during the reading.
<u>Saunter</u> "So he went sauntering down the street." "Oh, good! Some of you raised your hands. What word did you hear? Yes, 'sauntering.' 'So he went sauntering down the street.' " *Note:* If no one raises a hand, prompt them to listen for the word *sauntering* and reread the sentence. "Sauntering means walking. 'So he went walking down the street.' In the picture [*point*], you can see that the dog is sauntering, or walking down the street. Everyone say, 'sauntering.' " <u>Drenched</u> "The little white dog got drenched." "Oh, good! Some of you raised your hands. What word did you hear? Yes, 'drenched.' 'The little white dog got drenched.' " *Note:* If no one raises a hand, prompt them to listen for the word *drenched* and reread the sentence. "Drenched means really wet. 'The little white dog got really wet.' In the picture [*point*], you can see that the dog is drenched, or really wet. Everyone say 'drenched.' " <u>Timid</u> "Fluffy was timid, but he tried to be polite." "Oh, good! Some of you raised your hands. What word did you hear? Yes, 'timid.' 'Fluffy was timid, but he tried to be polite.' " *Note:* If no one raises a hand, prompt them to listen for the word *timid* and reread the sentence. "If you feel timid, it means you feel a little scared or shy about something. 'Fluffy felt a little scared and shy, but he tried to be polite.' In the picture [*point*], you can see that Fluffy looks timid or a little scared and shy. Everyone say 'timid.' "

FIGURE 6.4. Example vocabulary lesson plan for introducing new vocabulary during a read-aloud.

word's meaning and how it is typically used in text or language. The use of pictures can also provide context that illustrates a word meaning that can be particularly helpful for at-risk learners. Providing multiple contexts can be particularly impactful. This allows students to understand that a word can be used in various ways and can help to show the scope of a word's meaning.

Violet's Experience

Violet developed an anchor sentence to go along with each new word that she planned to teach. The sentences used the new word meaning in a way that would be easy for her kindergarten students to understand. She also found a picture example for each word that she posted on the wall and referred to whenever they discussed the new words. She thought the combination of example sentences and picture support, in addition to the student-friendly definition, would provide her students with a strong foundation for understanding the new word meanings. For example, Violet found a picture of a gymnast doing a backbend and explained to the students that the gymnast is flexible because she can bend her body easily. She posted the picture on the wall next to the word *flexible*. She also created an anchor sentence for that word that described the picture and demonstrated how to use the word in a sentence. The anchor sentence for flexible was "The flexible gymnast could easily bend her body all the way to the floor."

Teaching through Explicit Instruction

Students develop vocabulary knowledge in a variety of ways. Many words are learned through incidental exposure (Nagy & Herman, 1987). This occurs when a student encounters words through independent reading, listening to a book read aloud, engaging in a conversation, or through any other oral language experience. When students read or hear a word in these naturalistic situations, the surrounding context provides some level of information about a word's meaning. After many incidental encounters with words in different contexts, students gradually accumulate knowledge of these words and their meanings.

It is more difficult, however, for students who are at risk for reading difficulties to learn new vocabulary incidentally (Coyne et al., 2019). These students are less likely to read independently and so are less likely to encounter important academic vocabulary in text. Moreover, these students may have more difficulty leveraging the incomplete information about word meanings available during the incidental encounters they do experience. For example, they might not have sufficient background knowledge about a content area or have an incomplete understanding of other words within a passage. This lack of understanding would make it difficult to successfully infer meanings of unknown words. For many students, both those at risk and those who are typically developing, relying on incidental exposure may not result in full and complete knowledge of important academic vocabulary. Therefore, teachers should introduce some new vocabulary through explicit instruction (Archer & Hughes, 2010; Coyne & Koriakin, 2017). Although it is not possible to teach the meanings of all words directly, introducing essential academic vocabulary through explicit instruction optimizes the likelihood that all students will learn important words and their meanings (Archer & Hughes, 2010; Coyne & Koriakin, 2017).

Teaching vocabulary through explicit instruction means that teachers introduce new words and their meanings directly and do not assume that students will be able to guess or infer what words means. Explicit instruction involves providing definitions using clear and consistent language and modeling how words are used in different contexts by carefully selecting or developing examples that illustrate a word's meaning. When a new word is introduced using explicit instruction, a teacher indicates that the word is new to the class, pronounces the word clearly, provides a student-friendly definition, and models using the word in context.

Violet's Experience

Violet used explicit instruction to introduce new word meanings to her class. She decided to use the same routine to introduce each new word so that the students always knew what to expect and could easily follow along with the lesson. Her routine included the following: (1) she pronounced the word and clearly stated the definition while holding up a picture example illustrating the word, (2) she described how the picture showed the word's meaning, (3) she read the anchor sentence she created that demonstrated how the word could be used in a context that is understandable and relatable to her students, and (4) she had all of the students say the word and definition together.

Here is an example of explicit instruction for the word *flexible*:

1. "One of our new vocabulary words is *flexible*. Everyone say, 'flexible.' " [*Students say the word together.*] "If something is flexible, it bends easily. Everyone say, 'If something is flexible it bends easily.' " [*Students say the definition together.*]
2. [*Indicates the anchor picture of a gymnast.*] "In this picture, you can see that the woman is flexible because she is bending her back all the way over. She is able to bend easily."
3. [*Reads anchor sentence.*] "The flexible gymnast could easily bend her body all the way to the floor."
4. "Everyone say the word *flexible*." [*Students say the word together.*]

Providing Extended Instruction

Direct explicit instruction of vocabulary can help to build vocabulary knowledge for all students and is particularly important for those students who may be at risk. Direct instruction can involve a relatively quick and simple explanation of a word's meaning using a routine similar to the one described in the previous section. This type of instruction, sometimes referred to as "embedded" instruction (Coyne, McCoach, Loftus, Zipoli, & Kapp, 2009), results in measurable word learning beyond the learning that occurs incidentally (Penno, Wilkinson, & Moore, 2002). Although providing definitions and context can enable students to develop initial foundational knowledge of a word's meaning, it does not necessarily result in full and deep knowledge of that word. Students' knowledge of individual vocabulary words develops over time on a continuum from no knowledge to varying levels of partial knowledge to more complete and full knowledge (Nagy & Scott, 2000).

To ensure that students develop more complete and nuanced knowledge of important academic vocabulary, direct instruction can also include more extended activities that go beyond providing a definition and initial context. Extended vocabulary instruction includes interactive activities that allow students to process the words deeply. These activities may involve asking students to create a sentence using the word (e.g., "Tell me about a time when you saw something peculiar"), asking questions about the word that require knowledge of the word's meaning in order to respond correctly (e.g., "What is an example of a gigantic animal?"), asking students to identify examples and non-examples of the word (e.g., "Does this picture show something that is drenched?"), or having students categorize words and discuss how the new words are similar or dissimilar to other known words (e.g., "Which of our new words can we put together out of the following: *gigantic, drenched,* and *minuscule*? Why do *gigantic* and *minuscule* go together?"). Examples of extended vocabulary activities are included in Figure 6.5. Studies have shown that extended instruction leads to greater depth of word learning than incidental exposure or embedded instruction (Coyne et al., 2009; Loftus-Rattan, Mitchell, & Coyne, 2016). That does not mean that the other modes of instruction are not valuable. Extended instruction requires the most preparation and time to implement. It may be most beneficial to use a combination of approaches that includes reading aloud to your class, encouraging independent reading, providing quick, embedded instruction for some words, and providing extended instruction on another set of words.

Violet's Experience

Violet knows that the goal of intensive explicit vocabulary instruction is to ensure that her students not only learn definitions but also develop rich and nuanced knowledge of the words. She decides to use a variety of activities to encourage deep processing of the new word meanings. She develops picture-based and oral language-based activities that require her students to really think about what the words mean instead of relying on surface knowledge and memorization. For each activity, Violet prompts and encourages students to use extended language to interact with the new vocabulary words and one another, therefore maximizing engagement and opportunities to practice. Examples for the word *flexible* follow.

PICTURE EXAMPLES AND NON-EXAMPLES

Violet shows picture examples and non-examples for the word *flexible*. She instructs her students to show a thumbs-up for examples that show something that is flexible and a thumbs-down for examples that do not show something that is flexible:

Activity	Example
Asking students to create a sentence using the word	One time I saw a dog dressed up like a hot dog in a big hot dog bun! That was very peculiar or strange. Now it's your turn to tell me about a time when you saw something peculiar. Examples: "I saw someone walking on their hands. That was peculiar!"; "It is peculiar to eat spaghetti with maple syrup!"
Asking questions about the word that requires knowledge of the word's meaning in order to respond correctly	What is an example of a gigantic animal? Examples: "An elephant is gigantic"; "A blue whale is the biggest animal on Earth; it is gigantic!"
Asking students to identify examples and non-examples of the word	I'll show you some pictures and you will put your thumb up if the picture shows something that is drenched. Examples: a wet dog [*yes*], a dry fluffy dog [*no*], a kid coming out of the water [*yes*], a kid washing his hands [*no*], laundry in a washing machine [*yes*], a canoe on a lake [*no*].
Having students categorize words and discuss how the new words are similar or dissimilar to other known words	We are going to fill in this word web with words that tell about the size of something. Examples: *gigantic, enormous, miniscule, broad.*

FIGURE 6.5. Extended vocabulary activities.

> "We are going to look at some pictures and I want you to think about whether the picture shows something that is flexible, or bends easily, or if it shows something that is not flexible. If you see something that is flexible, put your thumb up and say, 'That's flexible!' If you see something that isn't flexible, put your thumb down and don't say anything."

- A person doing yoga
- A pencil [*not flexible*]
- A bendy straw
- A hose held in a loop
- A Lego block [*not flexible*]

MAKE A SENTENCE

Violet asks students to think of a time when they saw something that was flexible and describe it in a sentence using the word *flexible*. She used explicit instruction and modeled the activity for her students. She introduced the activity by saying the following:

> "We are going to take turns saying sentences with our new word: *flexible*. I want you to think of a time when you noticed that something was flexible and tell us about it. I'll go first. I like to use rubber bands because they are flexible and can bend

around things to hold them together. Now it's your turn, tell us about something that is flexible."

PICTURE SORT

Violet used the picture examples from the first activity to give her students an opportunity to sort the examples and non-examples into groups. She mixed the pictures together and instructed each student to place the pictures that showed something that is flexible in one pile and place the pictures that showed something that is not flexible in another pile:

> "We are going to use these pictures to play a game with our new word: *flexible*. I'm going to hand you the pile of mixed-up pictures and you will pick the top picture and decide if it shows something that is flexible, or bends easily. If it is flexible, put the picture here [*indicate where it goes*]; if the picture does not show something that is flexible, put the picture here [*indicate where it goes*]. I'll go first. I picked the picture of a straw. You can see that this straw is bending right here [*point*], so the straw is flexible. I will put the picture in the flexible pile. Now, it's your turn to pick a picture and put it into a pile."

Providing Feedback

Feedback is an important component of learning something new. Students need to know when they are on the right track and when they misunderstand something. One of the benefits of small-group instruction is that it allows teachers to provide more individualized feedback to all students. Feedback is particularly impactful when it is provided immediately after a student response so that any misunderstandings can be corrected right away. Additionally, feedback should both affirm correct responses and correct errors by using specific language. When correcting errors, an effective strategy is to provide the correct answer for the student and then allow the student another chance to practice the skill or demonstrate knowledge (Gersten et al., 2009). Another benefit of feedback during vocabulary instruction is that it can be used to encourage students to extend their language use by asking them to elaborate on their responses. Feedback, such as "That's right! Why is that an example of something that is *drenched*?" can get students talking about the new words beyond just giving yes or no responses. During vocabulary interventions, in addition to indicating whether a student response is correct or incorrect, feedback can be used to support student learning by providing individualized instruction, being responsive to individual students' needs, and eliciting student elaboration and extension.

Violet's Experience

Violet knows that her students will benefit from immediate, corrective feedback, so she thinks about ways she can provide this feedback during extended vocabulary activities.

She understands that different activities require different types of feedback but knows that she wants all of her responses to focus on the new word meaning and encourage extended language use. She also knows that it is sometimes difficult to provide specific supportive feedback on the fly, so she prepares for her lessons by developing a list of potential feedback based on student responses for each activity.

PICTURE EXAMPLES AND NON-EXAMPLES

If the students answer correctly by putting their thumbs up when a flexible picture is shown, Violet responds, "That's right! This picture does show something that is flexible, or bends easily."

If the students answer correctly by putting their thumbs down when a picture does not show something flexible, Violet responds, "That's right! This picture does not show something flexible because it does not bend easily."

If the students answer incorrectly by putting thumbs up when it is not a picture of something flexible, Violet immediately provides the correct answer and gives another opportunity to respond: "This doesn't show something flexible because this pencil can't bend easily. Does this picture show something that is flexible?"

MAKE A SENTENCE

If the student's sentence makes sense and describes something that is flexible, Violet follows up by confirming that response: "Yes, a soft stuffed toy could be flexible, or could bend easily." If the student's sentence is incorrect or the student doesn't respond, Violet provides assistance by asking the student questions and helps formulate a sentence: "Have you ever seen a garden hose? [*yes*] Could you bend the hose easily? [*yes*] Can you say that a garden hose is flexible?"

PICTURE SORT

If the student puts the picture in the right pile, Violet confirms the correct response and asks for elaboration: "That's right! Why does this picture go in this pile?"

If the student puts the picture in the wrong pile, Violet provides immediate corrective feedback and allows the student to try again: "This picture goes in the not-flexible pile because the block is hard and cannot bend. Try again. Where does this picture go?"

Reviewing Vocabulary

The ultimate goal of vocabulary instruction is to help students develop deep knowledge of words and retain this new vocabulary knowledge so it becomes a part of their usable vocabularies. In other words, we want students to be able to understand a word when they come across it in reading or conversation and we want them to be able to use these words correctly in their own writing and speaking. Research indicates that in order to establish strong, lasting representations of word meanings, students need to have repeated exposures to new vocabulary in supportive contexts (Nagy & Scott, 2000). Although we do not know exactly how many exposures to a new word are needed for most students, we do know that multiple exposures, over time, can help to increase the depth and flexibility of word learning (Zipoli, Coyne, & McCoach, 2010). Direct and explicit vocabulary instruction includes intentional review opportunities that ensure that students encounter target vocabulary in varied meaningful contexts through the day and over time.

Violet's Experience

Violet came up with two strategies to help students encounter the new words over time and review their meanings. First, she selected one previously taught word to include in each small-group vocabulary intervention session, ensuring that all previously introduced words were included equally in the review cycle. During the brief review, she would show the picture, read the definition and anchor sentence, and ask the students a question about the word (e.g., "Tell me about a time when you were *drenched*"). Second, she dedicated a part of the classroom wall for posting the words and pictures and referred to the vocabulary wall throughout the day. For example, a student might say, "Look at how easily this eraser can bend." In response, Violet would go over to the vocabulary wall and ask the students what word they could use to describe the eraser. She also created a space to keep track of how many times students used the new words during each school day. She found this to be very motivating for the students because they were excited to add new tallies to the chart.

ORAL VOCABULARY INSTRUCTION FOR STUDENTS IN THE UPPER-ELEMENTARY GRADES

The primary focus of this chapter has been on using oral language activities to support vocabulary development of students in the early elementary grades. It is important to note that these strategies can also be an effective approach for students in the upper-elementary grades. The emphasis on providing rich oral language experiences, along with opportunities to actively engage with words, can be beneficial for all students but is particularly important for those older students who are experiencing language and reading difficulties. These students are in a position where they are not likely to encounter complex vocabulary in their own reading but still need to work on building their vocabulary knowledge. For example, students in the upper-elementary grades who have difficulty with decoding and reading fluency may not be able to read grade-level texts that include sophisticated and complex vocabulary. However, these students' listening comprehension is often more developed than their reading abilities and therefore they can benefit from grade-appropriate oral language activities and experiences that include more advanced language and vocabulary. Therefore, the oral vocabulary activities described in this chapter can be tailored to be used with students in any grade. Older students will likely have a greater capacity to produce rich oral language responses. For example, a kindergarten student who is asked to make up a sentence using a vocabulary word might need high levels of scaffolding from the teacher to be able to produce a response that demonstrates a full understanding of a word meaning. Older students might have less difficulty with such a task and might enjoy these types of activities that allow for some creativity of expression more than a yes/no type of activity that is more supportive for younger students.

Another way to modify instruction for older students is to incorporate more opportunities to compare and contrast word meanings and discuss words with multiple meanings. Many young students have difficulty thinking about how words relate to other words. Older students might have an easier time holding multiple meanings in their mind while thinking about how they are similar or different. Using word webs or other graphic organizers can be a good way to help students understand relationships between words. One of the benefits of the strategies described throughout this chapter is that it is easy to modify the activities to meet the needs of students of various ages and abilities.

SUMMARY

Vocabulary knowledge is essential for successful reading. Students' understanding of words and their meanings is necessary for comprehending text that contains those words, and students' vocabulary knowledge and development in the early grades is one of the best predictors of overall reading achievement in elementary school, high school, and beyond. Extensive research provides compelling evidence that vocabulary instruction is effective, particularly for teaching the meanings of words that are targeted for instruction. In the early grades, vocabulary instruction occurs primarily through intentionally planned oral language activities, like teaching and discussing academic vocabulary that occurs in texts that are being read aloud to students and through whole-class and small-group interactive discussions about academic content and students' own experiences.

The most effective methods for teaching vocabulary are those consistent with an SL approach—for example, those that include highly explicit instruction, careful and purposeful selection of words to teach, and prompt and specific instructional feedback. Small-group intervention that supplements core programming intensifies instruction for students who are at risk for experiencing reading difficulties or those who do not respond to whole-class vocabulary instruction. It maximizes engagement, as well as opportunities to interact with new vocabulary and use extended language. Explicit vocabulary instruction is direct and extended, and includes (1) selecting important academic vocabulary to teach directly, (2) providing student-friendly definitions of target vocabulary, (3) introducing vocabulary in supportive and meaningful contexts, (4) explicitly teaching word meanings, (5) providing extended instruction that maximizes opportunities for students to interact with new vocabulary, (6) providing immediate corrective feedback, and (7) reviewing taught vocabulary across the school day and over time.

APPLICATION ACTIVITIES

Activity 1

A second-grade teacher, Mr. Chang, is looking for ways to include more vocabulary instruction throughout the day in his classroom. He already reads at least one book or chapter aloud as a part of their class routine. He decides that directly teaching the meanings of vocabulary words found in his read-alouds would be a relatively simple way to support his students' word learning.

PART 1

Below you will find a passage from a book that Mr. Chang is planning to read to his class. Select three to five words from this passage that you would recommend he target for instruction.

> Two friends, Kennedy and Zach, were playing on the soccer field near their school when something mysterious happened. A gust of wind came and off in the distance they saw something soar into the air. Kennedy and Zach looked at each other with confusion. What could that be? They took a deep breath and started moving toward the object with apprehension.

Answer

The following words could be good choices for instruction for typical second-grade classrooms: *mysterious, gust, soar, confusion,* and *apprehension.*

PART 2

Now that Mr. Chang has a list of vocabulary words to teach, he needs to develop student-friendly definitions. If you were teaching the meanings of the five target words from the passage, what definitions would you use?

Answer

Here are some examples of student-friendly definitions that Mr. Chang could use with his students.

Mysterious—hard to understand
Gust—a strong blast of wind
Soar—to fly fast

Confusion—not understanding something
Apprehension—feeling worried about what might happen

Activity 2

Mr. Chang has been introducing new vocabulary words through his read-alouds for a few months. Things have been going well and he thinks the students are benefiting from this type of structured vocabulary instruction. However, he is concerned about a few of his students who seem to be struggling to fully understand the new word meanings. What are some things that Mr. Chang could do to help support these students?

ANSWER

Mr. Chang might want to consider providing small-group intervention for the students who are not fully responding to classroom vocabulary instruction. He could meet with the students after a group of words is introduced through the storybook reading. This group could meet for 20–30 minutes in addition to the within-book instruction, with a goal of providing interactive, extended activities to allow the students to process those word meanings at a deeper level. Mr. Chang should provide explicit instruction and plan to incorporate multiple opportunities for the students to respond to questions about the words. Feedback should be immediate and clear. Finally, Mr. Chang should think about ways to review the new word meanings over time.

REFERENCES

Anderson, R. C., & Freebody, P. (1981). Vocabulary knowledge. In J. T. Guthrie (Ed.), *Comprehension and teaching: Research reviews* (pp. 77–117). Newark, DE: International Reading Association.

Archer, A. L., & Hughes, C. A. (2010). *Explicit instruction: Effective and efficient teaching.* New York: Guilford Press

Beck, I. L., McKeown, M. G., & Kucan, L. (2013). *Bringing words to life: Robust vocabulary instruction* (2nd ed.). New York: Guilford Press.

Biemiller, A. (2009). *Words worth teaching: Closing the vocabulary gap.* Columbus, OH: SRA/McGraw-Hill.

Coxhead, A. (2000). A new academic word list. *TESOL Quarterly, 34,* 213–238.

Coyne, M. D., & Koriakin, T. A. (2017). What do beginning special educators need to know about implementing intensive reading interventions for students with disabilities? *Teaching Exceptional Children, 49,* 239–248.

Coyne, M. D., McCoach, D. B., Loftus, S., Zipoli, J. R., & Kapp, S. (2009). Direct vocabulary instruction in kindergarten: Teaching for breadth versus depth. *Elementary School Journal, 110*(1), 1–18.

Coyne, M. D., McCoach, D. B., Ware, S., Austin, C., Loftus, S., & Baker, D. (2019). Racing against the vocabulary gap: Matthew effects in early vocabulary instruction and intervention. *Exceptional Children, 85,* 163–179.

Coyne, M. D., McCoach, D. B., Ware, S., Loftus-Rattan, S., Baker, D., Santoro, L., et al. (2021).

Supporting vocabulary development within a multi-tiered system of support: Evaluating the efficacy of supplementary kindergarten vocabulary intervention. Manuscript submitted for publication.

Coyne, M. D., Neugebauer, S., Ware, S., McCoach, D. B., & Madura, J. (2015). Vocabulary and its role in early comprehension development. In A. Debruin, A. Van Kleek, & S. Gear (Eds.), *Developing early comprehension: Laying the foundation for reading success* (pp. 19–34). Baltimore: Brookes.

Cunningham, A. E., & Stanovich, K. E. (1997). Early reading acquisition and its relation to reading experience and ability 10 years later. *Developmental Psychology, 33,* 934–945.

Elleman, A. M., Lindo, E. J., Morphy, P., & Compton, D. (2009). The impact of vocabulary instruction on passage-level comprehension of school-age children: A meta-analysis. *Journal of Research on Educational Effectiveness, 2,* 1–44.

Foorman, B., Beyler, N., Borradaile, K., Coyne, M., Denton, C. A., Dimino, J., et al. (2016). *Foundational skills to support reading for understanding in kindergarten through 3rd grade* [NCEE 2016-4008]. Washington, DC: National Center for Education Evaluation and Regional Assistance, Institute of Education Sciences, U.S. Department of Education.

Gardner, D., & Davies, M. (2014). A new academic vocabulary list. *Applied Linguistics, 35,* 305–327.

Gersten, R., Compton, D., Connor, C. M., Dimino, J., Santoro, L., Linan-Thompson, S., et al. (2009). *Assisting students struggling with reading: Response to intervention and multi-tier intervention for reading in the primary grades. A practice guide* [NCEE 2009-4045]. Washington, DC: Institute of Education Sciences, U.S. Department of Education.

Gough, P. B., & Tunmer, W. E. (1986). Decoding, reading, and reading disability. *Remedial and Special Education, 7*(1), 6–10.

Hiebert, E. H., Goodwin, A. P., & Cervetti, G. N. (2018). Core vocabulary: Its morphological content and presence in exemplar texts. *Reading Research Quarterly, 53*(1), 29–49.

Loftus-Rattan, S. M., Mitchell, A. M., & Coyne, M. D. (2016). Direct vocabulary instruction in preschool: A comparison of extended instruction, embedded instruction, and incidental exposure. *Elementary School Journal, 116*(3), 391–410.

Marulis, L. M., & Neuman, S. (2013). How vocabulary interventions affect young children at risk: A meta-analytic review. *Journal of Research on Educational Effectiveness, 6*(3), 223–262.

Nagy, W. E., & Herman, P. A. (1987). Breadth and depth of vocabulary knowledge: Implications for acquisition and instruction. In M. G. McKeown & M. E. Curtis (Eds.), *The nature of vocabulary acquisition* (pp. 19–36). Hillsdale, NJ: Erlbaum.

Nagy, W. E., & Scott, J. A. (2000). Vocabulary processes. In M. L. Kamil, P. B. Mosenthal, P. D. Pearson, & R. Barr (Eds.), *Handbook of reading research* (Vol. 3, pp. 269–284). Mahwah, NJ: Erlbaum.

Nation, K. (2019). Children's reading difficulties, language, and reflections on the simple view of reading. *Australian Journal of Learning Difficulties, 24*(1), 47–73.

Ouellette, G. P. (2006). What's meaning got to do with it: The role of vocabulary in word reading and word comprehension. *Journal of Educational Psychology, 98,* 554–566.

Penno, J. F., Wilkinson, I. A. G., & Moore, D. W. (2002). Vocabulary acquisition from teacher explanation and repeated listening to stories: Do they overcome the Matthew effect? *Journal of Educational Psychology, 94*(1), 23–33.

Sénéchal, M., Ouellette, G., & Rodney, D. (2006). The misunderstood giant: On the predictive role of vocabulary to reading. In S. B. Neuman & D. Dickinson (Eds.), *Handbook of early literacy* (Vol. 2, pp. 173–182). New York: Guilford Press.

Snow, C., Burns, M., & Griffin, P. (1998). *Preventing reading difficulties in young children.* Washington, DC: National Academies Press.

Spencer, M., Quinn, J. M., & Wagner, R. K. (2017). Vocabulary, morphology, and reading comprehension. In K. Cain, D. L. Compton, & R. K. Parrila (Eds.), *Theories of reading development* (pp. 239–256). Amsterdam: John Benjamins.

Stahl, S. A. (1986). Three principles of effective vocabulary instruction. *Journal of Reading, 29*(7), 662–668.

Stahl, S. A. (1991). Beyond the instrumentalist hypothesis: Some relationships between word meanings and comprehension. In P. Schwanenflugel (Ed.), *The psychology of word meanings* (pp. 157–178). Hillsdale, NJ: Erlbaum.

Wasik, B. A., Hindman, A. H., & Snell, E. K. (2016). Book reading and vocabulary development: A systematic review. *Early Childhood Research Quarterly, 37,* 39–57.

Zipoli, R., Coyne, M. D., & McCoach, D. B. (2010). Enhancing vocabulary intervention for kindergarten students: Strategic integration of semantically related and embedded word review. *Remedial and Special Education, 32*(2), 131–143.

FORM 6.1. Vocabulary Lesson Plan Template for Introducing New Vocabulary during a Read-Aloud

Step 1. Select three to five words from a book or text you are going to read aloud to your class.
Step 2. Create student-friendly definitions for each of the chosen target words.
Step 3. Introduce the target words to your class prior to reading the book.
Step 4. Teach the word meanings when you encounter them during the reading. *Note:* Remember to (a) provide the definition of the target word, (b) place the definition in the context of the sentence, (c) draw attention to any picture or contextual support that helps demonstrate the word meaning, and (d) have the students repeat the new word together.

CHAPTER 7

Structured Literacy Interventions for Oral Language Comprehension

Richard P. Zipoli
Donna D. Merritt

Kevin, a monolingual English-speaking third grader, is described by his classroom teacher as cooperative, eager to learn, and a capable conversationalist. In preschool, he received special education services from a speech–language pathologist (SLP). These supports continued through kindergarten and Kevin was exited from special education at the end of that grade, having met all of his individualized education program (IEP) goals and scoring in the average to low-average range on the diagnostic measures administered during his speech–language reassessment.

Kevin currently demonstrates accurate decoding and fluent reading, but impaired reading comprehension. Throughout grade 3, he has participated in differentiated small-group and individual instruction within general education to support reading comprehension, with an emphasis on activating prior knowledge, predicting, and summarizing. However, recent progress monitoring data indicate that he has not yet made sufficient improvement. The school's reading specialist reports that Kevin scored substantially below grade level in listening and reading comprehension on narrative passages from the Qualitative Reading Inventory–5 (Leslie & Schudt Caldwell, 2017), and he demonstrated particular difficulty when attempting to answer inferential questions. Moreover, his classroom teacher reports that Kevin appears to have difficulties following spoken instructions in the classroom. His rereferral to special education toward the end of the school year has prompted his team to recommend a comprehensive evaluation to clarify his learning strengths and weaknesses.

RESEARCH ON LANGUAGE COMPREHENSION DIFFICULTIES

Language comprehension is central to understanding spoken information in the classroom and essential for extracting meaning from text when reading. As noted in Spear-Swerling, Chapter 1, this volume, the *simple view of reading* posits that reading comprehension is the product of two broad areas of ability: word recognition and language comprehension (Hoover & Gough, 1990). This chapter addresses the learning needs of students who have difficulties with language comprehension, with a dual focus on sentence-level and discourse-level processing. These students' needs are addressed from a *developmental language perspective,* which emphasizes that written language (reading and writing), while not a simple by-product of oral language, shares many of the same foundations and processes needed for effective listening and speaking (Kamhi & Catts, 2012).

The intervention strategies presented in this chapter are especially relevant for students with two (of the three) common profiles of poor reading highlighted in Chapter 1. Students with *specific reading comprehension difficulties* (SRCD) have problems with reading comprehension despite intact phonological awareness and word recognition. Their deficits are typically attributable to weak language comprehension skills that interfere with understanding in both oral and written modalities. Students with a *mixed reading difficulties* (MRD) profile have poor word recognition and language comprehension, and their reading comprehension difficulties extend beyond what can be accounted for by weak word-reading skills alone (Spear-Swerling, 2015).

Students in many disability categories can have weak language comprehension. Those at risk for impaired comprehension include, but are not limited to, students with language impairment, learning disabilities, high-functioning autism, social (pragmatic) communication disorder, intellectual disability, and hearing impairment or deafness. Similarly, English learners and students who have not had sufficient opportunities to engage in communication-building experiences, because they are environmentally at risk or have complex medical or psychological needs, may have difficulty comprehending the language of instruction. Therefore, it is imperative for educators to closely monitor these learners for potential comprehension difficulties.

Assessment Issues

Despite growing recognition of the critical contributions that oral language skills make to reading comprehension, difficulties with oral language comprehension may go unnoticed (Cain & Oakhill, 2007), particularly when students have comparatively strong word-reading and spelling skills (Bishop & Adams, 1990). For example, Nation, Clarke, Marshall, and Durand (2004) analyzed the language and reading performance of a large sample of 8-year-old students. Among the children whose profiles were consistent with SRCD, most demonstrated low language ability and a substantial proportion met clinical criteria for language impairment. Of note, none of these students had been identified with language or reading impairment prior to the study. The investigators concluded that "serious reading and language impairments are not always obvious in children who have good phonological ability and appear, superficially at least, to read well" (p. 199).

A combination of code-based, listening comprehension and reading comprehension measures may help to identify students with SRCD or MRD (Spear-Swerling, 2015). However, assessors have historically lacked universal screening and progress monitoring probes of listening comprehension that have the brevity and technical adequacy of code-based measures (Zipoli & Merritt, 2017). Formal assessment of listening comprehension has also been recommended when testing students with suspected reading problems during comprehensive evaluations (Catts, Kamhi, & Adlof, 2012). Nonetheless, these measures may be missing from reading assessment batteries.

A *descriptive–developmental approach* can be effective for assessing and interpreting language difficulties. This method involves identifying specific patterns of strength and weakness across five language domains that are essential to listening and reading comprehension (Paul, Norbury, & Gosse, 2018). These domains are *phonology* (speech sounds), *morphology* (the smallest units of language that convey meaning, including prefixes and suffixes), *semantics* (which pertains to meaning, including vocabulary knowledge and figurative/nonliteral language), *syntax* (sentence-level word order and processing), and *pragmatics* (social communication) and *discourse*. Discourse consists of connected sentences organized into larger units of communication, such as conversation, spoken narratives, or written passages. Related skills that contribute to language comprehension include background knowledge, inferencing, comprehension monitoring, perspective taking, and specific features of literate language (Oakhill & Cain, 2007; Westby, 2012), as well as cognitive abilities, such as attention, auditory processing, working memory, processing speed, and executive functioning (e.g., Spear-Swerling, 2016). An advantage of systematically appraising skills across component language domains and cognitive–linguistic processes is that information on individual patterns of performance can then be used to plan developmentally appropriate and targeted interventions.

Guiding Principles for Intervention

Four principles inform the interventions described in this chapter. The first principle is that students with language difficulties will benefit from opportunities to practice and *integrate skills across multiple language modalities*: listening, speaking, reading, and writing (Paul et al., 2018). Speech signals, for example, are inherently fleeting. By "capturing" language in print, educators and clinicians can more explicitly introduce and stress key features of language, such as how conjunctions are used to formulate compound and complex sentences.

A second principle is that intervention should help students with comprehension weaknesses to improve their understanding of *literate language,* which is the more formal language style that characterizes classroom discourse and written language in textbooks. In contrast to everyday conversation, which is often about objects and events that are well-known to communication partners, literate language is often decontextualized, focusing on unfamiliar topics that are removed in place and time (Bruner, 1986). Literate language also has a high proportion of low-frequency words, complex syntactic forms, and abstract ideas (Benson, 2009).

The third principle is that *narrative skills may serve as a bridge to proficiency with literate language* (Westby, 2012). This is because stories have a structure that can be explicitly taught to students. In fact, research indicates that early narrative abilities predict later reading comprehension and success in school (Oakhill & Cain, 2007). However, students with SRCD and children who are language impaired (who may have an SRCD or MRD profile) often have deficits comprehending and producing spoken narratives (Cain & Oakhill, 2007; Paul et al., 2018). As discussed below, narrative intervention is particularly adaptable because instruction on related language skills (e.g., vocabulary, inferencing, and comprehension monitoring) can be strategically integrated while teaching story structure.

The fourth principle is that students with comprehension difficulties may be best served when assessment and intervention are implemented with *collaboration* among members of the student's educational team. The language and learning needs of students with impaired language comprehension are often complex. For example, advocating for partnerships to support reading comprehension, Ehren (2006) aptly noted that there could be "too much for any one professional to do" (p. 42). However, an interdisciplinary team affords a practical division of roles and responsibilities, wherein each professional brings highly specialized knowledge and skills. Coordination of services helps to avoid gaps or redundancy and promotes generalization of strategies across settings and content areas. Educational teams can also emphasize *curriculum-based intervention* by ensuring that their goals, activities, and materials are closely aligned with school curricula and achievement standards (Ehren & Whitmire, 2009).

INTERVENTIONS SUPPORTING ORAL LANGUAGE COMPREHENSION

Language specialists typically distinguish between oral and written language and between receptive (listening and reading comprehension) and expressive (speaking and writing) language. However, an alternate approach that differentiates *sound/word-level* skills from *sentence/discourse-level* skills (Nelson, 2010) has emerged from research and can also be helpful in educational practice. Interventions addressing sound/word-level skills are explored in Chapter 2 (phonological awareness; Al Otaiba, Allor, & Stewart, this volume), Chapter 3 (morphological knowledge; Kearns, Lyon, & Kelley, this volume), and Chapter 6 (vocabulary; Coyne & Loftus-Rattan, this volume). Instructional approaches for comprehension of expository text, a discourse-level skill, are addressed in Chapter 8 (Stevens & Austin, this volume). Therefore, the remainder of the current chapter discusses sentence/discourse-level skills (with a focus on narratives) that may need to be addressed in order to help students with SRCD or MRD improve their listening and reading comprehension.

Sentence-Level Intervention

> The results of Kevin's comprehensive special education evaluation indicate that he has solidly average word-reading and decoding skills. However, he presents with listening comprehension deficits at the sentence/discourse level that are negatively impacting his reading comprehension. He requires special education supports and services as a student with a learning disability consistent with an SRCD profile. The SLP reports that Kevin's performance was in the below-average to poor range on measures involving oral sentence comprehension, production, and processing, including the Following Directions, Formulated Sentences, and Recalling Sentences subtests of Clinical Evaluation of Language Fundamentals—Fifth Edition (CELF-5; Wiig, Secord, & Semel, 2013). Criterion-referenced assessment and informal probes corroborate that he has notable difficulties comprehending certain sentence structures. His classroom teacher also notes the frequent use of simple or "run-on" compound sentences in his written assignments, with occasional grammatical errors that are less likely when he speaks. Based on these findings, Kevin's educational team targets his understanding and use of difficult sentence structures, as described below.

Syntactic knowledge has been widely recognized as contributing to the understanding of spoken discourse and reading comprehension (e.g., Snow, Griffin, & Burns, 2005). For example, the Common Core State Standards (CCSS) for English Language Arts and Literacy state that students should be able to understand and produce simple, compound, and complex sentences by the end of third grade (National Governors Association and Council of Chief State School Officers, 2010). Unfortunately, educators may be underprepared to teach sentence comprehension and production (e.g., Moats, 2009), and many reading programs tend to neglect explicit instruction in sentence-level comprehension (Zipoli, 2017).

Potentially Confusing Sentence Structures

Four types of sentences are commonly challenging for elementary students with language comprehension difficulties: (1) passive sentences, (2) complex sentences with temporal and causal conjunctions, (3) sentences with center-embedded relative clauses, and (4) lengthy sentences with three or more clauses (e.g., Owens, 2016; Paul et al., 2018). Knowledge of these structures helps certified educators and SLPs, collectively referred to as interventionists in this chapter, to proactively anticipate and address potential sources of confusion.

Passive sentences are difficult for some students to understand. Consider the following two sentences. The first is written with an active voice (i.e., the subject performs the action), and the second is written with a passive voice (i.e., the subject is acted upon).

1. Army troops pursued Chief Joseph's men. [active voice]
2. Chief Joseph's men were pursued by army troops. [passive voice]

Although these two sentences have the same meaning, the second sentence may be more difficult to process if students fail to understand how small function words (*were* and *by*) are used to formulate a passive construction. Without this insight, they may misunderstand the sentence—based on their processing of the order of highly salient words—to mean "Chief Joseph's men pursued army troops." (The second sentence is also tricky because it is a reversible passive sentence, meaning that the noun phrases could be reversed, resulting in another passive sentence with a different meaning: "Army troops were pursued by Chief Joseph's men.")

Complex sentences that contain *temporal or causal conjunctions* are a second potential source of confusion. Consider the following two sentences:

1. Before the Revolutionary War started, the colonists were heavily taxed.
2. The colonist fought because he was drafted.

"The colonists were heavily taxed" is an independent clause because it can stand alone, whereas "Before the Revolutionary War started" is a dependent clause because it cannot stand alone. This dependent clause begins with a temporal conjunction (*before*), and it can also be referred to as an adverbial clause because it describes when an action occurred. The second sentence begins with an independent clause ("The colonist fought") that is followed by a causal conjunction (*because*) introducing an adverbial clause that describes why something happened ("because he was drafted"). These sentences might be confusing for students who do not understand the ordering effect of temporal or causal conjunctions. For example, a student might predominantly rely on the order of clauses in the first sentence (war started → colonists taxed), resulting in a failure to correctly understand the actual chronology of the events. Similarly, the order of the clauses or verbs in the second sentence (fought → drafted) does not correspond to the actual cause-and-effect relationship between events (drafted → fought). In typically developing children, accurate comprehension of the conjunction *because* in sentences may not develop until age 7, and consistent understanding in decontextualized contexts may not emerge until 10–11 years of age (Owens, 2016).

Center-embedded relative clauses are a third potential source of comprehension difficulty. Relative (adjective) clauses are dependent clauses that follow and modify a noun (Justice & Ezell, 2016; Owens, 2016). They are also introduced by relative pronouns, such as *who, that,* or *which*. Consider the following sentence:

The woman who followed the police officer asked a question.

What makes this complex sentence potentially difficult to process is the location of the relative clause "who followed the police officer," which separates the independent clause into two parts: "The woman" and "asked a question." Students with listening comprehension difficulties may not understand this sentence if they utilize a word-order strategy, misinterpreting the sentence as saying that the police officer asked a question. The likelihood of this confusion would increase among students with auditory processing or short-term memory weaknesses because of a recency effect, or tendency to process only the last few words of a sentence (Owens, 2016).

Finally, *long sentences with multiple clauses* may also be problematic for students with comprehension difficulties, especially those with weaknesses in attention, auditory processing, short-term memory, and/or executive functioning. The following sentence comes from *Moonshot: The Flight of Apollo 11* (Floca, 2009, p. 42), which is an example of a grade 3 CCSS informational text. "As Armstrong exited the Eagle he moved into position a camera that beamed to earth shadowy images of his climb down Eagle's ladder—and earth was watching."

> As Armstrong exited the Eagle [*dependent clause*]
> he moved into position a camera [*independent clause*]
> that beamed to earth shadowy images of his climb down Eagle's ladder [*dependent clause*]
> and earth was watching [*independent clause*]

This seemingly innocuous compound-complex sentence is composed of 27 words and four clauses, each of which communicates a distinct idea or proposition. It is not hard to appreciate the cognitive–linguistic resources needed to effectively process it. Interventionists can use informal probes or criterion-referenced judgment tasks to assess children's comprehension of potentially confusing sentence structures. For example, in order to assess a given student's comprehension of the sentence about Neil Armstrong, an interventionist might ask *directed questions,* such as "When was the camera moved into position?" and "What did people on earth see?" (See Paul et al., 2018, for information on criterion-referenced judgment tasks.)

Sentence-Level Intervention Strategies

Students who have difficulties unraveling sentences should receive explicit, systematic teaching with an emphasis on modeling and guided practice, utilizing specific strategies that can improve their ability to understand and produce challenging sentences (Zipoli, 2017). When supporting students who have difficulties with both word reading and language comprehension (i.e., an MRD profile), attempts should be made to work with sentences composed of words that students will be able to read automatically so that cognitive resources will not be diverted to decoding.

When a student has trouble understanding reversible passive sentences, the interventionist should first provide explicit instruction, explaining passive sentences that are written on a whiteboard, and comparing and contrasting them with sentences written in an active voice. Small function words can be made more visually prominent by presenting them in a **<u>bold</u>**, **<u>underlined</u>** font:

> Chief Joseph's tribe **<u>was</u>** pursued **<u>by</u>** the army troops.

A *directed questions* procedure can then be used to help the student more accurately and fluently discriminate between active and passive sentences (Carnine, Silbert, Kame'enui, & Tarver, 2010). Pairs of sentences with opposite meanings are presented, first in the active voice and then in the passive voice. After some initial modeling, students are engaged in guided practice with corrective feedback using three to five pairs of sentences. The following is an example of a directed questions procedure:

INTERVENTIONIST: I'll say a sentence and then ask you a question about it. . . . "Rebecca chased the dog." Who was chased?

STUDENT: The dog.

INTERVENTIONIST: Who did the chasing?

STUDENT: Rebecca.

INTERVENTIONIST: Yes. . . . Now I'll say a different sentence. . . . "Rebecca was chased by the dog." Who was chased?

STUDENT: Rebecca.

INTERVENTIONIST: Who did the chasing?

STUDENT: The dog.

Complex sentences containing certain temporal and causal conjunctions are sometimes challenging. Interventionists can design a two-part lesson that includes strategic integration of *sentence starters* (Hochman, 2011). First, for example, the conjunctions *before, after,* and *because* are written on a whiteboard. The interventionist then describes how these words can be used to describe the order of events and cause–effect relationships, modeling use of these conjunctions to formulate oral sentences about familiar daily routines.

During the second part of the lesson, the interventionist writes three sentences on the whiteboard, underlining the target conjunctions. Assume, for instance, that the following sentences from *A Drop of Water: A Book of Science and Water* (Wick, 1997) will be read soon as a part of the school district's third-grade science curriculum:

1. Before doing any experiments, make sure you take the following precautions. (p. 38)
2. After several minutes, you will see water condensing on the salt grains. (p. 39)
3. The molecules in the blue dropper break apart because they are pushed and pulled all over the jar by other water molecules. (p. 18)

The student is asked to read the paragraph where each sentence appears. A whiteboard and different colored markers are used to show how the same conjunction can introduce a dependent clause at either the beginning or end of the target sentence. For instance:

Make sure you take the following precautions before doing any experiments.

Next, the interventionist provides an opportunity for guided practice using sentence starters. The conjunctions *before, after,* and *because* are written vertically on a piece of paper and the student is asked to generate three original sentences pertaining to water or safety precautions (one starting with each respective conjunction). Once the sentences have been written, the student is asked to rewrite each sentence by moving the conjunction and dependent clause from the beginning to the end of the sentence, observing how the implied order of events or causal relationship is preserved.

Some students have problems understanding sentences with center-embedded relative clauses and/or lengthy sentences with multiple clauses. *Sentence combining* (Saddler, 2012), as well as a complementary *sentence decomposition* procedure (Balthazar & Scott, 2015), can be used to improve their ability to comprehend these sentences. Sentence combining is a particularly effective and versatile teaching strategy because it enhances reading comprehension, as well as understanding and use of complex sentences (Paul et al., 2018).

In order to enhance comprehension of sentences with center-embedded relative clauses, the interventionist can again design a two-part lesson that proceeds from explicit instruction to guided practice. First, relative clauses and relative pronouns are described, using a whiteboard and examples of sentences to explain and demonstrate how these clauses act like adjectives by modifying nouns. The following example is also taken from *A Drop of Water: A Book of Science and Water* (Wick, 1997, p. 28). The sentence is written on a whiteboard, placing the relative clause in brackets and underlining the relative pronoun introducing the clause:

Clouds [that produce snow] often contain both ice crystals and liquid droplets.

The interventionist then describes how the relative clause acts like an adjective by modifying the preceding noun: *clouds*. Next, the student is shown how the relative clause splits or separates the independent clause, which would otherwise stand alone:

Clouds often contain both ice crystals and liquid droplets.

At this point, the interventionist uses arrows, as illustrated below, to highlight how sentences with relative clauses in the center can be "tricky" because listeners or readers might be misled, thinking that it is the snow—rather than the clouds—that contains both ice crystals and liquid droplets:

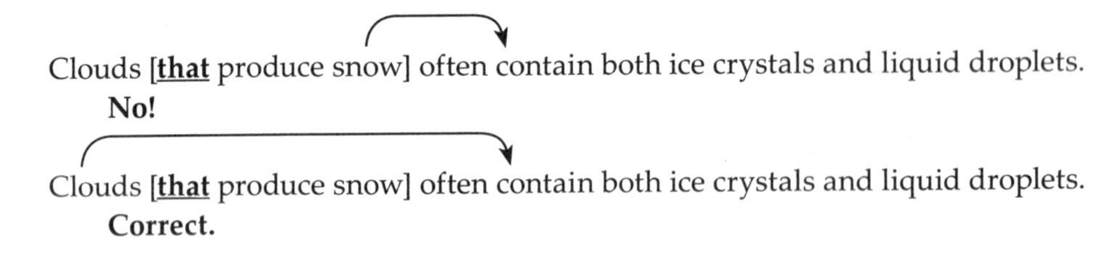

During the second part of the lesson, the student is given an opportunity to consolidate this insight through guided practice with cued sentence combining (Saddler,

2012). A different complex sentence structure from the same book is used for the exercise: " . . . water molecules [that cling to particles] form tiny ice crystals" (Wick, 1997, p. 28). Based on this wording, two "kernel" sentences are written on the board. First, the independent clause is written out as a simple sentence (see below). Then, the interventionist writes a second sentence with two clues: the relative pronoun *that* appears in parentheses at the end of the sentence and the information describing water molecules is underlined:

> Water molecules form tiny ice crystals.
> Water molecules <u>cling to particles</u>. (*that*)

The interventionist then scaffolds the student's attempt to combine the kernel sentences. Strategically combining these two kernel sentences into a more complex form that mirrors the original sentence from the science book deepens the student's understanding of how the center-embedded relative clause ("that cling to particles") simply describes "water molecules."

Many students with comprehension difficulties find it hard to make sense of lengthy sentences with three or more clauses. Again, either sentence combining or sentence decomposition—or a combination of both—can be used to promote sentence comprehension. The interventionist might start with sentence decomposition to promote awareness that longer, more complicated sentences often have several clauses that convey different ideas. To illustrate this, the following sentence from *A Drop of Water: A Book of Science and Water* (Wick, 1997, p. 9) could be written on a whiteboard:

> This sphere stretches because of the drop's weight and motion, but surface tension helps keep the drop together, as if it were held in an elastic skin.

The interventionist would explain how this sentence is made up of clauses that provide information about a water drop, writing each clause and modeling a "think-aloud" strategy to describe the information it conveys:

> This sphere stretches
> "This clause tells me something about the sphere. The sphere stretches."
>
> because of the drop's weight and motion
> "This clause tells me *why* the sphere stretches. The drop's weight and motion stretch the sphere."
>
> but surface tension helps keep the drop together
> "This clause tells me that surface tension helps to stop the water drop from breaking apart."
>
> as if it were held in an elastic skin.
> "This sentence compares the surface tension to an elastic skin. Both help to keep the contents inside."

Table 7.1 summarizes some potentially confusing sentence structures and selected intervention strategies that can be used to enhance students' understanding. Once students demonstrate the ability to use these sentence-level strategies during structured lessons, members of the educational team need to collaborate to ensure opportunities for strategy application during curriculum-based activities in the classroom (Balthazar & Scott, 2015). (The previous section provides a basic introduction to sentence-level intervention. For more comprehensive information on sentence-level assessment and intervention, syntactic structures, and sentence combining strategies, respectively, see Balthazar & Scott, 2015; Justice & Ezell, 2016; Saddler, 2012.)

Discourse-Level Intervention

Additional results from Kevin's comprehensive special education evaluation indicate that he also has discourse-level language difficulties that adversely impact his reading comprehension. His oral narrative abilities were below average on the Test of Narrative Language–2 (TNL-2; Gillam & Pearson, 2017). He had good recall of factual details—however, he made substantial comprehension errors in response to questions that required inferencing. Kevin's retold and self-generated stories were short, and he had minimal use of cohesive words, such as conjunctions. He often omitted content that conveyed the consequences of a character's actions. Other assessment results were also consistent with an SRCD profile, as Kevin had difficulty comprehending figurative language, or language with an implied meaning that differs from the surface meaning of the words (Gorman-Gard, 2002). Corroborating this finding, Kevin's team observed that he had difficulty understanding similes,

TABLE 7.1. Potentially Confusing Sentences

Sentence structure	Example	Effective intervention strategies
Reversible passive sentence	The lion was followed by the tourists.	Directed questions
Complex sentences containing dependent clauses that begin with temporal or causal conjunctions	Before multiplying, divide the two numbers. We hear thunder after we see lightning. Earth can support life because it has plenty of water and oxygen.	Sentence starters
Center-embedded relative clause	The catcher who tagged the runner was injured.	Sentence combining Sentence decomposition
Long sentences with multiple clauses	As a thunderstorm approaches, you should move inside of a building because cloud-to-ground lightning strikes can be dangerous when you are outdoors.	Sentence combining Sentence decomposition

metaphors, and idioms when discussing passages that he had heard or read. Based on these findings, his team focused their intervention on using academically relevant narratives to improve his discourse-level comprehension and expressive language skills. In anticipation of Kevin's promotion to fourth grade, and the expected language demands of the CCSS English Language Arts standards, his team also addressed inferencing and figurative language.

Narrative Structure

Story narratives have a substantial role in the transition from the contextualized, interactive, and informal language of home to the highly decontextualized, formal, abstract, and literate language of school (Benson, 2009; Bruner, 1986). As a more structured discourse form than conversation, stories are framed in predictable ways, including a *gist* or theme (i.e., content schema) and a *story grammar* structure (Stein & Glenn, 1979) that guide story comprehension and production. Story grammar combines a *setting* (time, place, central characters) and an *episode,* which is an event sequence that incorporates an *initiating event,* characters' *internal responses* to the event (including a plan), a series of temporally ordered *attempts* to reach the goal, a *consequence* (success or failure), and characters' emotional or evaluative *reactions.* Well-constructed children's literature typically includes all story grammar elements, although some components may need to be inferred. Story narratives also contain literate vocabulary (e.g., mental state verbs, such as *remember* or *think*) and cohesive words that conjoin meanings within and across the sentences of a text. These words can convey additive relations between ideas (e.g., *and*), signal temporal order (e.g., *next*), highlight causal connections (e.g., *since*), or specify contrastive associations (e.g., *however*). Thus, a coherent story has both a comprehensible structure and well-integrated cohesion among its parts.

Narrative Development

Narrative development follows a progression of stages delineated by Westby (2012). Young children typically tell stories identified as *descriptive sequences* that include characters, a setting, and basic actions. These evolve into *action sequences* in preschool, which include simple chronologically (but not causally) related events connected by strings of *then* or *and then.* Kindergarteners typically add in cause-and-effect relationships in their *reactive sequences,* using cohesive words, such as *so* or *because.* Those in grades 1 and 2 express a character's internal response (feeling) to an initiating event, as well as a goal, in their *abbreviated episodes.* By grades 3 and 4, students should comprehend and express *complete episodes* that include plans for reaching goals, attempts to resolve the situation, consequences, and reactions. *Elaborated episodes,* which include multiple event sequences or embedded episodes, develop in grade 4 and continue to expand in length and complexity, particularly in writing, throughout the school-age years. The CCSS generally parallel these stages of narrative development, with a primary K–3 focus on narrative structure, including identifying story grammar elements and retelling stories.

The discourse-level oral language competencies required for students to meet the narrative CCSS are broad in scope and are not explicitly delineated (Ehren & Whitmire, 2009). They are referred to as "language underpinnings," and are cumulative, with higher-level oral language skills building on lower ones. Table 7.2 lists some examples of the narrative language underpinnings of the CCSS that grade 3 students like Kevin need to comprehend and produce stories. Similar to sentence-level language, students are usually assumed to have these basic oral language competencies. However, educators may not be providing sufficient instruction in them, as teachers may be unaware of the importance of addressing these underpinnings (Moats, 2009).

Narrative Difficulties

Narrative comprehension weaknesses often coexist with poor narrative expression (Gillam, Gillam, & Reece, 2012), resulting in a cumulative negative impact on the development of literacy skills (McCardle, Scarborough, & Catts, 2001). Students with these language-based difficulties are typically better able to understand and recall the factual details of stories, such as a character's actions. In contrast, their ability to infer cause–effect relationships that are not stated explicitly is often problematic, as is their understanding of cohesive words (Liles, 1985; Merritt & Liles, 1987).

The stories produced by students with language-based difficulties usually have an overall cognitive organization. They typically establish setting information and introduce an event sequence but omit consequences. These students also tend to omit references to characters' goals, emotions, intentions, and thoughts. The sentences in their

TABLE 7.2. Examples of Grade 3 CCSS Sentence and Discourse-Level Narrative Language Underpinnings

Language comprehension

- Accessing content schema, a mental model for the facts and ideas represented in the topic or theme of the story.
- Identifying story grammar elements, recognizing the interrelationships among their parts, and retaining the structure in short-term memory.
- Acknowledging the perspective of different story characters.
- Understanding the meaning of sentence forms, ranging from simple to complex.
- Interpreting cohesive words that convey temporal order and cause–effect relationships, and using this knowledge to comprehend information between and across sentences.

Language production

- Retrieving essential content about the topic of the story.
- Recalling the salient components of a story to retell it in a coherent way.
- Organizing information within story grammar episode structures.
- Generating stories from various stimuli (e.g., a shared event, picture, sequence of pictures, curricular texts).
- Representing the perspectives of different story characters.
- Producing complex, sequential ideas using correct sentence forms.
- Using a range of cohesive words representing temporal and cause–effect relationships relevant to the context, within and across sentences.

stories are short, less complex, have more grammatical errors, and fewer different or unique words. They also use fewer cohesive words that connect temporal and causal ideas, frequently resulting in stories that are ambiguous (Liles, 1985; Merritt & Liles, 1987; Westby, 2012).

Narrative Intervention Strategies

Elementary school students must be able to comprehend and produce coherent, chronologically ordered, causally connected, and decontextualized narratives (Ukrainetz, 2015). This may be elusive for students like Kevin, who have core listening comprehension difficulties consistent with SCRD, as well as for students with MRD. However, narrative intervention can improve these discourse-level weaknesses (Spencer & Petersen, 2020). The method presented in this chapter simultaneously addresses narrative comprehension and expression, and it includes a planning phase and a sequence of six instructional steps. It uses contextualized literature-based approaches (Merritt, Culatta, & Trostle, 1998; Ukrainetz, 2015; Westby, 2012), as opposed to traditional language remediation using isolated tasks that are not tied to the school curriculum. This methodology is consistent with the findings of Gillam and colleagues (2012), who reported that students who received contextualized language intervention significantly outperformed those who received decontextualized intervention on both sentence- and discourse-level measures. Throughout this narrative intervention, students are engaged in learning activities that provide scaffolded support, numerous opportunities for oral responses, and immediate feedback. Multiple language skills (i.e., the language underpinnings) are targeted, promoting enhanced access to the general education curriculum. The methodology does not explicitly address vocabulary development (see Coyne & Loftus-Rattan, Chapter 6, this volume) or written language (see Lambrecht Smith & Haynes, Chapter 9, this volume), although these language components would also be embedded within a comprehensive, integrated approach.

Prior to initiating the six-step instructional sequence described below, interventionists should plan out the intervention by selecting an academically relevant grade-level narrative and previewing the text. The narrative intervention examples described below use *Charlotte's Web* (White, 1952), a CCSS grades 2–3 exemplar text, which captures the adventures of Wilbur the pig within episodes that have salient narrative structures and strong emotional appeal. The intent of specialized instruction is to target gaps in a student's learning, teaching skills and strategies that transfer beyond a particular text. Thus, it is not necessary or advisable for interventionists to teach an entire text or even the content of the narrative, per se. That is the role of the general education teacher. Instead, the interventionist can select parts of texts that provide good examples of language skills that need to be addressed and create lessons that provide explicit instruction in those skills. Considerations include the story structure, complexity of sentences, and literate language forms. Within the planning phase, it is also advisable to determine what story content is clearly stated (e.g., setting information, events, and attempts) in contrast to implicit ideas that require inferencing and may need more explicit instruction.

Effective narrative intervention requires students to think and talk about stories. As such, interventionists should provide instruction that is primarily oral and reciprocal. Scaffolded interactions, with opportunities for many guided oral language exchanges, help students to connect information within and across story episodes and relate to characters' motivations and feelings. Throughout the instruction, it is important to balance questions with explanations and clarifications, so that the intervention focuses on explicit teaching.

STEP 1. READ THE TEXT OUT LOUD

Interventionists can begin the instruction by reading the text to the students, using intonation, gestures, and pauses to allow for processing time. *Rereading the text* will enhance familiarity and strategic use of think-alouds will support *comprehension monitoring* (McClintock, Pesco, & Martin-Chang, 2014). This involves interrupting the reading to clarify images that the story evokes, linking previously established content to new information, and making the text personally relevant. Emphasis should also be given to words, phrases, or sentences that are difficult and impact meaning. For example, the adult could explain the "hullabaloo" that frightened Wilbur, when he escaped his pigpen in chapter 3 of *Charlotte's Web* (White, 1952), as the roar of animal noises.

STEP 2. TEACH NARRATIVE STRUCTURE AND STORY GRAMMAR RELATIONSHIPS

It is essential for interventionists to provide explicit instruction in story grammar. This can initially involve naming, defining, and explaining the function of *story grammar elements,* using brief examples from classic children's stories and then transitioning to a grade-level curricular text. Interventionists can begin by highlighting examples of each element, naming each story part, and explaining the concept and relating it to the story schema—stressing how the parts relate within the organization of the story. For example, in *Charlotte's Web* (White, 1952), Wilbur follows the advice of the overbearing goose (initiating event) and imagines an escape from his pigpen (internal response). He then pushes a loose board (attempt) and escapes to the apple orchard (consequence), where he becomes confused and scared (reactions). Additional story components can be introduced until all of the elements have been taught and learned. At this juncture, interventionists can expand instruction to other episodes within the same story.

Visual and tactile cues representing the story grammar elements, such as icons represented within *The Story Grammar Marker* (Moreau, 2008b), can help students to internalize a story schema, understand relationships among story grammar elements, and support generalization of learning to new texts. A variety of nonlinguistic representations (Marzano, Pickering, & Pollock, 2001) can be used to make narrative structure and relationships among story grammar elements more explicit. Visual cues that use mental imagery provide a foundation from which the student can organize and construct a coherent mental model of the text's meaning. These representations can take any graphic form (e.g., story map, story wheel, story board), as long as a narrative schema is clearly depicted. The purpose of the visual representations is to orient students to the structure of the narrative and reduce the cognitive load inherent in narrative tasks. Several instructional approaches can be used, including a *cloze story map* in which students, who are scaffolded as they generate the missing elements, fill in some story grammar elements. A *running story map* can also be constructed by the interventionist (see Figure 7.1) or co-constructed by the adult and students (Merritt et al., 1998). This approach involves simultaneously talking and writing words, phrases, or simple drawings reflecting story grammar content and connections.

The presence of a visual model alone does not ensure comprehension. Regardless of the format used, the most important guiding principle for this instruction is to "talk about" and "talk through" the information that has been visually represented. Interventionists can provide further reinforcement of story schema—for example, by referencing the visual representations when asking directed questions based on the organization of story grammar. An interventionist might point to an icon depicting an attempt while asking, "What did Wilbur do when he felt lonely and wanted a friend?" Pointing to the icon for the consequence, a follow-up question might be "What happened when Avery tried to knock Charlotte down?"

STEP 3. PROVIDE INSTRUCTION IN TEMPORAL ORDERING AND CAUSE–EFFECT RELATIONSHIPS

For students with good decoding, such as Kevin, interventionists can reinforce the timeline of events in a story, helping them to arrange *story strips* containing segments of episode content in a correct temporal sequence. The instruction can begin by explicitly teaching the meanings of temporal words that signal the passage of real time (e.g., *next, suddenly*) and then offering them in a word bank. Students can then practice inserting these words into the story strips displaying the sequence of events. For example:

1. [*first*] The sheep warned Wilbur that he would become smoked bacon by autumn.
2. [*then*] Wilbur started to worry when he realized that he might die.
3. [*meanwhile*] He talked to his only friend, Charlotte.
4. [*and then*] She told him that she would protect him.
5. [*finally*] She told him to stop asking questions and go to sleep.

A running story map or a co-constructed map can also reinforce temporal and cause–effect relationships. As illustrated in Figure 7.1, conjunctions (those stated in the text and those implied) can be integrated into the graphic representation, while talking about them in relation to the content and visually highlighting them. It is helpful to signal the meaning of the conjunctions with symbols—for example, a thin arrow (→) to convey a temporal relationship and a thick arrow (➔) for cause and effect. Additive conjunctions (e.g., *and, also*) are a good starting point for this instruction, as they are easiest for students to comprehend, followed by contrasting conjunctions (e.g., *but, however*). Temporal and then causal conjunctions could be introduced next. Students can then be provided with opportunities to summarize story segments in order to help them internalize temporal ordering.

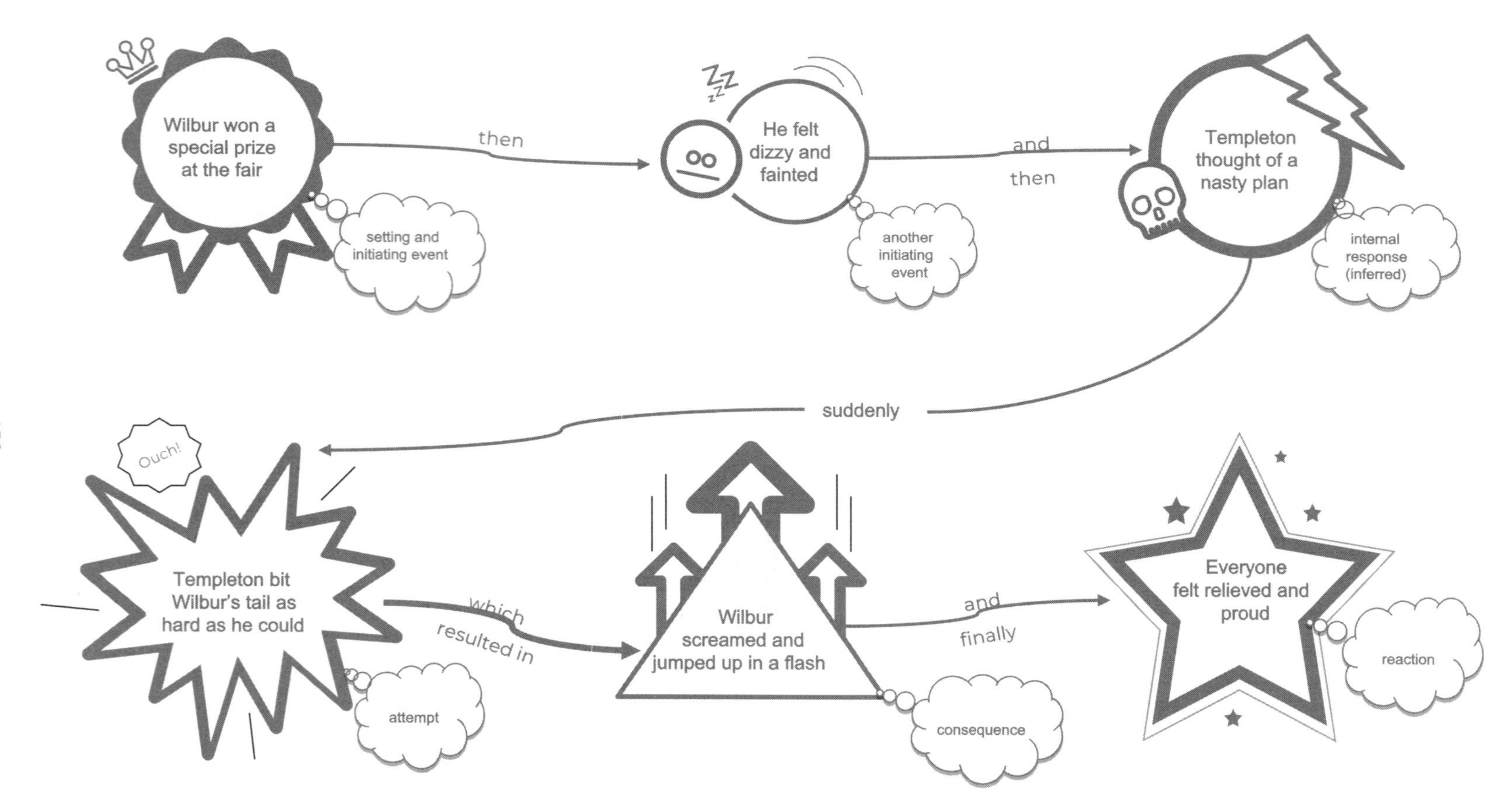

FIGURE 7.1. Example of a running story map.

STEP 4. MODEL AND SCAFFOLD RETELLING OF EPISODE STRUCTURES

Retellings enhance story comprehension, as well as expressive language skills. Interventionists can begin this instructional step by referencing the graphic representation of the episode, thus reducing the cognitive demand for recall. The adult first models episode retelling, giving added emphasis to story grammar elements or the literate language features that are most adversely impacting comprehension. For example, exaggerated prosody can be used to emphasize words that indicate the characters' reactions. As story retelling can be daunting to some students, it can be advantageous to shift to narrative production in a nonthreatening way (e.g., "Let's tell the story together"). It is important to scaffold this learning by providing as much support as the student needs to be successful, then gradually fading the support as the student produces more coherent retellings. It can also be helpful for students to retell a story in a round robin format, using the visual representation as a guide.

STEP 5. CO-CONSTRUCT PARALLEL STORIES

Story generation is more challenging than story retelling for typically developing students and for those with language-based learning difficulties (Merritt & Liles, 1989). Students benefit from opportunities to co-construct their own stories, which can begin by referring back to the reactions of characters in a previously taught story. Interventionists can encourage students, through discussion, to relate these reactions to a personal experience or a vivid memory. For example, the adult could say, "I had an experience once like Wilbur's, when I was lonely and confused and felt 'out of sorts.' Can you think of a time when you were confused or were somewhere you didn't want to be?" Subsequently, the instruction can transition to co-constructing a parallel fictional story. It is advisable to plan out the story schema by asking the students to generate the more concrete aspects of the story first, including a problematic event or situation, a potential list of actions, and probable consequences with a focus on logical, temporal, and cause–effect relationships. Open-ended questions are particularly effective as prompts (e.g., "I wonder what might happen next?") or choices can be provided if needed. Students can select cohesive words from a word bank and incorporate these into a visual representation. Characters' emotions and internal states can then be highlighted, while eliciting increasingly higher-level vocabulary (e.g., *bewildered*). Interventionists might also demonstrate how to create additional "branches" to the story, using a consequence or a character's reaction to prompt another initiating event that generates a more complex story line. The eventual goal is for students to independently generate their own stories.

STEP 6. MONITOR STUDENT PROGRESS

Data should be collected at scheduled intervals to inform instruction and determine a student's progress toward IEP goals. A story episode from a curricular text can be used, asking the student to retell as much of the story as possible without any prompts or cues. Alternatively, the student can be asked to generate an original story, a more difficult task, using a stimulus that offers minimal contextual cues (e.g., a single picture or a story stem). The structure of the child's stories can be analyzed using research-informed progress monitoring tools, such as Monitoring Indicators of Scholarly Language (MISL; Gillam, Gillam, Fargo, Olszewski, & Segura, 2017) or measures designed by Moreau (2008a). Alternatively, grade-level narrative listening tasks from CUBED—Narrative Language Measures (NLM): Listening protocols (Petersen & Spencer, 2018) can be used to gather data from story retelling and generation tasks, as well as responses to factual and inferential questions. NLM protocols are free downloadable benchmark assessment tools that were designed to be used in general education within a tiered intervention process, but can also be used to document student progress in special education. Based on the student's data, interventionists can repeat the intervention cycle with a new curricular text, adjusting learning objectives and the intervention focus as indicated.

An overview of this narrative instructional sequence is presented in Table 7.3.

TARGETING RELATED LANGUAGE SKILLS

Students with impaired listening comprehension often need support for related language difficulties, including inferencing skills and understanding figurative language

TABLE 7.3. Narrative Instructional Sequence

Step 1. Read the text out loud	Read the story episode with intonation, gestures, and pauses, allowing for ample processing time. Reread, using a "think-aloud" strategy to clarify content.
Step 2. Teach narrative structure and story grammar relationships	Provide explicit story grammar instruction, using visual and tactile cues to represent the global organization of the story episode and the interrelationships among the elements.
Step 3. Provide instruction in temporal ordering and cause–effect relationships	Visually highlight the sequence of events and cause–effect relationships with symbols. Provide opportunities to summarize episodes in order to help students internalize the story sequence.
Step 4. Model and scaffold retelling of episode structures	Support narrative production by scaffolding students' episode retellings, using graphic representations and emphasizing story grammar elements.
Step 5. Co-construct parallel stories	Transition to student-generated stories by planning out a story schema and mapping story grammar elements with an emphasis on logical temporal and cause–effect relationships. Highlight characters' emotions and internal states through discussion and visual representations.
Step 6. Monitor student progress	Use story retelling and/or generation tasks to gather progress monitoring data (e.g., number of story grammar elements and number of complete episode structures).

(Oakhill & Cain, 2007; Westby, 2012). Strategies targeting these skills can readily be integrated within narrative discourse lessons. (Interventionists are also encouraged to apply and reinforce the sentence comprehension strategies presented earlier when working with passages from authentic texts.)

Inferencing

Think-alouds are a powerful strategy for improving students' inferencing skills (Kispal, 2008). The interventionist first models the strategy by reading a passage out loud, intermittently stopping to verbalize thoughts about the content. For example, using "The Last Day" chapter in *Charlotte's Web* (White, 1952), the interventionist could make comments such as "I wonder how Charlotte knew that her children would be safe after she died? I think that it's because she watched Templeton, the rat, rescue her egg sac and her good friend, Wilbur, carry it with him into his crate." The interventionist might then invite students to share a thought about the same content. After demonstrating the think-aloud procedure, the interventionist asks students to answer specific questions that prompt them to generate their own inferences. For example, "What is Charlotte really telling Wilbur when she says that she won't see the arrival of her five hundred and fourteen children?"

Inferences that explain characters' reactions can also be strengthened by supporting a think-aloud strategy with a *perspective map*, as described by McTigue, Douglass, Wright, Hodges, and Franks (2015). An event sequence in a story is captured in a visual representation from the perspective of two (or more) characters by generating words representing their implied reactions in thought bubbles and connecting these to story grammar elements. For example, the perspective map might show that Wilbur felt "panicky" and "desperate" as he sought Templeton's help in returning Charlotte's egg sac to the farm. In contrast, Templeton was "indifferent" to Charlotte's situation, and he also felt "unappreciated."

Having students apply the think-aloud strategy with instructional scaffolding has several advantages. Students learn how to relate content to what is already known, locate context clues, consider multiple alternatives or perspectives, identify sources of confusion, and apply repair strategies (Spector, 2006). Student responses to think-aloud questions may also help interventionists to identify where comprehension breakdowns are occurring (Laing & Kamhi, 2002) and what types of inferences are challenging (e.g., how a character is feeling vs. the likely consequence of a character's attempts; Kispal, 2008).

Figurative Language

Figurative language can be taught using a two-step sequence that combines explicit instruction with guided practice using grade-level curricular texts as a supportive context for learning (Paul et al., 2018). For example, as an initial step, an interventionist could provide definitions of three targeted forms: similes, metaphors, and idioms. Examples of each form would be used to demonstrate how speakers and writers use these devices to make language more vivid and interesting. In the next step, the interventionist would focus on examples of targeted forms found within familiar passages from a curricular text. For example, the following sentences from *Charlotte's Web* (White, 1952) could be written on a whiteboard with key words underlined:

1. The asparagus patch looked like a silver forest. [*simile,* p. 77]
2. "I'm scared to death," whispered Mrs. Zuckerman. [*idiom,* p. 155]

For the first sentence, the students would be asked whether the asparagus patch was actually a silver forest, drawing their attention to the comparison being made. Then, the interventionist could ask them to consider and explain why the author might have chosen to use this simile. It may be necessary to scaffold this discussion, focusing on common features of an asparagus patch and a forest (e.g., long, slender growth extending up to the sky), perhaps using pictures to activate or enhance background knowledge. A similar procedure can be used with the second sentence by asking the students whether Mrs. Zuckerman really died, and then engaging them in a dialogue about the intended meaning of the idiom and why the author might have chosen to use it.

SUMMARY

According to the simple view of reading, listening comprehension makes a unique and important contribution to reading comprehension. Nevertheless, students' listening comprehension skills are sometimes neglected during reading assessment and intervention. When listening comprehension is impaired, interventionists can collaborate to strategically target component language skills that support reading comprehension. While many reading programs include a focus on morphology and vocabulary knowledge, sentence-level confusions tend to be overlooked and may need to be considered during intervention. At the discourse level, narrative intervention can be used to help students to effectively transition to the formal, abstract, decontextualized, and literate language that is widely used in classrooms and written text. Narratives serve as an ideal "bridge" to comprehension and use of more complex discourse genres (i.e., expository text or persuasive writing) because stories have a predictable structure that can be explicitly taught. Related language skills that may need to be targeted include inferencing and understanding of figurative language.

This chapter focused on the language-based difficulties of readers with SRCD or MRD profiles. Students with SRCD demonstrate average or better word recognition skills but below-average oral language comprehension. The strategies described for improving sentence/discourse-level comprehension can be integrated with reading comprehension strategies in order to optimally support readers with an SRCD profile. In order to support readers with MRD, these language-based strategies may be combined with interventions addressing word reading and reading comprehension as part of a comprehensive program.

Application Activities

Activity 1

An interventionist is using curriculum-based narrative intervention approaches with fourth-grade students with listening and reading comprehension difficulties, several of whom have documented difficulties with sentence-level processing and comprehension. Which of these sentences from *Charlotte's Web* (White, 1952) is the most likely to be misunderstood? What sentence-level intervention strategies could be used to improve their understanding of this sentence type? Explain your answers.

1. The goose chuckled.
2. The kitchen table was set for breakfast, and the room smelled of coffee, bacon, damp plaster, and wood smoke from the stove.
3. He looked cute when his eyes were closed because his lashes were so long.
4. When Mr. Arable returned to the house half an hour later, he carried a carton under his arm.

ANSWER

Sentence 1 is a simple sentence; it has one independent clause that can stand alone. Sentence 2 is a compound sentence; it has two independent clauses. Sentence 4 is a complex sentence that contains an independent clause, preceded by a dependent clause that describes when Mr. Arable carried the carton. Sentence 3 may be the most difficult for students with language difficulties to process. It is a complex sentence with three different clauses: an independent clause ("He looked cute") followed by two adverbial clauses ("when his eyes were closed" and "because his lashes were so long"). Note that the effect ("He looked cute") appears *before* the cause ("because his eye lashes were so long"). This might confuse students who have a shallow understanding of the ordering effect of the causal conjunction *because*. Anticipating potential difficulty, the interventionist could ask, "Why did Wilbur look cute?" If the student responds inaccurately, the sentence could be analyzed by applying sentence-decomposition and sentence-combining strategies.

Activity 2

Mrs. Lambert, a second-grade teacher, is using a story map with blank boxes labeled "Beginning," "Middle," and "End." Some students in her class are unsure about what story information to capture in the boxes. What instructional design features could be added to make this story map instruction more explicit?

ANSWER

The beginning, middle, and end of a story can be difficult for students to distinguish, as some of this content may be amorphous or need to be inferred. The missing factor in this instruction is explicit systematic teaching and learning of developmentally appropriate story grammar elements paired with clear visual representations. This instruction provides a common vocabulary for labeling story parts, highlighting temporal and causal connections, guiding story comprehension, and anchoring retelling. Consistent with this approach, additional prompts, icons, or questions can be added within each box of the story map to support comprehension. For example, the following question might be added to the end box: "How did the character feel about the consequence?"

Activity 3

Arianna, a fifth grader receiving special education supports and services, produced the following oral retelling of a multiepisode adventure story entitled *Buried Alive* (Merritt & Liles, 1987):

> "Jim was riding his truck for a long, long time. And it was snowing a lot. So then he turned off the road. And then it really came down. He slept for a long time, for a couple of hours. The snow was covering the truck. And he couldn't breathe good and he got scared."

What stage of narrative development most closely aligns with this story sample? What should be targeted in Arianna's narrative intervention?

ANSWER

Arianna's retold story readily meets the criteria for an action sequence as she introduces a character and actions that are structured within a simple chronological sequence. Her use of the conjunction *so* suggests an emerging understanding of cause–effect relationships, and use of the word *scared* implies that she is also developing insight into a protagonist's internal response. Therefore, her story retell suggests that Arianna is in the process of transitioning to reactive sequences and abbreviated episodes. Her narrative intervention should simultaneously address oral and written language, supporting this transition to reactive sequences and abbreviated episodes. This can be done by targeting consistent use of temporal forms and causal words, initiating events, mental state verbs and feeling words (to convey internal states), characters' goals, and consequences.

REFERENCES

Balthazar, C. H., & Scott, C. M. (2015). The place of syntax in school-age language assessment and intervention. In T. A. Ukrainetz (Ed.), *School-age language intervention: Evidence-based practices* (pp. 279–333). Austin, TX: Pro-Ed.

Benson, S. E. (2009). Understanding literate language: Developmental and clinical issues. *Contemporary Issues in Communication Science and Disorders, 36,* 174–178.

Bishop, D. V. M., & Adams, C. (1990). A prospective study of the relationship between specific language impairment, phonological disorders, and reading retardation. *Journal of Child Psychology and Psychiatry, 31,* 1027–1050.

Bruner, J. (1986). *Actual minds, possible worlds.* Cambridge, MA: Harvard University Press.

Cain, K., & Oakhill, J. (2007). *Children's comprehension problems in oral and written language: A cognitive perspective.* New York: Guilford Press.

Carnine, D. W., Silbert, J., Kame'enui, E. J., & Tarver, S. G. (2010). *Direct instruction reading* (5th ed.). Boston: Merrill.

Catts, H. W., Kamhi, A. G., & Adlof, S. M. (2012). Defining and classifying reading disabilities. In A. G. Kamhi & H. W. Catts (Eds.), *Language and reading disabilities* (3rd ed., pp. 45–76). Upper Saddle River, NJ: Pearson.

Ehren, B. J. (2006). Partnerships to support reading comprehension for students with language impairment. *Topics in Language Disorders, 26*(1), 42–54.

Ehren, B. J., & Whitmire, K. (2009). Speech–language pathologists as primary contributors to response to intervention at the secondary level. *Seminars in Speech and Language, 30*(2), 90–104.

Floca, B. (2009). *Moonshot: The flight of Apollo 11.* New York: Atheneum Books.

Gillam, R. B., & Pearson, N. A. (2017). *Test of Narrative Language–2.* Austin, TX: Pro-Ed.

Gillam, S. L., Gillam, R. B., Fargo, J. D., Olszewski, A., & Segura, H. (2017). Monitoring indicators of scholarly language: A progress-monitoring instrument for measuring narrative discourse skills. *Communication Disorders Quarterly, 38*(2), 96–106.

Gillam, S. L., Gillam, R. B., & Reece, K. (2012). Language outcomes of contextualized and decontextualized language intervention: Results of an early efficacy study. *Language, Speech, and Hearing Services in Schools, 43,* 276–291.

Gorman-Gard, K. A. (2002). *Figurative language: A comprehensive program.* Eau Claire, WI: Thinking Publications.

Hochman, J. C. (2011). Composition: Evidence-based instruction. In J. R. Birsh (Ed.), *Multisensory teaching of basic language skills* (pp. 405–426). Baltimore: Brookes.

Hoover, W. A., & Gough, P. B. (1990). The simple view of reading. *Reading and Writing, 2,* 127–160.

Justice, L. M., & Ezell, H. K. (2016). The syntax handbook: Everything you learned about syntax but forgot (2nd ed.). Austin, TX: Pro-Ed.

Kamhi, A. G., & Catts, H. W. (2012). *Language and reading disabilities* (3rd ed.). Upper Saddle River, NJ: Pearson.

Kispal, A. (2008). *Effective teaching of inferencing skills for reading: Literature review.* Slough, UK: National Foundation for Educational Research.

Laing, S. P., & Kamhi, A. G. (2002). The use of think-aloud protocols to compare inferencing abilities in average and below-average readers. *Journal of Learning Disabilities, 35*(5), 437–448.

Leslie, L., & Schudt Caldwell, J. (2017). *Qualitative Reading Inventory* (5th ed.). Upper Saddle River, NJ: Pearson.

Liles, B. Z. (1985). Cohesion in the narratives of normal and language-disordered children. *Journal of Speech and Hearing Research, 28,* 123–133.

Marzano, R. J., Pickering, D. J., & Pollock, J. E. (2001). *Classroom instruction that works: Research-based strategies for increasing student achievement.* Alexandria, VA: ASCD.

McCardle, P., Scarborough, H. S., & Catts, H. W. (2001). Predicting, explaining, and preventing children's reading difficulties. *Learning Disabilities Research and Practice, 16,* 230–239.

McClintock, B., Pesco, D., & Martin-Chang, S. (2014). Thinking aloud: Effects on text comprehension by children with specific language impairment and their peers. *International Journal of Communication Disorders, 49*(6), 637–648.

McTigue, E., Douglass, A., Wright, K. L., Hodges, T. S., & Franks, A. D. (2015). Beyond the story map. *Reading Teacher, 69*(1), 91–101.

Merritt, D. D., Culatta, B., & Trostle, S. (1998). Narratives: Implementing a discourse framework. In D. D. Merritt & B. Culatta (Eds.), *Language intervention in the classroom* (pp. 277–330). San Diego, CA: Singular.

Merritt, D. D., & Liles, B. Z. (1987). Story grammar ability in children with and without language disorder: Story generation, story retelling, and story comprehension. *Journal of Speech and Hearing Research, 30*, 539–552.

Merritt, D. D., & Liles, B. Z. (1989). Narrative analysis: Clinical applications of story generation and story retelling. *Journal of Speech and Hearing Disorders, 54*, 438–447.

Moats, L. C. (2009). Still wanted: Teachers with knowledge of language. *Journal of Learning Disabilities, 42*(5), 387–391.

Moreau, M. R. (2008a). *Data collection & progress monitoring process: Linking MindWing's tools to the teaching–learning cycle*. Springfield, MA: MindWing Concepts.

Moreau, M. R. (2008b). *Story grammar marker*. Springfield, MA: MindWing Concepts.

Nation, K., Clarke, P., Marshall, C. M., & Durand, M. (2004). Hidden parallels between poor reading comprehension and specific language impairment? *Journal of Speech, Language, and Hearing Research, 47*, 99–211.

National Governors Association and Council of Chief State School Officers. (2010). Common Core State Standards. Washington, DC: Author.

Nelson, N. W. (2010). *Language and literacy disorders: Infancy through adolescence*. Boston: Allyn & Bacon.

Oakhill, J., & Cain, K. (2007). Introduction to comprehension development. In K. Cain & J. Oakhill (Eds.), *Children's comprehension problems in oral and written language: A cognitive perspective* (pp. 3–40). New York: Guilford Press.

Owens, R. E. (2016). *Language development: An introduction* (9th ed.). Upper Saddle River, NJ: Pearson.

Paul, R., Norbury, C., & Gosse, C. (2018). *Language disorders from infancy through adolescence: Listening, speaking, reading, writing, and communicating* (5th ed.). New York: Elsevier.

Petersen, D. B., & Spencer, T. D. (2018). *CUBED—narrative language measures (NLM): Listening*. Laramie, WY: Language Dynamics Group.

Saddler, B. (2012). *Teacher's guide to effective sentence writing*. New York: Guilford Press.

Snow, C. E., Griffin, P., & Burns, M. S. (2005). *Knowledge to support the teaching of reading: Preparing teachers for a changing world*. San Francisco, CA: Jossey-Bass.

Spear-Swerling, L. (2015). *The power of RTI and reading profiles: A blueprint for solving reading problems*. Baltimore: Brookes.

Spear-Swerling, L. (2016). Listening comprehension, the Cinderella skill: Giving the neglected stepchild her due. *Perspectives on Language and Literacy, 43*(3), 9–15.

Spector, C. C. (2006). *Between the lines: Enhancing inferencing skills*. Greenville, SC: Super Duper Publications.

Spencer, T. D., & Petersen, D. B. (2020). Narrative intervention: Principles to practice. *Language, Speech, and Hearing Services in Schools, 51*(4), 1081–1096.

Stein, N. L., & Glenn, C. G. (1979). An analysis of story comprehension in elementary school children. In R. O. Freedle (Ed.), *Current topics in early childhood education* (Vol. 2, pp. 261–290). New York: Ablex.

Ukrainetz, T. A. (2015). Telling a good story: Teaching the structure of narratives. In T. A. Ukrainetz (Ed.), *School-age language intervention: Evidence-based practices* (pp. 335–377). Austin, TX: Pro-Ed.

Westby, C. E. (2012). Assessing and remediating text comprehension problems. In A. G. Kamhi & H. W. Catts (Eds.), *Language and reading disabilities* (3rd ed., pp. 163–225). Upper Saddle River, NJ: Pearson.

White, E. B. (1952). *Charlotte's web.* New York: Harper & Row.

Wick, W. (1997). *A drop of water: A book of science and wonder.* New York: Scholastic.

Wiig, E. H., Secord, W. A., & Semel, E. (2013). *Clinical evaluation of language fundamentals–5.* Upper Saddle River, NJ: Pearson.

Zipoli, R. P., Jr. (2017). Unraveling difficult sentences: Strategies for enhancing reading comprehension. *Intervention in School and Clinic, 52*(4), 218–227.

Zipoli, R. P., Jr., & Merritt, D. D. (2017). Risk of reading difficulty among students with a history of speech or language impairment: Implications for student support teams. *Preventing School Failure: Alternative Education for Children and Youth, 61*(2), 95–103.

CHAPTER 8

Structured Reading Comprehension Intervention for Students with Reading Difficulties

Elizabeth A. Stevens
Christy R. Austin

Mr. Romero, a special education teacher, provides Tier 2, small-group intervention to fifth-grade students with reading disabilities and reading difficulties. His students decode adequately but have specific reading comprehension difficulties. Mr. Romero tries to support his students' content-area learning by using informational texts focused on grade-level topics in social studies and science. Unfortunately, his students have difficulty understanding what they read because of limited background knowledge on the science and social studies topics, limited vocabulary understanding, difficulty monitoring for meaning while reading and identifying key ideas in the text, and difficulty integrating key ideas to summarize text after reading. Mr. Romero wonders what he can do to support his students' reading comprehension. He knows that middle and high school students are expected to read and understand text independently, and he worries students won't succeed in learning important social studies and science content unless their reading comprehension improves. Mr. Romero wants to plan instruction to support students' expository text reading, but also wants to align his instruction to the students' upcoming social studies unit on the early American westward expansion.

Mr. Romero is not alone in worrying about his students' reading comprehension—many upper-elementary and middle grade intervention teachers worry about their students' reading comprehension. Like Mr. Romero, many teachers may not know where to start because improving reading comprehension can be a daunting task. Furthermore, there are many reading comprehension strategies available for different comprehension-related skills, such as predicting, generating inferences, visualizing, and retelling. One concern with strategy instruction is that the process may be taxing on students' working memory because many at-risk students have limited working memory (Compton, Fuchs, Fuchs, Lambert, & Hamlett, 2012). Students have to memorize the acronym, the associated steps for each letter of the acronym, what each step means and how to apply it, and utilize the strategy independently while reading. Another concern with strategy instruction is that teachers may teach these strategies (e.g., making a prediction) as isolated skills, disconnected from text and content learning.

We provide teachers with several important guidelines when planning for reading comprehension intervention. First, instead of teaching comprehension strategies (i.e., students memorize the acronym, the steps in the acronym, and how and when to apply it), we recommend that teachers select a few evidence-based practices shown to improve understanding for upper-elementary and middle grade students, and implement these practices throughout the school year, providing ample opportunities for practice with high-quality feedback. Second, we recommend selecting practices that support students' background and vocabulary knowledge, and integration of key ideas across sections of text, as these practices are rooted in theoretical frameworks for reading comprehension (Gough & Tumner, 1986; Kintsch, 1988; Kintsch & van Dijk, 1978). Third, we suggest teaching practices that support text processing, meaning the practices are implemented and practiced while students read and engage with text. Teaching practices that support text processing also involve text-based discussion so that students can integrate new ideas and content with previously learned content. This also avoids emphasis on strategy use in isolation, separate from text or important content.

In this chapter, we provide teachers with an instructional framework for providing reading comprehension intervention to students in the middle grades. The practices are organized based on when they are implemented: before reading text, during reading text, and after reading text. We explain each practice, briefly describe the research supporting the practice, and then provide a model on how to implement the practice using text. We utilize a sample fifth-grade social studies text on Lewis and Clark's exploration to demonstrate how to use each practice with text (see Figure 8.1; Radner, 2005; *http://teacher.depaul.edu*). We focus on practices used with informational texts, as students are generally familiar with narrative text structure in the elementary grades; students are less familiar with expository text structure, but they are required to read and understand these texts as part of their content-area learning.

BEFORE READING: PRACTICES THAT WORK

Before reading informational texts, skilled readers activate prior knowledge about the text topic and make predictions about new information they are likely to learn (Klingner, Vaughn, Arguelles, Hughes, & Leftwich, 2004; Vaughn, Klingner, et al., 2011).

American Explorers

1. More than 200 years ago, in 1804, two explorers made an important journey. They were named Meriwether Lewis and William Clark. Today, people know a lot about the places they visited, but 200 years ago there were no maps of that part of the United States. They would travel by boat most of the way and they would make the first maps of that part of our country. They were going to trace where a great river went. The river they were mapping is a very big one called the Missouri River. They wanted to find out where it went. They hoped it would take them to the ocean.
2. They took many people with them to help with the exploration. There were more than 40 people on the trip. They also carried many supplies, including a lot of food. They hoped they would find food along the way, but this was long ago and they did not know what the territory would be like. The explorers had three boats to carry them and their supplies. It was summer when they started on this long trip.
3. They traveled slowly, each day traveling a short distance because they had to row their boats on the river. They would only travel a few miles every day. They traveled for months and were still far from their destination. In winter it was difficult to travel, so they camped along the river. There they would wait for spring when traveling would be easier. Snow and ice made it very hard to travel in winter.
4. Native Americans helped them along the way. They helped them get food, and they showed them where places were. The explorers had never been to this area before, so they were not sure where to find food or even where the river went. The Native Americans had lived there for many years, so they knew the area and how to survive there, even in the hard winter.
5. A Native American woman named Sacajawea helped them travel. She became their guide, and she traveled with them for months. It was hard work for everyone, including Sacajawea. The explorers needed her help to find their way to the West. They wanted to find out how to get to the ocean.
6. As they traveled, they made maps. Their maps showed the way the river went. It passed through grasslands, and then they were in mountains. When they got to the mountains, they had to leave their boats and walk.
7. It took more than a year for the explorers to get to the ocean. When they got there, they had made maps that would help many people. But they had to bring the maps back. It had taken more than a year to make this first part of the trip. It also took a long time to get back. When the explorers came back, in 1806, they had been gone two years, and people said they were heroes. They would not make such a great journey again. They had done their job.
8. Their maps would help people settle in the new land. Long after their trip, people would build roads to the west. They would travel quickly by car. Today people can travel their route by plane. If you look out the window from the plane you will see those high mountains and, you will see what a difficult journey it was.

FIGURE 8.1. Sample fifth-grade social studies text used to demonstrate each instructional practice. From Radner (2005). Reprinted with permission.

Activating prior knowledge prepares readers to map their existing knowledge onto the new knowledge and vocabulary they will acquire through reading. Struggling readers often possess limited background knowledge about the text topic, and therefore may have a difficult time activating prior knowledge. For struggling readers, teachers may need to build students' background knowledge prior to reading. Background knowledge can be built by using various forms of media, such as pictures, maps, or videos. In addition, background knowledge can be built by providing an overarching big idea related to the unit of instruction or through a teacher previewing the text and providing a brief explanation of important concepts or ideas (Vaughn et al., 2013). Finally, informational texts include a large number of academic vocabulary words that are critical for comprehension. Good readers are able to use their prior knowledge and context clues to acquire new vocabulary knowledge through reading. However, poor readers benefit from explicit vocabulary instruction prior to reading informational text. We provide a detailed description of two instructional practices that support reading comprehension prior to reading: a routine for building background knowledge and explicit vocabulary instruction. Building students' content and vocabulary knowledge provides a Velcro for new content to "stick" to.

Building Background Knowledge

Background knowledge is an important predictor of reading comprehension (Alexander, Kulikowich, & Schulze, 1994; Shapiro, 2004), but many students demonstrate insufficient background knowledge for comprehending expository texts (e.g., Kieffer, 2012). Recht and Leslie (1988) conducted a seminal study investigating how prior knowledge about baseball influenced seventh- and eighth-grade students' reading comprehension on a passage about baseball. Findings demonstrated that prior knowledge about baseball resulted in better reading comprehension of the passage. Students with high reading ability but low background knowledge about baseball were no more able to retell or summarize the passage than students with low reading ability and low background knowledge about baseball. While word reading is necessary for reading comprehension, this study suggested that background knowledge is also important. One method for building students' background knowledge prior to reading includes four steps: (1) summarize the unit's big idea, (2) position the new learning with students' prior learning, (3) use a visual to tell students important information they need to know prior to reading the text, and (4) provide a comprehension question to offer a purpose for reading the text (Vaughn et al., 2013).

Building Background Knowledge in Action

We recommend situating expository text reading within larger themed units. By providing students with many opportunities to read expository text passages that relate to a central unit or theme, students can develop deep background knowledge that facilitates comprehension of complex texts. It is tempting to spend a substantial amount of time building students' background knowledge—however, we encourage teachers to complete this routine in 5 minutes or less. The majority of the instructional time should be spent actually reading and discussing the text. Because of this, it is important for teachers to plan *how* they will build background knowledge prior to teaching the lesson. For other practices described in this chapter (e.g., main idea generation, question writing), we recommend using an explicit instruction framework in which the teacher gradually releases responsibility to students (modeling, guided, and independent practice). For building background knowledge, however, this routine should always be teacher led because the teacher is situating new learning with prior learning and providing key information that students need to know prior to reading. This is teacher led, but students can engage in this part of the lesson by responding to teacher questions and prompts.

Prepare Your Model Lesson

First, the teacher identifies a unit of study related to science or social studies. Next, the teacher identifies expository text passages at students' instructional reading level that relate to the unit of study and cover the important topics required for the particular unit. Selecting text students can read accurately ensures that attentional resources can be devoted to comprehension rather than decoding. Once all expository text passages are identified, the teacher writes a big idea statement that relates to the unit overall. Then, the teacher places the expository text passages in a logical order to introduce the related topics. After, the teacher writes a sentence connecting what students learned in the previous lesson and what students can expect to learn from the current lesson. This helps to situate the new content with students' prior knowledge from previous lessons. The teacher selects a visual to use when explaining important information that students need to know prior to reading the text. The visual might be provided with the text, or the teacher may need to select one (e.g., map, photograph, a short video clip). Using the visual, the teacher provides a simple explanation of the content in one to three sentences. Finally, the teacher states a question that provides the students with a purpose for reading the passage.

Teach to Build Students' Background Knowledge

At the start of the lesson, remind students of the big idea for the unit. For example, the expository passage about Lewis and Clark could be part of a larger social studies unit related to the westward expansion of settlers into the American West. The teacher might state, "Throughout this unit, we have been learning about westward expansion—how people settled land west of the Mississippi River in early America." Next, remind students of what they learned during the previous lesson, and what they can expect to learn from the current lesson. For example, if during the previous lesson students learned about the Louisiana Purchase, the teacher might say, "In our last lesson, you learned about the Louisiana Purchase, which allowed the United States to buy the territory of Louisiana from France in 1803. Today, you will learn about two

American explorers—Lewis and Clark—who explored the western United States by following the Missouri River in 1804." After that, the teacher uses a visual—in this case, two maps—to explain important content that students need to know prior to reading: "Lewis and Clark were very important in the early 1800s because they explored the land along the Missouri River [*locate the Missouri River on a map from the 1800s time period*]. Today we have maps showing all of the land in the United State [*point to the map of the United States*], but back then there were no maps of the Missouri River. Lewis and Clark explored and created maps of these areas [*point*], which helped people move to and settle there." Finally, ask students a question that will set a purpose for reading: "While you read, think about this question: 'How did Lewis and Clark's exploration help early Americans settle new land in the West?' We'll answer this question after reading."

Explicit Vocabulary Instruction

Vocabulary knowledge is highly correlated with reading comprehension, and the relationship between vocabulary and comprehension increases as students get older (Cunningham & Stanovich, 1997; Tannenbaum, Torgesen, & Wagner, 2006; Torgesen, Wagner, & Rashotte, 1997). Expository texts include a large number of academic vocabulary words. Good readers acquire new vocabulary words through independent reading. Good readers also use context clues (Watts, 1995) or glossaries (Swanson et al., 2017) to determine the meaning of previously unfamiliar words. However, these methods for acquiring new vocabulary words do not provide students with the number of exposures required to demonstrate mastery of a new word's meaning (Ausubel & Youssef, 1965). In addition, struggling readers do not effectively acquire new vocabulary knowledge through independent reading. For struggling readers, explicit vocabulary instruction supports students' understanding of new vocabulary words and their comprehension of the text (Elleman, Lindo, Morphy, & Compton, 2009; Harmon, Hedrick, & Wood, 2005). We recommend that teachers use an essential words routine, in which teachers preteach the meanings of important words using a semantic map and a routine (see Figures 8.2 and 8.3). For each word, the teacher provides a student-friendly definition of the word, presents synonyms or related words, and leads a discussion about a visual representation of the word (i.e., "How does this photograph help you remember the meaning of the word?"). Next, the teacher provides two examples of the word in context. One example relates to students' everyday lives and the other example relates to the unit of study or passage. Finally, students practice using the word in a brief turn-and-talk discussion. The teacher poses a question to pairs of students who turn and answer the question with a peer. Each partner has an opportunity to respond, and the teacher may provide a sentence stem to answer the question or model answering the question before students answer in partners. We recommend that teachers provide instruction on the definition, illustration, and example sentences prior to reading, and return to the map after reading for the turn-and-talk discussions. This ensures that students have some familiarity with the text content when they answer the turn-and-talk questions.

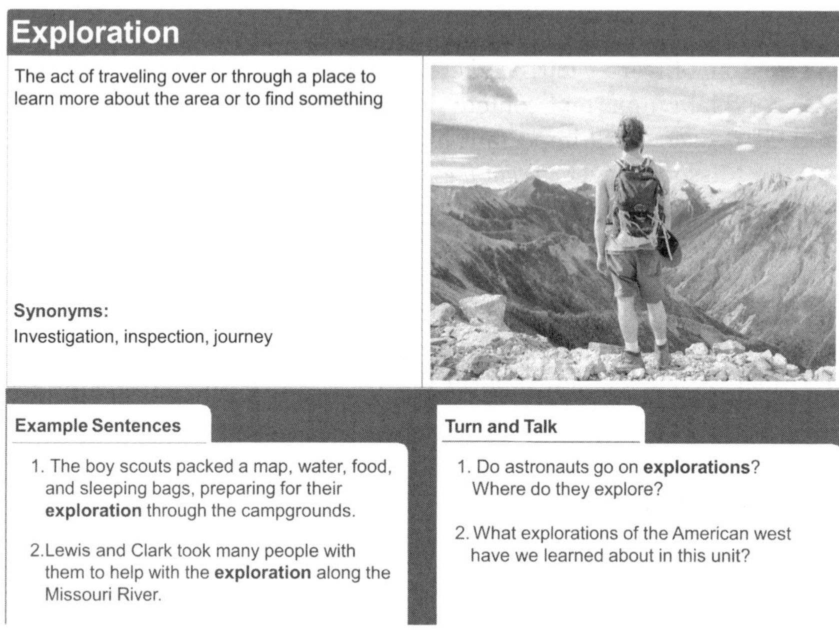

FIGURE 8.2. Sample vocabulary map to teach the word *exploration*. Reprinted with permission from The University of Texas at Austin/The Meadows Center for Preventing Educational Risk.

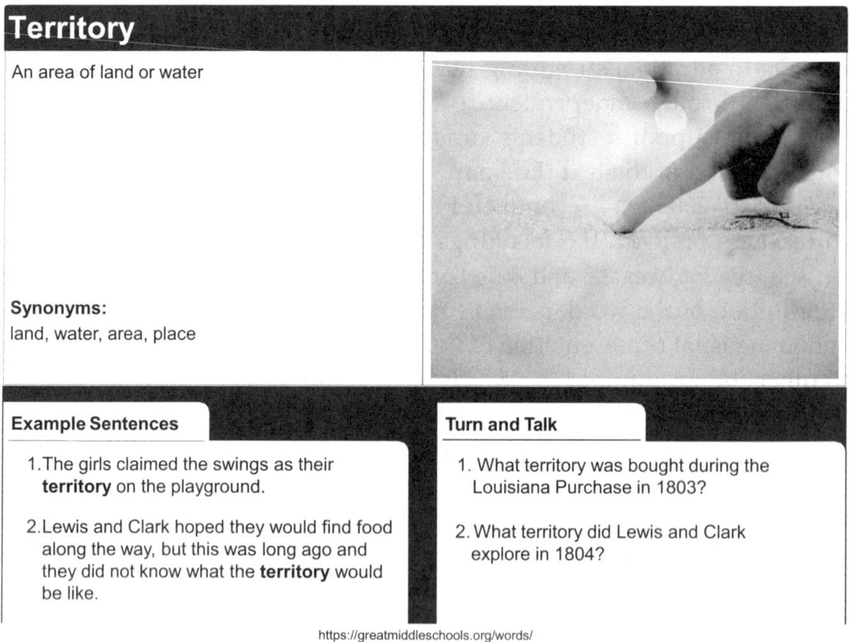

FIGURE 8.3. Sample vocabulary map to teach the word *territory*. Reprinted with permission from The University of Texas at Austin/The Meadows Center for Preventing Educational Risk.

Explicit Vocabulary Instruction in Action

Teachers follow three steps to explicitly teach the meaning of unfamiliar words: (1) select two to three essential words students need to know for the target expository passage, (2) prepare a vocabulary map graphic organizer for each word, and (3) use the vocabulary map to teach each vocabulary word to students (see *greatmiddleschools.org/words* for a downloadable, blank version of the vocabulary map). We recommend that teachers utilize the principles of explicit instruction to teach the meaning of target vocabulary words (Archer & Hughes, 2010). The following sections are teacher led but involve student responses through questioning: student-friendly definition, illustration, synonyms, and example sentences. By using a brisk pace and providing multiple opportunities for the student to respond, teachers can increase student engagement. The turn-and-talk (see the "After Reading: Practices That Work" section) is student led and provides opportunities for students to practice using and applying the word in context. Allowing students to immediately practice applying their new vocabulary terms gives teachers the opportunity to provide immediate feedback on students' understanding of word meanings.

Prepare Your Model Lesson

First, the teacher selects two to three essential words that are critical to understanding the expository passage. Focus on words you anticipate are not already a part of the students' prior knowledge that are essential to understanding the main idea of the text or the big idea of the unit. By selecting words that are central to the main idea of the passage or big idea of the unit, students will be exposed to these words repeatedly and the repeated exposures will help students develop and retain deep vocabulary knowledge. It is also important to consider words that may have multiple meanings across content areas (e.g., equal in mathematics vs. equal in social studies). In the Lewis and Clark passage, we selected the words *exploration* and *territory* because these words are critical for understanding the passage and relate to the larger unit focused on the early exploration of American Western territories. We limit instruction to two to three words so that students can develop depth of vocabulary knowledge through repeated exposure, discussion, and practice opportunities with each word. Once you have selected the terms, prepare a vocabulary map for each word. Developing vocabulary maps takes time, so teachers may want to work collaboratively to divide and conquer. There are websites that provide access to free images for the illustration section (e.g., *www.pixabay.com*); teachers can also use the advanced search feature in Google to identify images designated for free use. Then, deliver explicit vocabulary instruction for each vocabulary map.

Explicitly Teach the Target Vocabulary Words

The *before reading* portion of the vocabulary maps includes the target word, a student-friendly definition, a picture to visually represent the word, synonyms, and example sentences (see Figures 8.2 and 8.3 for sample vocabulary maps for *exploration* and *territory*). The teacher projects an image of each vocabulary map for the small group to see and provides each student with a copy of the map. To teach the word *exploration,* the teacher might say, "The word is *exploration.* What word? [*exploration*] Exploration means the act of traveling over or through a place to learn more about the area or to find something. How does this picture help us remember the meaning of the word *exploration*? [It helps us remember that exploration means traveling or going through a new place to learn more about it. This man is traveling through the mountains—he might be learning more about the mountains, or he might be looking for something.] Synonyms, or words that have similar meaning, include *investigation, inspection,* and *journey.* How is the word *investigation* related to *exploration*? [In an investigation you search for something, and if you're on an exploration, you might also search for something.]"

The example sentences on the vocabulary map can be used to provide students with correct usages of the word. One example sentence relates to students' everyday lives, and the other sentence relates to the unit of study or the target passage. "Read Sentence 1 with me: 'The boy scouts packed a map, water, food, and sleeping bags, preparing for their exploration through the campgrounds.' Why would the boy scouts go on an exploration of the campgrounds? [e.g., to learn more about the area, to look for a specific place] Why would they need supplies for their exploration? [They might need food and water because they will be gone for a while/overnight, they are using the map to find a specific place or to keep from getting lost, they need sleeping bags because the exploration will take several days, so they will stay overnight.] Good. Read Sentence 2 with me: 'Lewis and Clark took many people with them to help with the exploration along the Missouri River.' Why would Lewis and Clark need people to go with them on their exploration of the Missouri River? [e.g., to help carry supplies, to help look for things, to help draw pictures of the land/create the maps]."

At this point, the teacher might stop and check students' understanding of the word by asking example and non-example questions. For the Lewis and Clark text passage, the teacher may use the following example and non-example questions: "If you go play in the backyard, are you going on an exploration? If an American explorer traveled somewhere no one had ever been before, did they embark on an exploration?" These questions allow the teacher to provide immediate affirmative or corrective feedback to shape students' understanding of the target word. After completing these steps, students are ready to read the passage with their new vocabulary knowledge to support reading comprehension. Refer to the "After Reading: Practices That Work" section to learn more about how to use the turn-and-talk prompts after students read the passage.

DURING READING: PRACTICES THAT WORK

During reading, skilled readers actively engage with the text by thinking about the ideas in the text while they are reading, integrating new information with their existing knowledge about a topic, and connecting key ideas across sections of text (Duke & Pearson, 2008; Pressley, 2006). Good readers also monitor for understanding; when meaning breaks down, the reader takes an action to repair that misunderstanding, such as rereading the text (Goldman, 2012). Struggling readers do not engage in consciously processing the text while reading; they might passively read the words without actively trying to construct meaning. We provide two instructional practices that support struggling readers with consciously processing the meaning of the text as they read: generating main idea statements and writing questions. These practices teach students to monitor their understanding while reading and to repair misunderstandings to improve reading comprehension.

Main Idea Generation

Generating main ideas is an important subskill for summarizing texts but presents challenges for students with reading difficulty. Main idea generation can be challenging for students because they have difficulty identifying the most important information; instead, students choose a fact that is particularly interesting to them or identify a detail (Stevens & Vaughn, 2020). Teaching students to generate main ideas is challenging for teachers because teachers may be unsure about showing students *how* to find the main idea of a text rather than simply asking them to *find it*.

One way to support students is by using a paraphrasing process, which is a set of brief steps students follow to identify the main topic and the most important information about that topic (Stevens, Park, & Vaughn, 2019). Get the Gist is a three-step paraphrasing process in which students stop after reading a paragraph or a section of text to (1) identify the main "who" or "what" in the text, (2) tell the most important information about the "who" or "what," and (3) combine answers to Steps 1 and 2 to write the gist using a complete sentence (see Figure 8.4; Klingner, Vaughn, & Schumm, 1998). Get the Gist has been examined in multicomponent reading intervention studies and intervention studies targeting main idea generation (e.g., Stevens, Vaughn, House, & Stillman-Spisak, 2020; Vaughn, Wexler, et al., 2011).

Main Idea Generation in Action

We recommend using an explicit instruction framework for teaching students how to write gist statements (Archer & Hughes, 2010). After modeling [*I do*] Get the Gist, it is important to provide opportunities for guided [*we do*] and independent [*you do*] practice. During guided practice, the teacher and the students write gist statements together, following the three-step process. Instead of showing students each step in the process using a think-aloud, the teacher walks students through the process by reminding them of each step (e.g., "What do we do first? What do we do next? Write your gist"). Making progress with main idea generation—and eventually summarizing—will take time. Teachers should provide additional modeling as needed across different text types and content areas.

Prepare Your Model Lesson

First, the teacher prepares an introductory lesson to model the practice for students. Select a short, expository passage written on students' independent reading level that addresses a familiar topic. As students learn the practice, they should focus on learning and applying the steps rather than struggling to read the text. Next, divide the text into sections or paragraphs. Students will stop reading at these predetermined points in the text to write their gist statements. Finally, prepare a target gist statement for each section using the three-step paraphrasing process. This is an important step in preparing the model lesson as it helps the teacher to prepare for potential challenges students may encounter (e.g., difficulty finding the "who" if there are two or more persons discussed in the section of text) and how to address those challenges.

Teach Get the Gist

When you introduce the practice, set a purpose for learning by explaining that Get the Gist will help students to think about what they are reading while they read. It will also help them to remember the most important information in the passage. Introduce the practice by explaining what students will do at each step. Provide each student with a copy of the text, a gist log, and a Get the Gist cue card (see Figure 8.4; see Form 8.1 at the end of the chapter for a reproducible version of the Get the Gist Log). Then, model Get the Gist by reading a section of the text aloud and showing students how to carry out each step in the process. For example, in Paragraph 1 of "American Explorers" (Radner, 2005), the teacher might think aloud: "First, I need to tell who or what this section is about. This paragraph talks mostly about the explorers named Lewis and Clark [write on gist log]. Next, I ask myself what is the most important information about Lewis and Clark? Lewis and Clark created the first maps of the Missouri River [write on gist log]. Last, I'll combine my answers to Steps 1 and 2 to write the gist: 'Lewis and Clark made the first maps of the Missouri River' " (see Figure 8.7 for a completed gist log for the passage).

After modeling the process for students, facilitate guided practice where the teacher generates gist statements with students' help and then independent practice where students write gists independently. During guided and independent practice, the interventionist should provide feedback for students on the accuracy of their gist statements. If students have difficulty with the process, there are several ways to provide scaffolding (Stevens & Vaughn, 2020). First, encourage students to use headings or subtitles as these often provide clues as to the most important information in the text. If students identify a detail rather than the most important information, encourage them to reread to find the most important information in the text. Finally, if gist statements are too long or students copy sentences directly from the text, you may need to model how to write the main idea in a concise way, putting the information into your own words. Additional resources for teaching Get the Gist can be found at *greatmiddleschools.org*.

Get the Gist Log

Student(s): ______________________

Class and Period: ______________ Name of Text: ______________

Section	Step 1: Who or what is this section about?	Step 2: What is the most important information about the "who" or "what"?	Step 3: Write gist statement.

Get the Gist Strategy

Step 1: Who or what is this section about?

Step 2: What is the most important information about the "who" or "what"?

Step 3: Write your gist statement by combining information from Steps 1 and 2.

Remember, your gist should

- include only the most important information,
- leave out unnecessary details, and
- be a complete sentence.

FIGURE 8.4. Get the Gist cue card and log. Reprinted with permission from The University of Texas at Austin/The Meadows Center for Preventing Educational Risk.

Question Writing

Another way to support students' comprehension during reading is through question writing. Often the teacher does the heavy lifting by asking all of the questions. In this practice, however, the onus is on students to write and answer their own questions. Question writing encourages the reader to reflect on the content in a particular section of text, to make connections across ideas within the text, and to make connections among texts or between the text and the reader's prior knowledge (Palinscar & Brown, 1984; Stevens, Murray, Fishstrom, & Vaughn, 2020). This practice promotes content learning and encourages students to actively engage in close reading of the text, monitor for meaning, and participate in text-based discussions about the content (Stevens, Murray, et al., 2020; Vaughn, Wexler, et al., 2011). Teachers can evaluate students' reading comprehension based on the quality of the question asked and whether or not it can be answered in the text.

Teachers can support students with generating different levels of questions, ranging from lower-level, literal questions to higher-level, inferential questions. We recommend teaching students to write two question types: specific and wide questions (see Figure 8.5). Specific questions can be answered in one word or sentence in the passage and begin with one of the following question words: *who, what, when, where, why,* or *how.*

Writing Questions While I Read

While I read, I stop every once in a while to see whether the information makes sense.
I check my understanding by challenging myself to ask a question, just like a teacher does.

Question Type	Description	Possible Stems	Examples
Specific Questions 	• Questions can be answered in one word or one sentence. • Answers can be found word-for-word in the text.	• Who • What • When • Where • Why • How	ELA: In *Number the Stars*, why did Annemarie's parents burn their newspaper? Science: What is the largest ocean? Social studies: How many original colonies were there?
Wide Questions 	• Questions can be answered using information from multiple places in the text. • Questions can be answered by making inferences (combining your prior knowledge with information from the text). • Answers require one or more sentences.	• Who • What • When • Where • Why • How • Describe • Explain • Summarize	ELA: Explain how the setting in chapters 7 and 8 contrasts with the city setting of previous chapters. Science: Describe some of the dangers associated with earthquakes. Social studies: How was the experience of the Jamestown colonists different from what they expected?

FIGURE 8.5. Question types. Reprinted with permission from The University of Texas at Austin/The Meadows Center for Preventing Educational Risk.

Wide questions can be answered using information from multiple places in the text, using information from the text and the reader's prior knowledge, or using information from the current text and another text. Wide questions begin with one of the following question words or stems: *who, what, when, where, why, how, describe, explain,* or *summarize.* As with Get the Gist, the question writing practice consists of three steps (see Figure 8.6). First, students read a section of the text independently, with a peer, or as part of a whole-group read-aloud. Next, students pause after reading a section of text to write a question. During this step, students identify important information or facts in the text and turn that information into a question (e.g., if the fact describes a reason, students might turn this into a "why" question). Last, students record their question and answer on a log, citing evidence from the text that supports their answer (see Figure 8.6; see Form 8.2 at the end of the chapter for a reproducible version of the Question Log).

Question Writing in Action

We recommend using an explicit instruction framework for teaching students how to write questions during small-group reading comprehension intervention (Archer & Hughes, 2010). This includes preparing a model lesson, teaching the model lesson, and providing guided and independent practice opportunities for students to write and answer questions, and engage in text-based discussion. We suggest teachers provide two modeling lessons: one for specific questions and one for wide questions (see Figure 8.5). Students will likely master specific questions more easily than wide questions; teachers should monitor students' progress with wide questions and provide additional modeling as needed to demonstrate asking and answering higher-level questions that require synthesis of information across the text, among texts, and between the text and the reader's background knowledge.

Question Log

Student(s): __________

Class and Period: __________ Name of Text: __________

Question	Answer	Text Evidence

The Question Writing Practice

How is it done?

Step 1: Students read a text or learn new information, either in small groups, pairs, or independently.

Step 2: Students pause at regular intervals to generate their own questions and write the questions in a log or notebook.

Step 3: Students answer their questions and cite text evidence.

FIGURE 8.6. Question log and steps for question generation. Reprinted with permission from The University of Texas at Austin/The Meadows Center for Preventing Educational Risk.

Prepare Your Model Lesson

We suggest similar guidelines for preparing a question writing model lesson as those provided for Get the Gist: select a text on a familiar topic at the students' independent reading level, divide the text into sections, and write questions and answers for each section using different question stems.

Teach Question Writing

When you introduce the practice, set a purpose for learning by explaining that question writing will help students to stop, think about what they have read, remember the important information, make connections among ideas in the text, and make connections between ideas in the text and what students already know. Next, introduce the steps for writing questions while reading. While explaining the steps, it is important to post the steps somewhere in the room or provide students with a cue card listing the steps (see Figure 8.6). Explain to students that they will create their own question and provide the answer to that question using evidence—or information—directly from the passage. When modeling specific questions, read aloud a section of text. Stop at the end of the section, identify an important fact, turn that fact into a question, and record the question on the log. Complete the process by answering the question and citing text evidence. For example, in Paragraph 3 of "American Explorers" (Radner, 2005), the teacher might think aloud: "A specific question can be answered in one word or one sentence in the text. Paragraph 3 says 'snow and ice made it very hard to travel in winter.' This fact tells the reason traveling was difficult in the wintertime, so I'm going to ask a 'why' question: 'Why was traveling difficult for Lewis and Clark during winter?' " Underline the fact to verify that the answer is located in one place in the text and record the question, answer, and text evidence on the question log. Continue this process as you read through additional sections of text, modeling how to write specific questions using various question stems.

When modeling wide questions, follow a similar process. When introducing wide questions, explain that wide questions ask about big ideas in the text rather than an isolated fact in one sentence. Wide questions can be answered using different parts of the same text, using the current text and another text, or using the text and information the reader has already learned. Read aloud a section of text and show students how to locate information in various places in the text to write a question. For example, after reading Paragraphs 4 and 5 of "American Explorers" (Radner, 2005), the teacher might think aloud: "Wide questions ask about a big idea in the text and the answer can be found in multiple places. Paragraph 4 tells about how the Native Americans helped explorers find food and locate the river. Paragraph 5 tells about how Sacajawea guided the explorers as they traveled [underline these facts in the passage]. All of these facts explain how the Native Americans helped Lewis and Clark, so I will write a 'how' question: 'How did the Native Americans help the explorers?' " As with specific questions, record the question, answer, and text evidence on the question log and continue the process as you read additional sections of text.

AFTER READING: PRACTICES THAT WORK

After reading, instructional practices provide students with an opportunity to reflect on the important content of the entire passage. We provide two instructional practices that support struggling readers with reflecting on the meaning of the passage after reading: the turn-and-talk routine as part of explicit vocabulary instruction (i.e., return to the vocabulary map) and summarizing.

Application of Vocabulary Words in Action

Application of vocabulary knowledge allows students to develop and retain deep vocabulary knowledge that can be used in their speech and writing. We recommend developing a routine for turn-and-talk to maximize instructional time and support students in applying their vocabulary knowledge in conversation. To maximize instructional time, assign partners for the unit. Identify Partner A and Partner B in each pair. This allows the teacher to prompt either Partner A or Partner B to answer first and prevents students from wasting time discussing who will go first. For each prompt, provide students with a brief amount of time to share their response with a partner. Remember to keep instruction brisk so that students remain engaged. Each student requires 1 minute or less to share their response to the prompt.

Prepare Your Model Lesson

The vocabulary maps developed prior to implementing the lesson include two prompts for students to turn and talk to a partner about the target vocabulary words. The first prompt can relate to students' everyday lives or experiences. The second prompt can relate to the target text passage of the larger unit. While students share, monitor student responses to provide immediate affirmative or corrective feedback. After, ask several students to share their responses aloud with the small group. For more information on developing the vocabulary maps, refer to the "Before Reading: Strategies That Work" section.

Teach the Turn-and-Talk Routine

For the word *exploration,* the teacher may state, "Do astronauts go on explorations? Where do they explore? Turn and talk to your partner to answer this prompt. Partner A goes first, then Partner B." Then the teacher listens to student responses. If the teacher heard a student reply, "Astronauts go on explorations to space, or they may go on explorations to the moon," the teacher would respond, "Yes. That is correct. Astronauts go on explorations in outer space. Excellent!" If the teacher heard a student reply, "Astronauts do not go on explorations," the teacher would respond, "An exploration is the act of traveling somewhere to learn more about the area. Where do astronauts travel? [student: 'space']. Do they learn more about outer space by traveling there? [student: 'yes'].

That means that astronauts go on explorations to outer space. Try answering again: 'Do astronauts go on explorations?' "

Providing this immediate corrective feedback to students reinforces the definition of the target word and helps students understand how to utilize the target word correctly. Students would continue this process by answering the turn-and-talk Prompt 2, which addresses content related to the passage (i.e., "What explorations of the American West have we learned about in this unit?"). This question, in particular, supports text-based discussion, as students have read the passage and can apply their knowledge of the word and the content to answer the prompt. The teacher can call on one or two pairs to share their responses to the questions with the small group.

Summarizing

Summarizing text is an important part of reading comprehension because it demonstrates that students can integrate key ideas (i.e., main idea statements) across longer sections of text to provide a global understanding of the passage (Stevens et al., 2019). Studies examining interventions for summarization resulted in improved reading comprehension outcomes for students with reading difficulty (Stevens et al., 2019). Furthermore, summarizing is recommended by experts to improve the reading comprehension of upper-elementary and middle grade readers (e.g., Institute of Education Sciences Practice Guide for Improving Adolescent Literacy; Kamil et al., 2008). This practice helps students to remember and organize the most important information in the text (Stevens & Vaughn, 2019). Working collaboratively with a partner or group to summarize text after reading provides an opportunity for text-based discussion. Students describe their understanding of key ideas in the text, use information from the passage to support their thinking, and adjust their thinking with input from other readers in the group (Goldman, Snow, & Vaughn, 2016). This process supports struggling readers, as it facilitates the integration and synthesis of information in the text.

Summarizing in Action

There are two ways to summarize text after reading. One way to summarize the text is for students to generate a wrap-up statement (one to two sentences) that provides a passage-level gist. If students have learned to write gist statements during reading, the wrap-up is easy to implement, as they follow the same steps but consider the entire passage—that is, (1) identify the main "who" or "what" in the text, (2) tell the most important information about the "who" or "what," and (3) combine answers to Steps 1 and 2 to write the gist using a complete sentence.

Another way to summarize text is for students to write a paragraph that includes an introductory sentence, supporting details, and a concluding sentence explaining the most important information from the passage. If students generate gist statements during reading, then they have already completed most of the hard work to summarize the text. Get the Gist facilitates summary writing because it is easy for students to integrate those gist statements into a summary of the entire text (Klingner et al., 2004; Vaughn, Klingner, et al., 2011). First, students write an introductory sentence by writing a passage-level gist. They identify the main who/what of the entire passage and the most important information about the who/what. Then, students organize their existing gist statements into the body of the summary. Students might be able to include the existing gists without any editing—however, it may be necessary to combine some of the gists or even restate them in order to improve the flow of the paragraph. Finally, students write a concluding sentence by restating the introductory (passage-level) gist in a different way. We recommend that teachers use a gist-to-summary graphic organizer (see a downloadable, fillable template at *greatmiddleschools.org*) so that students can write their gists on the left-hand side of the page and view them easily for integration into the summary paragraph on the right-hand side of the page. Students may need several opportunities for guided practice in which the teacher and the students craft the summary together and with support; once students learn the process, they can work independently or in collaborative learning groups to write summaries thereafter.

Prepare Your Model Lesson

First, the teacher prepares an introductory lesson to model summary writing for students. Ideally this will occur over two lessons. In Lesson 1, the students read the passage and write gist statements for each paragraph or section during reading. In Lesson 2, students organize the previously written gists to write a summary of the entire passage. Select an expository passage with at least five paragraphs, written on students' independent reading level, that addresses a familiar topic. Remember that as students learn the practice, you want them to focus on learning and applying the summarizing steps rather than struggling to read the text, so texts need to be at students' instructional or independent reading levels. Next, prepare a target, passage-level gist statement that will serve as the introductory sentence—be sure to use the three-step paraphrasing process for generating a gist. After that, organize the existing gists (i.e., from Lesson 1) that will serve as the body of the summary. You might be able to use four to five gist statements in the body of your summary. In some cases, you will need to reorder the gists or combine gists to make the information clear and concise. This is an important step in preparing the model lesson, as it helps the teacher plan for showing students how to combine two gists, eliminate a gist that may not fit in the paragraph, or rewrite a gist in a more concise way. Finally, identify a target concluding sentence by restating the introductory sentence.

Teach Summarizing

Assuming students have already read the passage and generated gists in the previous lesson (i.e., using a gist-to-summary graphic organizer; see *greatmiddleschools.org* for a sample organizer), set a purpose for learning by explaining that summary writing helps students reflect on the most important information in the text and develop a "big picture" understanding of the text. Explain to students that they will use their previously generated gists for the bulk of the summary—most of the hard work is already done! Start by modeling the first step for students: writing the topic sentence by generating a gist for the entire passage. Using the passage "American Explorers" (Radner, 2005; see Figure 8.1), the teacher might think aloud: "The first sentence in a summary is the introductory sentence that introduces the topic to the reader and tells the most important information about the entire passage. I'm going to use Get the Gist steps, but this time I'll think about the whole passage. First, this passage talks mostly about the explorers named Lewis and Clark. Next, the most important idea about Lewis and Clark is that they created the first maps of the Missouri River. Last, I'll combine my answers to write the introductory sentence on my gist-to-summary log: 'Lewis and Clark were explorers who made the first maps of the Missouri River' " (see Figure 8.7 for a completed gist log for the passage).

Next, show students how to insert their previously written gists into the body of the summary: "The gists for Sections 2 and 3 tell about Lewis and Clark's preparations for the journey and how the trip was long and difficult [write Gists 2 and 3 on the

Main Idea (Gist) Statements	**Brief Summary**
Section 1: Lewis and Clark made the first maps of the Missouri River. Section 2: Lewis and Clark traveled to unknown territory, so they brought their own supplies. Section 3: Travel was slow due to the river and winter weather. Section 4: Native Americans helped Lewis and Clark get food and navigate the land. Section 5: Sacajawea helped Lewis and Clark find their way to the West. Section 6: Lewis and Clark made maps showing where the river went. Section 7: Lewis and Clark returned home with maps that would help many people. Section 8: Lewis and Clark's maps helped people settle in the West.	Lewis and Clark were explorers who made the first maps of the Missouri River. They were traveling to an unknown territory, so they took supplies with them. Their travel was slow due to the river and harsh winter weather. Native Americans, like Sacajawea, helped Lewis and Clark get food, navigate the land, and find their way to the West. As they traveled, Lewis and Clark made maps showing where the river went. They returned home with maps that would help many people. Lewis and Clark were considered heroes because their maps allowed many people to settle in the West.

FIGURE 8.7. Gist to summary for "American Explorers." This brief summary was written by using the gist statements in the order they were already written. However, the gists for Sections 4 and 5 were combined, as were the gists for Sections 7 and 8. Finally, some light editing was applied so that the sentences "flowed" in a way that makes sense. Reprinted with permission from The University of Texas at Austin/The Meadows Center for Preventing Educational Risk.

summary log]. I can combine Gists 4 and 5 into one sentence because they tell about the same idea. I'll write, 'Native Americans, like Sacajawea, helped Lewis and Clark get food, navigate the land, and find their way to the West' [write the combined gist for Sections 4 and 5 on the summary log]. Next, I'll write Gist 6, which tells what they did throughout their journey: they made maps of the river. I can combine Gists 7 and 8 to explain that when they returned home, their maps helped many people" [write the combined gist for Sections 7 and 8 on the summary log).

Finish modeling the summary writing process by showing students how to write a concluding sentence by restating the introductory sentence: "The concluding sentence ends the paragraph and reminds the reader of the big idea for the entire passage. We can write our concluding sentence by restating the introductory sentence in a different way. I'm going to restate the introductory sentence by writing, 'Lewis and Clark were considered heroes because their maps allowed many people to settle in the West' " [write the concluding sentence on the summary log].

After modeling the process for students, facilitate guided and independent practice where students work in groups or pairs to write summaries using their gist statements. The interventionist should provide feedback to students on their introductory sentence (passage-level gist), the body (i.e., organizing previously written gists, combining gists as needed), and the concluding sentence (restating the introductory sentence in a different way).

SUMMARY

Before, during, and after reading practices support students in comprehending expository texts. Before reading, teachers build students' background knowledge by identifying a big idea for the unit of study, situating new content with previously learned content, and explaining key information using a visual. Teachers also support students' comprehension by explicitly teaching target vocabulary words. During reading, teachers show students how to identify main ideas using Get the Gist and how to generate and answer specific and wide questions. After reading, teachers explicitly teach students to summarize what they have read and apply their knowledge of new vocabulary through turn-and-talk discussions. These before, during, and after practices—when used consistently—have been proven effective in supporting the content learning and reading comprehension of struggling readers.

> After learning about the evidence-based before, during, and after reading practices for supporting students' reading comprehension, Mr. Romero had the direction he needed to plan instruction to support students' reading comprehension of expository texts, while also aligning his instruction to the upcoming fifth-grade social studies unit on early American westward expansion. Mr. Romero noticed that his before, during, and after comprehension instruction resulted in improvements in students' background knowledge,

vocabulary, main idea generation, question generation, and summarization. Student progress was not immediate. To achieve mastery, students required substantial explicit instruction and review, but Mr. Romero now feels confident that students are progressing and demonstrating the comprehension skills necessary for success in middle school, high school, and beyond.

Application Activities

Activity 1

Explain some of the concerns about reading comprehension strategy instruction and provide evidence-based practices to support readers' comprehension before, during, and after reading.

ANSWER: One concern with strategy instruction is that the process may be taxing on students' working memory (Compton et al., 2012). Students have to memorize the acronym, the associated steps for each letter of the acronym, what each step means and how to apply it, and utilize the strategy independently while reading. Another concern with strategy instruction is that teachers may teach these strategies (e.g., making a prediction) as isolated skills, disconnected from text and content learning. Instead of teaching strategies, we recommend that teachers select two to three practices that can be implemented throughout the school year, providing ample opportunities for students to practice with feedback. Explicit vocabulary instruction, building background knowledge, main idea generation, question generation, and summary writing support students' knowledge building and integration of key ideas across sections of text. Finally, these practices are implemented while students read and engage with text, thus supporting text-based discussions.

Activity 2

Consider the "American Explorers" passage. Plan further before, during, and after reading instruction using the following prompts:

1. Identify a picture, video, or map you could use to build students' background knowledge before reading the passage.

   ANSWERS: *https://en.wikipedia.org/wiki/Lewis_and_Clark_Expedition#/media/File:Map_of_Lewis_and_Clark's_Track,_Across_the_Western_Portion_of_North_America,_published_1814.jpg*

   https://en.wikipedia.org/wiki/Lewis_and_Clark_Expedition#/media/File:Carte_Lewis_and_Clark_Expedition.png

2. Identify a student-friendly definition, two synonyms, an illustration, and two example sentences for the vocabulary word *territory*.

   ANSWER: See Figure 8.3 for a completed map for the word *territory*.

3. Prepare a gist statement for Section 5.

   ANSWER: See Figure 8.7 for a completed gist log.

4. Identify a specific question and a wide question for Sections 7 and 8.

   POSSIBLE ANSWER (SPECIFIC QUESTION): How long did Lewis and Clark's journey last?

   POSSIBLE ANSWER (WIDE QUESTION): Why did people refer to Lewis and Clark as heroes?

ACKNOWLEDGMENTS

The authors have no conflicts of interest to disclose. This research was supported by the Institute of Education Sciences, U.S. Department of Education, through Grant R305A170556 to The University of Texas at Austin. The opinions expressed are those of the authors and do not represent views of the Institute or the U.S. Department of Education.

REFERENCES

Alexander, P. A., Kulikowich, J. M., & Schulze, S. K. (1994). How subject-matter knowledge affects recall and interest. *American Educational Research Journal, 31*(2), 313–337.

Archer, A. L., & Hughes, C. A. (2010). *Explicit instruction: Effective and efficient teaching.* New York: Guilford Press.

Ausubel, D. P., & Youssef, M. (1965). The effect of spaced repetition on meaningful retention. *Journal of General Psychology, 73*(1), 147–150.

Compton, D. L., Fuchs, L. S., Fuchs, D., Lambert, W., & Hamlett, C. L. (2012). The cognitive and academic profiles of reading and mathematics learning disabilities. *Journal of Learning Disabilities, 45*(1), 79–95.

Cunningham, A. E., & Stanovich, K. E. (1997). Early reading acquisition and its relation to reading experience and ability 10 years later. *Developmental Psychology, 33*(6), 934–945.

Duke, N. K., & Pearson, P. D. (2008). Effective practices for developing reading comprehension. *Journal of Education, 189*(1/2), 107–122.

Elleman, A. M., Lindo, E. J., Morphy, P., & Compton, D. L. (2009). The impact of vocabulary instruction on passage-level comprehension of school-age children: A meta-analysis. *Journal of Research on Educational Effectiveness, 2*(1), 1–44.

Goldman, S. R. (2012). Adolescent literacy: Learning and understanding content. *The Future of Children, 22*(2), 3–15.

Goldman, S. R., Snow, C., & Vaughn, S. (2016). Common themes in teaching reading for understanding: Lessons from three projects. *Journal of Adolescent and Adult Literacy, 60*(3), 255–264.

Gough, P. B., & Tunmer, W. E. (1986). Decoding, reading, and reading disability. *Remedial and Special Education, 7*(1), 6–10.

Harmon, J. M., Hedrick, W. B., & Wood, K. D. (2005). Research on vocabulary instruction in the content areas: Implications for struggling readers. *Reading and Writing Quarterly, 21*(3), 261–280.

Kamil, M. L., Borman, G. D., Dole, J., Kral, C. C., Salinger, T., & Torgesen, J. (2008). *Improving adolescent literacy: Effective classroom and intervention practices: A practice guide* [NCEE No.

2008-4027). Washington, DC: National Center for Education Evaluation and Regional Assistance, Institute of Education Sciences, U.S. Department of Education. Retrieved from *http://ies.ed.gov/ncee/wwc*

Kieffer, M. J. (2012). Before and after third grade: Longitudinal evidence for the shifting role of socioeconomic status in reading growth. *Reading and Writing, 25*(7), 1725–1746.

Kintsch, W. (1988). The role of knowledge in discourse comprehension: A construction-integration model. *Psychological Review, 95*, 163–182.

Kintsch, W., & van Dijk, T. A. (1978). Toward a model of text comprehension and production. *Psychological Review, 85*, 363–394.

Klingner, J. K., Vaughn, S., Arguelles, M. E., Hughes, M. T., & Leftwich, S. A. (2004). Collaborative strategic reading "real-world" lessons from classroom teachers. *Remedial and Special Education, 25*(5), 291–302.

Klingner, J. K., Vaughn, S., & Schumm, J. (1998). Collaborative strategic reading during social studies in heterogeneous fourth-grade classrooms. *Elementary School Journal, 99*(1), 3–22.

Palinscar, A. S., & Brown, A. L. (1984). Reciprocal teaching of comprehension-fostering and comprehension-monitoring activities. *Cognition and Instruction, 1*(2), 117–175.

Pressley, M. (2006). *Reading instruction that works: The case for balanced teaching* (3rd ed.). New York: Guilford Press.

Radner, B. (2005). *American explorers*. Retrieved from *http://teacher.depaul.edu*

Recht, D. R., & Leslie, L. (1988). Effect of prior knowledge on good and poor readers' memory of text. *Journal of Educational Psychology, 80*(1), 16–20.

Shapiro, A. M. (2004). How including prior knowledge as a subject variable may change outcomes of learning research. *American Educational Research Journal, 41*(1), 159–189.

Stevens, E. A., Murray, C., Fishstrom, S., & Vaughn, S. (2020). Using question generation to improve reading comprehension for middle grade students. *Journal of Adolescent and Adult Literacy, 64*(3), 311–322.

Stevens, E. A., Park, S., & Vaughn, S. (2019). A review of summarizing and main idea interventions for struggling readers in grades 3 through 12: 1978 to 2016. Remedial and Special Education, 40(3), 131–149.

Stevens, E. A., & Vaughn, S. (2019). Interventions to promote reading for understanding: Current evidence and future directions. In J. Dunlosky & K. Rawson (Eds.), *Cambridge handbook of cognition and education* (pp. 381–408). New York: Cambridge University Press.

Stevens, E. A., & Vaughn, S. (2020). Using paraphrasing and text structure instruction to support main idea generation. *Teaching Exceptional Children, 53*(4), 300–308.

Stevens, E. A., Vaughn, S., House, L., & Stillman-Spisak, S. (2020). The effects of a paraphrasing and text structure intervention on the main idea generation and reading comprehension of students with reading disabilities in grades 4 and 5. *Scientific Studies of Reading, 24*(5), 365–379.

Swanson, E., Stevens, E. A., Scammacca, N. K., Capin, P., Stewart, A. A., & Austin, C. R. (2017). The impact of tier 1 reading instruction on reading outcomes for students in grades 4–12: A meta-analysis. *Reading and Writing, 30*(8), 1639–1665.

Tannenbaum, K. R., Torgesen, J. K., & Wagner, R. K. (2006). Relationships between word knowledge and reading comprehension in third-grade children. *Scientific Studies of Reading, 10*(4), 381–398.

Torgesen, J. K., Wagner, R. K., & Rashotte, C. A. (1997). Prevention and remediation of severe reading disabilities: Keeping the end in mind. *Scientific Studies of Reading, 1*(3), 217–234.

Vaughn, S., Klingner, J. K., Swanson, E. A., Boardman, A. G., Roberts, G., Mohammed, S. S., et al. (2011). Efficacy of collaborative strategic reading with middle school students. *American Educational Research Journal, 48*(4), 938–964.

Vaughn, S., Swanson, E. A., Roberts, G., Wanzek, J., Stillman-Spisak, S. J., Solis, M., et al. (2013). Improving reading comprehension and social studies knowledge in middle school. *Reading Research Quarterly, 48*(1), 77–93.

Vaughn, S., Wexler, J., Roberts, G., Barth, A. A., Cirino, P. T., Romain, M. A., et al. (2011). Effects of individualized and standardized interventions on middle school students with reading disabilities. *Exceptional Children, 77*(4), 391–407.

Watts, S. M. (1995). Vocabulary instruction during reading lessons in six classrooms. *Journal of Reading Behavior, 27*(3), 399–424.

FORM 8.1. Get the Gist Log

Student(s): ______________________________

Class and Period: ______________________ Name of Text: ______________________

Section	Step 1: Who or what is this section about?	Step 2: What is the most important information about the "who" or "what"?	Step 3: Write gist statement.

FORM 8.2. Question Log

Student(s): ______________________________

Class and Period: ____________________ Name of Text: ____________________

Question	Answer	Text Evidence

(continued)

Question Log *(page 2 of 2)*

Question	Answer	Text Evidence

CHAPTER 9

Structured Language Interventions for Written Expression

Susan Lambrecht Smith
Charles Winthrop Haynes

Ryan is a sixth grader who has been receiving special education services for decoding and spelling since third grade when he was diagnosed with dyslexia. He can fluently decode a fifth-grade text—however, his reading comprehension is at the second-grade level. Ryan demonstrates age-appropriate listening comprehension skills and receptive vocabulary, yet his ability to name pictures is in the low average range and his sentence formulation skills are below average.

Ryan excels at sports and enjoys board games that require visual–spatial analysis. He is a friendly and talkative student who is interested in science and robotics. Ryan often talks about outdoor activities that he enjoys with friends and family. In school, Ryan participates during hands-on activities, such as science labs, but his teachers have noticed that he is often off task during language arts exercises that involve reading. His output is very limited during writing exercises.

In science class, Ryan and his classmates were introduced to biodiversity and explored several habitats and organisms that live in them. Students were assigned by the teacher to "Pick your favorite habitat. Answer the following question about your habitat: 'How do the animals in your ecosystem survive? Make sure you address the biodiversity of important animal and plant species.' " Ryan chose to write about tidal pools because he lives close to the ocean and has spent time exploring the seashore with his family. He and his classmates were presented with a general outline and had access to resource materials. In response to this assignment, Ryan wrote the following paragraph:

> TIDAL POOLS
>
> Tidal pools have lots of aminals. And starfish there too. When the water goes out, it leaves a pool with mostly plants are seeweed. Branacles can hurt your feet.

Ryan's difficulties, characterized by weaknesses in word-, sentence-, and text-level expression, provide a window into how writing can break down in children with reading- and language-related issues. In a meta-analysis of studies examining writing proficiency in children with learning disabilities (LD), Graham, Collins, and Rigby-Willis (2017) observed that for virtually every writing outcome (writing quality, vocabulary, grammar and syntax, organization, spelling, conventions, and motivation), children with LD underperformed relative to typically developing peers.

TEACHING WRITING: THE BIG PICTURE

While competence in writing appears to be at the forefront of educational concerns at the national level, there is little consensus on how writing skills should be taught. National core curriculum standards for written language (Common Core State Standards for Written Language [CCSS-WL]) were introduced in 2012 to provide consistent guidelines for grade-level writing expectations (Graham, Gillespie, & McKeown, 2013; Troia & Olinghouse, 2013). However, Graham and colleagues observed that these standards do not address strategy instruction and are not content centered. Furthermore, in the early grades, teaching is often focused on conventions of writing (e.g., punctuation), and may ignore other parts of the writing process, such as sentence construction. On a more general level, evidence-based practice is also not embedded in curricular competencies (Troia & Olinghouse, 2013).

While our sixth-grader Ryan enjoys interacting with friends at school and engages in academic activities that are experience based, he is at high risk for developing negative attitudes and reduced motivation for writing. In a meta-analysis of writing characteristics of children with LD, Graham and colleagues (2017) found that children in this group indeed had lower motivation. This may be compounded by the possibility that a reading disability places a "cognitive burden" on the process of writing (Costa, Edwards, & Hooper, 2015).

Koutsoftas (2016) found that while students with language-learning disabilities (LLD) benefited from instruction in planning, as did typically developing writers, they needed targeted instruction for language production skills. As such, access to instruction addressing these multiple components of writing becomes critical for students with reading and related language difficulties. In a review of effective writing intervention for students with LLD, Al Otaiba, Rouse, and Baker (2018) stressed that struggling writers should have instruction that is systematic, transparent, and explicit. Later in this chapter, we provide concrete examples of how to teach writing in a structured, systematic, and explicit way that gives the student a specific strategy for each step of writing. Such approaches provide linguistic and cognitive support for a range of learners, including struggling writers who may not have a diagnosed disability in reading.

WRITING AND ITS RELATIONSHIP TO STRUCTURED LITERACY

Models of writing development emphasize the integration of a wide array of cognitive and linguistic resources (e.g., Berninger et al., 2002; Graham, 2018; Hayes, 2012). Individual variables, such as attention, working memory, and executive control, interact with long-term memory resources (e.g., background knowledge) and production processes (e.g., spelling and handwriting) to support translation of ideas into writing (Graham, 2018; Hayes, 2012). Emotions, physical state, and personality traits modulate these processes. More recently, Graham proposed a "writer-within-community model," where community is defined as "a group of people who share a basic set of goals and assumptions and use writing to achieve their purposes" (p. 259). Children with deficits in cognitive or linguistic skills may struggle to access writing as a social activity. Undeniably, writing is a complex behavior, thus any effective approach to writing instruction should take these multiple components into account.

The International Dyslexia Association (IDA) defines Structured Literacy (SL) as a teaching approach that is explicit, systematic, cumulative, and multisensory. In SL practice, language is viewed as a multimodal enterprise, involving speaking, writing, listening, and reading. The ensuing sections of this chapter focus on describing a comprehensive, structured approach to teaching writing based on the work of Jennings and Haynes (2018). To clarify terminology, many studies use the terms *learning disability*, *language-learning disability*, and *developmental language disorder* (DLD) interchangeably. While studies recruiting children with LD may have a portion of participants who do not have any language issues, this comprises a small segment of children with LD. For the purposes of the following discussion, we refer to LLD as the source of both reading and writing problems. Below, we review some challenges facing children with reading and language-related difficulties, and note research supporting effective interventions at the word, sentence, and text levels.

WRITING IN CHILDREN WITH READING- AND LANGUAGE-RELATED DIFFICULTIES: WHAT WORKS

Word-Level Findings

Despite having rich background knowledge about tidal pools, our student Ryan relies on nonspecific vocabulary (*water*) and uses copular verbs (*is/are*) or high-frequency words (*live, hurt*). For children like Ryan, poor productivity is a hallmark of their writing and is evidenced by fewer words, limited vocabulary specificity or diversity, and issues with spelling (Gregg, Coleman, Davis, & Chalk, 2007; Morken & Helland, 2013).

While overall length of text detracts from writing quality in this population, lack of complexity of vocabulary is also highly related to their reduced writing quality (e.g., Graham et al., 2017; Gregg et al., 2007). Critically, children with oral and written language weaknesses are at high risk for building adequate vocabulary knowledge to support text comprehension and writing. Subsequent gaps in writing productivity may increase over time, leading to "Matthew effects" (Wood, Schatschneider, & Wanzek, 2020), such that struggling writers fall further behind—in contrast, the writing of children with stronger vocabulary skills builds exponentially over time.

Based on their review of effective vocabulary interventions, Elleman, Oslin, Griffin, and Myers (2019) recommend that vocabulary be taught in context, including exploring background knowledge related to a topic, and intentionally targeting words that are important to the meaning of a text. Even though Ryan had some background experience with tidal pools, he did not directly respond to the prompt "How do the animals in your ecosystem survive?" Both *ecosystem* and *survive* were key vocabulary words that could have guided his writing. Integration of topical vocabulary provides students with multiple ways to build semantic networks (Elleman et al., 2019; McKeown, Crosson, Moore, & Beck, 2018; Wright & Cervetti, 2017). Additionally, students need to be engaged in active processing through guided discussions in which they talk about the vocabulary and context, and use the same words in writing (Elleman et al., 2019; Lawrence, Francis, Paré-Blagoev, & Snow, 2017; McKeown et al., 2018; Wright & Cervetti, 2017).

Finally, while Ryan enjoys interacting with friends at school and engages in experience-based academic activities, he is at high risk for developing negative attitudes, including reduced motivation for engaging in writing. In their 2017 meta-analysis, Graham and colleagues found that children with LD had lower motivation—this is not a trivial consideration. For struggling writers, translating thoughts into writing begins with strategies for accessing and generating necessary word forms so that phrases and sentences become rich and meaningful. Thus, high-interest topics and texts are a critical component of both vocabulary and writing instruction. Motivating environments for teaching vocabulary can be established through high-interest topics that lend themselves to debate and opinion (e.g., Lawrence et al., 2017). Jennings and Haynes (2018) also highlight the power of a personal narrative for engaging beginning writers.

Sentence-Level Findings.

In Ryan's writing sample, his sentence structures are primarily simple and lack elaboration with prepositional phrases or descriptors. Sentence-level writing involves the ability to translate thoughts into syntactic sequences, a skill that emerges as early as first grade (Berninger, Nagy, & Beers, 2011). Not surprisingly, children with LD demonstrate problems with grammar and syntax, as well as sentence writing fluency (Graham et al., 2017). Berninger and colleagues (2011) found that, in a subset of early-elementary schoolchildren, thoughts were not realized completely, resulting in sentence fragments or run-on constructions. This is consistent with Houck and Billingsley's (1989) observations that compared to typically developing peers, children with LD appeared to produce more sentence fragments and fewer sentences overall.

Evidence for Sentence-Level Interventions

While sentence skills are a key predictor of writing quality, schools seldom teach students how to combine words and phrases into complete sentences. Decontextualized teaching of the abstract "rules" of grammar is largely ineffective for improving students' sentence writing skills, particularly in children who struggle with reading and writing. Saddler and Graham (2005) effectively utilized a sentence-combining approach in which explicit structures were taught in a sequence moving from simple sentences to more complex sentences with embedded clauses. Students may find using conjunctions to create compound sentences with the word *and* fairly easy but may need explicit instruction for embedding an adverb (e.g., She walked on the ice. She walked carefully. → She walked carefully on the ice). Saddler and Graham provide an example of teaching embedded adverbial clauses: "They all cheered. The movie stopped." → "They all cheered when the movie stopped" (p. 46). A meta-analysis indicated that explicit teaching of sentence combining not only improved this skill but improved story quality and writing complexity (Saddler, Ellis-Robinson, & Asaro-Saddler, 2018). Other research has used single-case experimental design to examine the inclusion of writing fluency via timed tasks at the paragraph and sentence levels (Datchuk, Wagner, & Hier, 2020). Results indicated that using both direct instruction (e.g., explicit teaching of sentence structures) and embedded planning strategies followed by timed practice increased students' writing sequences.

Paragraph-Level Findings

The overall organizational structure of Ryan's paragraph shows that he struggles with discourse planning. There is no clear topic sentence, ideas do not have a logical sequence, and some facts do not relate to the writing prompt. While Ryan can name some of the animals that live in tidal pools, he does not include additional relevant information that would elaborate on the response. He does not refer at all to the second part of the prompt that asks for how animals adapted to their habitat.

Competent paragraph-level writing has "flow" that can be attributed to macro-level elements, such as genre structure (e.g., narrative, compare/contrast vs. opinion essays), coherent organization, and micro-discourse elements, such as intersentence cohesion. Cohesion may include devices such as connectives, but it also overlaps with semantics since pronouns and synonyms are employed. Intrasentence cohesion is achieved when focal sentences are followed by facts and/or events that are clearly related and provide additional information. Children who have a profile of poor reading comprehension and relatively strong word recognition may also produce weak written narratives, particularly in areas related to use of more advanced connectives and cohesion (Carretti, Motta, & Re, 2016). These cohesive elements are absent in Ryan's sample.

Finally, while Ryan provides a title ("Tide Pools"), he does not provide a topic sentence or conclusion that gives the reader a summary of the information. Instead, his paragraph is a collection of largely disjointed facts. Children with reading- and language-related difficulties often struggle with the organization and planning needed to write a well-constructed paragraph. These children demonstrate issues with cognitive demands related to executive function for self-regulating different components of writing—they lack strategies for approaching planning and have limited procedural knowledge of the writing process (Harris & Graham, 2013). Such needs can be met through explicit and systematic teaching of strategies for organizing text-level writing.

Evidence for Paragraph-Level Intervention

There is a significant body of evidence showing that Self-Regulated Strategy Development (SRSD) is an effective writing approach for students with LD (see Harris & Graham, 2013). SRSD is a framework for teaching writing that fuses explicit instruction in strategies for writing with steps for leading students to monitor their use of these strategies. Initially students are engaged in developing background knowledge about writing genres and setting goals for writing. Teachers then actively model a strategy (e.g., pick ideas, organize notes, write and say more [POW]) by talking through the process. Students memorize the strategy with the help of mnemonics and initially collaborate with the teacher in applying the strategy to their writing. Independent performance is achieved when they are able to use self-regulation strategies without teacher support (Graham, Harris, & Troia, 2000; Mason, Harris, & Graham, 2011). Lane and colleagues (2011) found that students with behavioral and writing difficulties who received SRSD instruction made gains in elements and quality of writing over controls who received other process-oriented instruction. More recently, Hebert, Bohaty, Nelson, and Roehling (2018) found that a modification of SRSD with explicit teaching of text frameworks was effective for improving the quality of expository writing for struggling students. While the use of graphic organizers as a "structure" is commonly found in educational practice, interventions that incorporate explicit instruction along with these visual supports have been found to be the most effective (see Peterson, Fox, & Israelsen, 2020).

A COMPREHENSIVE APPROACH TO STRUCTURED WRITTEN LANGUAGE INSTRUCTION

The literature reviewed thus far has shown effective approaches to strategy instruction for writing targeting vocabulary, sentence-level structures, and planning, organizing, and revising text. The use of oral language in the service of written language intervention is mission critical. Indeed, the link between oral language and writing is well established in children with and without LLD (Dockrell & Connelly, 2009). A language-based approach benefits a range of students: those with a primary weakness in word recognition, those who have mixed profiles that include weaknesses related to receptive and expressive language, and those students for whom executive functioning impacts writing.

The comprehensive approach outlined in this chapter draws upon a structured writing intervention described by Jennings and Haynes (2018) in which students are taught *explicit* strategies for word-, sentence-, and paragraph-level writing. This approach emphasizes that written language activates a synthesis of speaking, listening, reading, and writing. Hence, all modalities are employed when engaging in the writing process. The elements of this procedure are *cumulative,* with a context for writing established at the beginning, including background knowledge and priming of topic-related vocabulary. Additional teaching of semantic mapping at the word level facilitates enriched vocabulary contributing to cohesion and coherence of writing. This progresses to *systematic* teaching of sentence and micro-discourse-level structures. Explicit *strategies* for planning and organization of text-level writing build upon previous word-, sentence-, and phrase-level instruction. A binding principle of this comprehensive approach is that lessons are topic centered so that meaningful vocabulary may be employed in structured activities for each component of writing.

In a recent report published by the IDA dedicated to structured approaches to reading and writing, we outlined hands-on word-, sentence-, and paragraph-level strategies exemplifying key elements of our comprehensive approach. In the next section, we resurface elements of that text (Haynes, Lambrecht Smith, & Laud, 2019, pp. 22–28), adapting and augmenting them with additional practical techniques based on our clinical application of the research summarized above (Jennings & Haynes, 2018; Lambrecht Smith, Haynes, Laud, Larrivee, & Perrigo, 2019).

Word-Level Strategies and Techniques

Leverage Topic-Centered Vocabulary and Concepts

Students benefit from structured language activities that incorporate vocabulary drawn from academic topics, or themes (Myhill, Jones, & Lines, 2018). When language exercises are not topic centered, students must randomly shift between different mental schemas. Figure 9.1 illustrates a "decontextualized" sentence exercise: one with no focal topic or theme. In this writing activity, the topic shifts from banking to seagulls to plumbing. This random shifting of topics taxes word retrieval, word finding, and working memory, and does not allow the student to practice and build semantic associations for learned topical vocabulary. Compare this approach with the "contextualized" exercise

Directions: Add a "where phrase" to each sentence.

1. A wealthy banker reviewed accounts ______________________________.
2. Screeching seagulls flew ____________________________________.
3. The skilled plumber installed pipes ____________________________.

FIGURE 9.1. Decontextualized or nontopical writing exercise.

Directions: Complete these sentences about scenes we discussed from the film we saw about beekeeping. Add a "where phrase" to each sentence:

The industrious worker bees carried golden pollen ______________________________.

A teenage beekeeper placed honey-filled frames ______________________________.

Several excited scout bees danced ______________________________.

FIGURE 9.2. Contextualized exercise (topic: beekeeping).

in Figure 9.2, which employs thematic vocabulary and concepts based on recent classroom instruction. We have selected the topic of beekeeping to add thematic variety for our readers and return to the topic of tide pools for application to Ryan's case at the end of this chapter.

The task in Figure 9.2 is accompanied by a visual stimulus that allows the learner to focus on a central topic, as well as practice key vocabulary and concepts related to the theme of interest. This frees cognitive resources for the central task of formulating spatial prepositional phrases. Whenever possible, teachers should employ key thematic vocabulary, constructing sentence-, paragraph-, and essay-level exercises using the same set of key words. This systematic use of new vocabulary in meaningful sentence contexts helps to consolidate learning of those words (Beck, McKeown, & Kucan, 2013).

Employ Noun and Verb Boxes

For grade school students and older struggling writers, teachers can help students learn to construct "noun and verb" boxes and fill them with selected topical vocabulary. For example, in a third-grade class focused on the topic of beekeeping, a teacher might guide students' retrieval of the topical vocabulary of interest, as illustrated in Figure 9.3.

Students learn to generate noun and verb boxes in the margins of their papers and refer to these boxes for important words to include in their sentence- and paragraph-level writing. It is important to note that students with LD and/or limited background knowledge may generate only a few high-frequency nouns and verbs, so it is incumbent

Noun	**Verb**
queen bee	*laid*
brood chamber	*contained*
scout bees	*signaled*
pollen	*filled*
honey	*dripped*

FIGURE 9.3. Brainstormed noun and verb boxes (topic: beekeeping).

on instructors to build on students' prior knowledge and current reading level by adding lower-frequency, more specific vocabulary to students' foundation of familiar words.

Link Oral Chaining with Phonetic Spelling

Many learners avoid using important words when they are difficult to say or spell. Chaining—having students orally building words (*ent-*, *ento-*, *entomol-*, *entomolo-*, *entomologist*)—can help learners pronounce multisyllabic vocabulary words. This practice supports learners' articulatory mastery, and thus ownership of key vocabulary. Chaining can be linked with phonetic spelling, having the student count the syllables, draw a line for each syllable, and then spell each syllable as it sounds. While this strategy does not replace systematic spelling instruction, it helps poor spellers to get their words on paper. (See Haynes et al., 2018, for details.)

Use Cueing Techniques and Strategies for Supporting Retrieval

Some students struggle to find the words they want. Teacher-provided cues include, but are not limited to, visual (picture), gestural (mimed verb or action of target noun), semantic (definition), and phonologic/graphemic (first sound or letter of a word). Cues students can employ by themselves include visualizing (trying to envision the object or action) and making semantic associations, such as recalling time, use, or location. (See Haynes & Jennings, 2018, for details.)

Teach Semantic Feature Mapping

Meanings of topical nouns or verbs can be explored and elaborated through semantic feature mapping. Semantic features are specific, component meanings associated with words. For example, Figure 9.4 is a semantic feature map for the key noun *hive tool*, from our beekeeping theme.

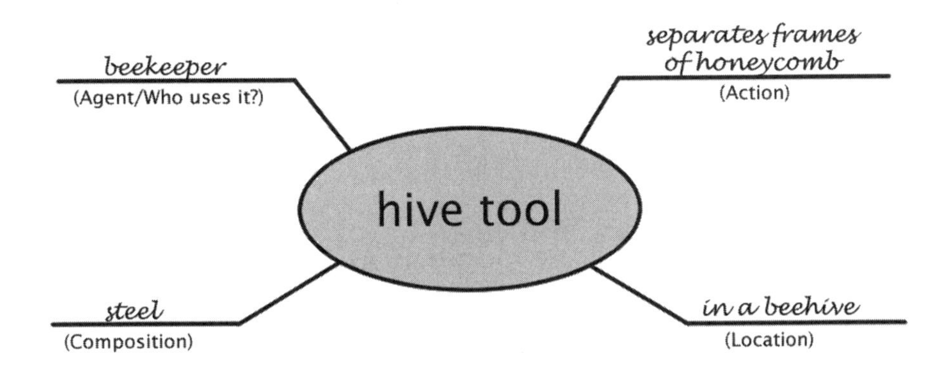

FIGURE 9.4. Semantic feature map.

When students identify and discuss the semantic features of a key noun or verb, they build a network of meaningful relationships around that word. These semantic associations resurface to support language formulation at the sentence level.

Sentence-Level Strategies and Techniques

Tap Semantic Feature Knowledge to Support Sentence Formulation

When students analyze the semantic features of a key noun, it sets them up to formulate meaningful sentences that reuse those same features. For example, consider the feature mapping done for "hive tool" in Figure 9.4 above and how the features can reemerge at different levels of sentence development:

- *Level 1:* The beekeeper uses a hive tool.
- *Level 2:* The beekeeper used the steel hive tool to separate frames in the beehive.
- *Level 3:* Standing next to the beehive, the beekeeper pried apart brood frames with his sharp steel hive tool.

In the Level 1 example, the features "beekeeper" and "uses a hive tool" resurface almost exactly. In contrast, in the Level 3 example—a complex sentence—the semantic features are used less directly and more flexibly, and additional vocabulary is inferred.

Teach Using a Sentence Hierarchy

According to SL principles, sentence instruction needs to be incremental and sequential, moving from simple to more complex. Table 9.1 provides a sample sentence hierarchy that incorporates previously introduced topical vocabulary from our beekeeping theme. Students with language impairment are often confused by formal grammatical terms, such as *noun phrase, predicate,* and *temporal adverbial phrase*. For this reason, simplified terms (*noun, verb, where phrase*) can help these students identify sentence parts and develop rudimentary syntactic awareness. The earlier-presented noun and verb box exercise (see Figure 9.3) provides key topical vocabulary for struggling writers to reference. In addition, the kernel noun (N) + verb (V) elements set up a range of simple sentence patterns. As students become more facile with recognizing and producing sentence parts, conventional terms can be introduced, as appropriate.

Introduce Flexibility

After learners show mastery of a given pattern, they can learn to experiment with moving elements around in that pattern. For example, after the N + V + where pattern is automatic, the student can be introduced to moving the where phrase to the beginning of the sentence: "The beekeeper located the hives on a hill next to the orchard" → "On a hill next to the orchard, the beekeeper located the hives." This experimentation at the

TABLE 9.1. Sentence Hierarchy

Structure	Example (topic: bees)
N + V	Bees swarmed.
N + V "where phrase" (where)	The beekeeper stood next to her hive.
N + is/are + V + Adj	The hive tool is sharp.
Adj + N + V + where	Angry bees flew toward the bear.
Adj + N + V + "when phrase" (when)	Several scout bees returned at dusk.
Adj + N + N + V + where + when	The energetic queen laid eggs in the brood chamber throughout the day.
Adj + Adj + N + V + where + when	Several aggressive bears attacked the hives in the orchard one sunny day.
Adj + N + V + where + *and* + (Art) + N + V + where	Hardworking beekeepers separated the hive chambers and bees landed on their bee hats.
Adj + N + V + where + *because* + (Art) + N + V + where	The hungry bees flew toward the field because the nectar dripped from the flowers there.
Adj + N + V + where + *but* + (Art) + N + V + where	Active bees flew toward our apple trees, but rain landed on their wings.
"When clause" + Adj + N + V + where	Before the customers arrived, the industrious shopkeepers placed packages of honeycomb on the shelves.
Adj + N + V + where + "who/which/that clause"	Nervous bees swarmed around the beekeepers, who donned their bee hats.
Adj + N + "who/which/that clause" + V	The queen, who was surrounded by worker bees, filled the brood chambers with bee larvae.

Note. N, noun; V, verb; Adj, adjective; Art, article. From Jennings and Haynes (2018, p. 84). Adapted with permission from the authors and Landmark School Outreach Program.

phrase level shifts semantic emphasis and provides the opportunity for learners to consider subtle differences in meaning that occur with changes in word order.

Reinforce Target Patterns Using Listening, Speaking, Reading, and Writing Modalities

Listening and reading tasks require students to monitor for the teacher's examples of correct versus incorrect sentences, while speaking and writing tasks ask students to retrieve vocabulary, as well as self-monitor their own productions. Following are sample, topical exercises for students working on the N + V + where (where prepositional phrase) sentence pattern. Teachers need to model the target behaviors before each exercise so that students understand what is expected. Examples of theme-centered exercises for receptive and expressive modalities are outlined in Table 9.2.

In sum, repeated practice with sentence patterns in multiple modalities helps students to internalize the forms, and the linking of recognition (listening and reading) with production (speaking and writing) tasks prepares students to self-monitor their production at the multisentence level (Jennings & Haynes, 2018). The continued use of topic-centered words provides students with repeated opportunities to recognize and use key vocabulary meaningfully within sentences.

Consolidate Sentence Skills with Fluency Drills

Repeated, timed practice writing sentences helps students to consolidate skills and become more fluent with producing isolated sentences. In addition, this repeated practice positively influences word order and sentence writing at the text level (see Datchuk et al., 2020). In our own practice, we have students create topical noun and verb boxes, copy a developmentally appropriate target sentence structure from the board (e.g., N + V + where), and then engage them in "sentence slams" in which they write as many sentences as possible within a 3-minute time constraint. Each student's number of correct target sentences per slam can serve as an informal progress monitoring tool.

TABLE 9.2. Receptive and Expressive Sentence Exercises

A. Listening (receptive: taps recognition and monitoring)

Procedure: Teacher displays the selected target sentence pattern noun + verb + where on the board. Students listen to teacher's production of theme-centered sentences and identify correct ("C") versus incorrect ("X"). If incorrect, the student then corrects the sentence so it follows the pattern. For example:

TEACHER: The beekeeper stood . . .

STUDENT: [*Marks on paper "X – where" and corrects the teacher's sentence to include the missing element.*] The beekeeper stood next to the hive.

B. Reading (receptive: taps recognition and monitoring)

Procedure: Same as for Task A, but with written stimuli.

C. Speaking (expressive: taps oral production)

Procedure: Teacher displays target sentence pattern noun + verb + where on the board and names a topical noun. The student orally formulates a sentence that follows the pattern. For example:

TEACHER: Bears . . .

STUDENT: Bears stole honey from the hive.

D. Writing (expressive: taps written production)

Procedure: Same as for Task C, but requires written formulation.

Note. From Jennings and Haynes (2018, p. 84). Adapted with permission from the authors and Landmark School Outreach Program.

Provide Visual Scaffolding

Students with deficits in language formulation often have trouble organizing their writing on the page. An effective remedial strategy is to employ templates to visually scaffold oral and written production. Figure 9.5 provides a simple example of how a template can visually scaffold an expanded kernel sentence with boxes.

A common teaching experience is to employ a sentence template, observe that a student has mastered a given sentence pattern using the template, and then be disappointed when the student fails to use the pattern correctly in spontaneous writing. In such cases, it is important to remember that children with language difficulties need scaffolds, like boxes and category labels, removed *gradually.* This same teaching principle—systematic application and removal of scaffolding—applies to any kind of cueing system that one uses to support language learning.

Micro-Discourse Strategies and Techniques

"Micro-discourse" refers to two- to four-sentence "chunks" of text. Important micro-discourse skills are (1) producing semantic flow (cohesion) from sentence to sentence and (2) using varied detail sentences for elaboration.

Support Semantic Flow through the Cohesive Tie Strategy

Struggling writers often overuse key topical nouns, which results in uninteresting writing that lacks semantic flow. Here is an example lack of flow within a student's sequential narrative:

> Next, the *queen bee* lays her eggs. This *queen bee* lays hundreds of eggs into cells inside the brood chamber. The *queen bee* may live three or four years.

Problems with semantic redundancy can be addressed by first modeling, and then having students memorize and apply the cohesion circle strategy illustrated in Figure 9.6.

Following is an example in which the student has applied the strategy to the queen bee sequence:

> Next, the queen bee lays her eggs. This amazing insect lays hundreds of eggs into cells inside the brood chamber. She may live three or four years.

Adj	N	V	Where	When
Massive	*bee swarms*	*gathered*	*in a pine tree*	*at sunset.*

FIGURE 9.5. Visual scaffolding for sample sentence pattern.

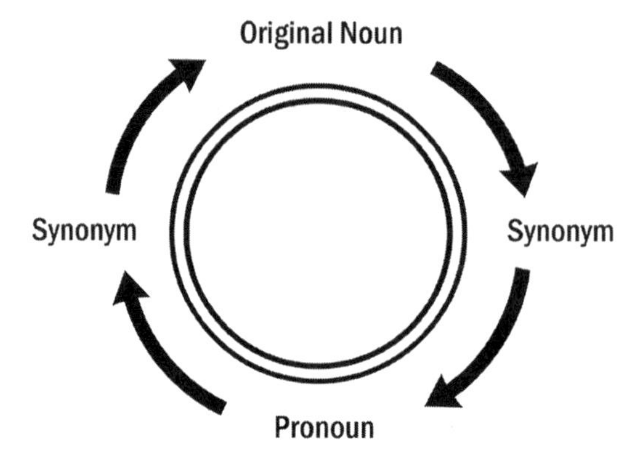

FIGURE 9.6. Cohesion circle strategy. From Jennings and Haynes (2018, p. 144). Adapted with permission from the authors and Landmark School Outreach Program.

In order for the cohesion circle strategy to be effective, students should first generate lists of synonyms and pronouns for the selected topical noun. For example, prior to generating the text above, the student would first list words or phrases, such as *queen bee, amazing insect,* and *she*. While the strategy is a powerful visual reminder, students need reminders to use this strategy flexibly, "listening" to the text they have written to make sure the cohesive ties "sounds right." Learners can also use the strategy image for analyzing texts they or peers have written: Students recall the image, draw it on paper, underline key nouns in topic sentences in the text, and then proofread the text for semantic flow.

Promote Rich Elaboration through Use of the Detail Circle Strategy

Students who struggle with writing often fail to provide salient and varied details to support points they want to make. These students benefit from incrementally learning the "detail circle," a mnemonic device that aids their recall of types of details (see Figure 9.7).

The detail circle is organized into basic-level details (1–4) and advanced-level details (5–8). When introducing the detail circle, the teacher first writes only the basic-level details into the circle, and then provides a topic sentence with key nouns underscored. Then, the teacher models how to add one or two relevant fact detail sentences with semantic cohesive ties in each underscored sentence. Each detail sentence elaborates on one or more of the underscored key nouns in the preceding sentence using the cohesion circle strategy to vary key vocabulary—for example:

- Teacher topic sentence: The queen bee lays eggs in the brood chamber.
- First relevant fact detail: This amazing insect lays up to two thousand of them in a single day.
- Second relevant fact detail: Most of her offspring develop into worker bees.

The three-sentence micro-discourse "chunk" looks like this:

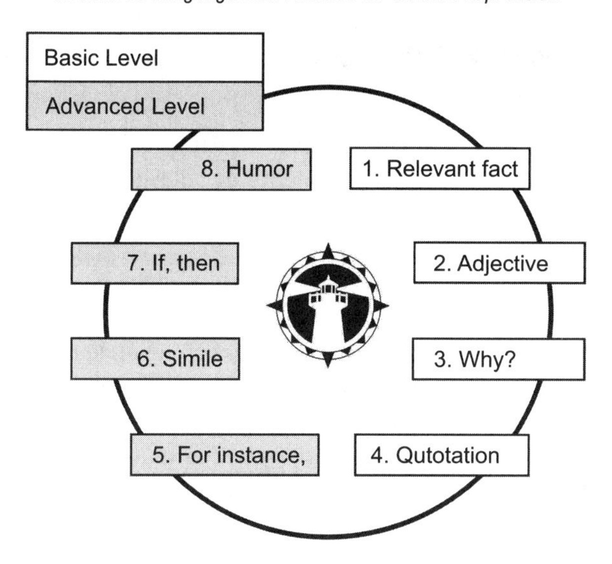

FIGURE 9.7. Detail circle strategy. From Jennings and Haynes (2018, p. 148). Reprinted with permission from the authors and Landmark School Outreach Program.

> The queen bee lays eggs in the brood chamber. This amazing insect lays up to two thousand of them in a single day. Most of her offspring develop into worker bees.

Initially, learners memorize the detail circle with only the basic-level details. They recall and draw the circle in the margin of their paper and use this mnemonic to guide their recall of varied detail sentences. First, they formulate details in micro-discourse exercises of two to three topic-centered sentences, and then within the familiar discourse environment of the personal sequence narratives. Initially, students master elaborating sequences (first, then, next, after that, and finally) in narratives—after that they apply their detail skills to expanding expository paragraphs and essays.

Paragraph-Level Principles, Strategies, and Techniques

A main purpose of teaching word-, sentence- and micro-discourse-level skills is to support students' paragraph-level writing. Principles for teaching paragraph-level writing are:

1. Employ oral rehearsal prior to writing.
2. Prepare students with theme-centered sentence expansion and/or sentence combining.
3. Teach the sentence at the core of each paragraph type.
4. Scaffold paragraph components (introductory and concluding sentences, paragraph body).

Strategies for supporting these principles are described below.

Prepare Students for Writing with Oral Rehearsal and Topical Sentence Instruction

When students struggle with paragraph-level writing, it is important for teachers to self-check whether they have engaged students in adequate oral rehearsal and topic-centered instruction at the sentence level.

Teach Sentences That Support Paragraph Logic

Before being expected to convey logic at the paragraph level, learners first need to learn to communicate logic at the sentence level. Standard expository paragraph types—such as descriptive, enumerative, comparison–contrast, and sequential process—often have at their core a specific type of sentence and logic. For example, descriptive expository paragraphs typically contain sentences with prenominal adjectives (*industrious queen bee, golden honey, buzzing worker bees*) and adjective stacking (*several pesky bears, sweet golden honey, exuberant young beekeeper*), enumerative sentences have words that signal number (*first, second, third*), comparison–contrast paragraph sentences denote contrast (*while, although, . . . but, . . . however*), and sequential-process paragraph sentences include words or phrases that indicate temporal transition (*first, then, next, after that, finally*). When students have mastered the logic of the sentence, they are better able to convey the logic of the paragraph.

Scaffold Paragraph Structure

Students with LLD typically do not intuit patterns of language through incidental exposure. With respect to discourse-level writing, they need to internalize reliable strategies for formulating sentences to begin and end their paragraphs. Sentences that comprise the body of the paragraph may also need to be scaffolded or supported. Figure 9.8 illustrates a generic framework for scaffolding an enumerative or persuasive paragraph. In this paragraph-level exercise, the student is responding to the prompt, "What are different jobs honeybees have that support the activity of the hive?"

SRSD makes use of mnemonic strategies, such as the TIDE acronym, to support the development of elaborated expository structures with topic + idea + detail + idea + detail + idea + detail + end (Mason, Reid, & Hagaman, 2012). In Figure 9.8, the left-hand margin illustrates our adaptation of TIDE to provide the overall structure for the student's elaborated paragraph. Students transition to memorizing this acronym, writing it in the margin of their paper and eventually dropping this self-cue as automaticity is gained. The framework first lists the prompt, so that the student knows what the teacher or audience is looking for, and the title is scaffolded by the embedded reminder to use words that tell "what the prompt asks for." In turn, the topic sentence is supported by the generic starter "There are different/several/many + [key noun from prompt] + [outcome that prompt asks for]." This starter might elicit the topic sentence "There are different jobs honeybees have that help the hive." Enumeration words—*first, second,* and

Prompt: "What are different jobs honeybees have that support the activity of the hive?"

Name: ______________________ Date: ______________

Title: Jobs of Bees in the Hive

Note: [what prompt asks for]

T (Topic)	There are different jobs honeybees have that help the hive. (Scaffold): There are different/several/many + [key noun from prompt] + [outcome that prompt asks for].
I (Idea)	First, there are drones, and their job is to mate with the queen bee.
D (Detail)	After the drones have mated, the worker bees kick them out of the hive.
I (Idea)	Second, the queen's job is to lay one to two thousand eggs each day.
D (Detail)	She lays one tiny egg in each cell, and these eggs turn into larvae.
I (Idea)	Third, there are guard bees that sit at the entrance to protect the hive from invaders.
D (Detail)	When a bee from a different hive tries to enter the hive to steal honey, these guards attack it.
E (End)	In conclusion, there are several important roles that honeybees play in helping the hive to stay healthy. (Scaffold): In conclusion, + [paraphrase of the prompt] + [comment on benefits or challenges].

FIGURE 9.8. Object description framework.

third—are overlearned to help students remember to list their key ideas. In the initial phases, the student can be required to recall, write in the margin, and apply the cohesion and detail circles to aid provision of meaningful details and reduce their use of redundant terms within their paragraph. The concluding sentence is supported by the scaffold "In conclusion, + [paraphrase of the prompt] + [comment on benefits or challenges]," which is overlearned. The cohesion circle acts as a mnemonic to help the student remember to avoid redundant terms when paraphrasing from their topic sentence. The enumerative/persuasive paragraph framework described here differs from typical graphic organizers in its greater number and variety of scaffolds employed to support the writer.

Scaffolding of paragraph components should vary according to the type of paragraph being taught. For example, a comparison paragraph would require different supports for topic, body, and concluding sentence than the enumerative/persuasive paragraph described above. When teaching at the paragraph level, it is critical to consider the different types of cues needed for a given student or group of students and then plan for how to systematically remove the scaffolding as mastery is demonstrated (Haynes & Jennings, 2006, pp. 15–16).

SUMMARY

Oral language skills provide a foundation for reading and writing. While writing is a complex activity that can be daunting for students with dyslexia and related LLD, there are many helpful strategies that teachers and students can use. A foundational cross-cutting principle is to use topical vocabulary as content for language-learning exercises. Given structured, systematic teaching that exploits synergies between listening, speaking, reading, and writing, struggling writers can learn to write independently and effectively at the word, sentence, micro-discourse, and paragraph levels. Below, we return to our case of Ryan and demonstrate how many of the above strategies might be applied to address objectives within a structured lesson plan to provide support for his writing.

APPLICATION ACTIVITIES

The following steps outline a 2-hour lesson plan for our case study, Ryan. The topic of this plan centers on the initial prompt provided by Ryan's teacher: "How do the animals in your ecosystem survive?" This lesson is intended to be administered to an individual student. However, sections may be adapted for small-group or whole-class instruction and could be extended to a topical unit that may take place over 1–2 weeks. A summary of the lesson plan with steps and objectives for each level is provided in Table 9.3.

1. Prereading Activity or "Brainstorming" (Including Word Categories)

In this first activity, Ryan will brainstorm nouns, verbs, and/or prepositional phrases related to the topic when given topically related pictures. Ryan will copy these into his word boxes at first, and then add more words later after reading (e.g., *seaweed, floats, after the tide goes out*). See Figure 9.3 for an example.

Rationale: Since Ryan has experience exploring tidal pools with his family, this is a potentially rich source of known vocabulary. In this activity, he will view a colorful, detailed picture of a tide pool and begin to use his vocabulary boxes.

2. Passage Reading with Writing Prompt

Prior to reading or listening to the passage, Ryan will read the prompt and state what he needs to look for while he reads. The teacher will restate the prompt ("How do the animals in your ecosystem survive?") and Ryan will copy it onto a piece of paper. The passage about tide pools (*https://oceanservice.noaa.gov/facts/tide-pool.html*) is then read to Ryan and he is prompted to read along with the teacher.

TABLE 9.3. Summary Lesson Plan: Tidal Pools

Area targeted	Task
1. Prereading activity (activate prior knowledge)	*Objective:* Given pictures and/or a video of a tidal pool, Ryan will brainstorm at least eight total nouns, verbs, and where/when phrases relating to the topic.
2. Review writing prompt and passage reading	*Objective:* Ryan will read the prompt and explain what he needs to look for as he reads, then listens to the passage: *https://oceanservice.noaa.gov/facts/tide-pool.html* *Prompt:* How do the animals in your ecosystem survive?
3. Postreading vocabulary review	*Objective:* Given the text, Ryan will brainstorm and add at least 15 total nouns, verbs, and where/when phrases relating to the topic in his vocabulary boxes.
4. Postreading concept mapping	*Objective:* Given a concept and related reading, Ryan will generate three ideas and three related fact details to add to his concept map.
5. Postreading semantic feature analysis of key vocabulary	*Objective:* Given a graphic organizer and key words from the text, Ryan will correctly identify key semantic features of a selected term from the text with moderate scaffolding from the instructor.
6. Sentence-level practice: use of key nouns and concepts in target sentence structure(s)	*Objective:* Given models, a structured graphic organizer, and related vocabulary, Ryan will formulate at least five targeted sentences that follow the pattern (article) + N + V + where + when.
7. Sentence level: micro-discourse cohesion	*Objective:* Given a theme-related starter sentence, Ryan will generate a relevant adjective detail in a second sentence.
8. Word level: micro-discourse cohesion	*Objective:* Given the key vocabulary term *tide,* Ryan will complete the cohesion circle using at least two synonyms and one pronoun.
9. Text-level writing	*Objective:* After reviewing the prompt, Ryan will use the structured graphic organizer to generate an eight-sentence paragraph.

Rationale: The purpose of this lesson is to elicit expressive language (oral and written) rather than to assess fluent decoding. Selection and presentation of the passage section is a critical consideration in this case because Ryan has a primary diagnosis of dyslexia. The passage may be modified for students with severe word recognition issues. In Ryan's case, the passage was also read aloud to him so that he could focus on the content. For students with reading- and language-related issues, support for understanding the content of the passage is critical so that they can write about it later. After reading, Ryan will be asked whether there are any other key vocabulary words that he might add to his vocabulary boxes from brainstorming.

3. Postreading Concept Mapping and Prompt Analysis

In this activity, the teacher will repeat the prompt, "How do the animals in your ecosystem survive?" and ask Ryan to rephrase it or to identify key words in the prompt. Through guided discussion, Ryan will identify key nodes and his teacher will transcribe the central focus of the concept map "Survival in Tide Pools" (see Figure 9.9).

Rationale: Note that this type of prompt leads to the formulation of an enumerative (listing) type of paragraph structure. Using a visual structure for three key ideas and related details, the teacher or Ryan fills out the map with the nodes for ideas and relevant details. Systematic questioning ("What comes next?" or "Why do we need to do this?") helps make the mapping approach transparent.

4. Post-reading Semantic Feature Analysis of Key Vocabulary

In this step, the teacher will provide or model visually the semantic map (e.g., see Figure 9.4) for Ryan to draw. In this case, the verb *retreat* is used, as this is less frequent in the lexicon and has utility for responding to the prompt. In this case, the categories are synonyms (*withdraw, ebb*), who/what does this (*tides, armies*), where does this happen (*ocean, shoreline, battlefield*), and antonyms (*advance, flow, move forward*).

Rationale: Semantic features analysis will help Ryan capitalize on key vocabulary and strengthen semantic relationships for terms that may be more complex and/or critical to later cohesion work.

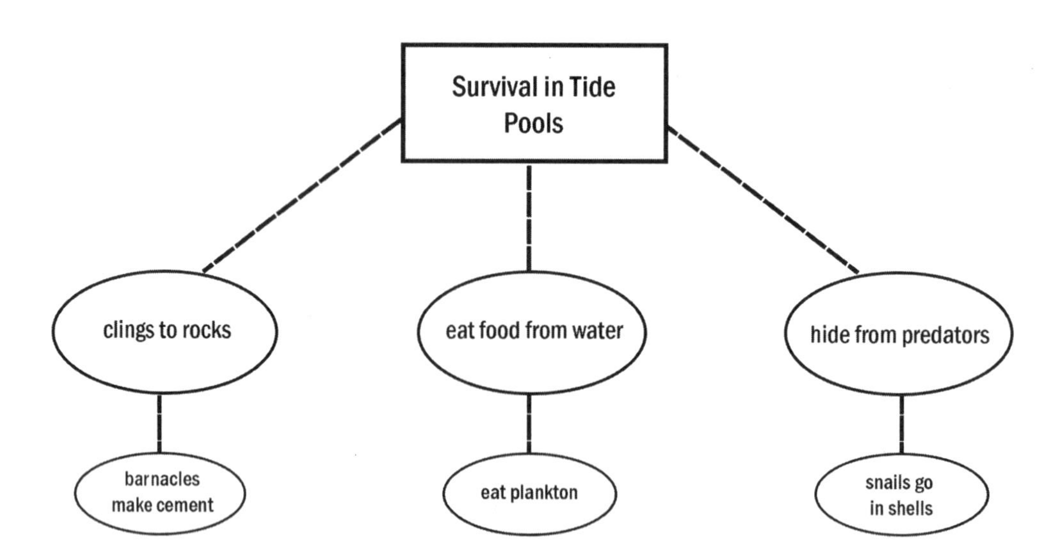

FIGURE 9.9. Enumerative concept map for ideas and details.

5. Sentence-Level Practice: Use of Key Nouns and Concepts in Target Sentence Structure(s)

Using models and a structured graphic organizer, Ryan will formulate sentences that follow the target pattern "(article) + N + V + where/when," using his vocabulary boxes (see Figure 9.5 for example). The teacher will start with a model sentence (e.g., "The barnacles stick to the bottom of the pool") and then guide Ryan to write several more sentences using that pattern.

Rationale: Given Ryan's use of primarily kernel sentences, the purpose of this activity is for Ryan to internalize an expanded kernel sentence structure. Reuse of key topical vocabulary maintains a meaningful context for sentence formulation. These sentences may also relate to nodes on the concept map.

6. Micro-Discourse: Building Cohesion with Vocabulary

The teacher will instruct Ryan in explicit strategies for building intersentential cohesion using vocabulary from the word boxes from the first step of the lesson. Ryan will draw the cohesion circle (see Figure 9.6) in the margin of his paper. The teacher may give Ryan the key word *tide*, which occurs frequently in his paragraph. He is prompted to provide a pronoun for the "tide" (*it*) and synonyms (*ocean, water, sea*).

Rationale: Previous lessons have introduced the cohesion circle, so Ryan is familiar with the visual prompt and understands that he will generate both pronouns and synonyms for key vocabulary. In preparation, Ryan may be asked, "What do we need to do to make sure our writing is interesting?" This question links the strategy to this specific component of writing.

7. Micro-Discourse: Building Cohesion with Elaboration

The teacher will then guide Ryan to include an adjective detail (see Figure 9.7) using the following script:

> The teacher says, "Last week we learned how to add a fact detail to our ideas to make a better paragraph. Here is an example: 'The beachgoers decided to leave after lunch.' Fact detail: 'A fog rolled in from the ocean.' What fact did we add here? That's right; the fog rolled in. What does that make you think? Yes, the sun goes away, and it feels cold. You are using words that make us think about how that feels. What feels cold? Yes, the sand. I'm thinking I will use the verb *feels* to describe the sand." The teacher writes the adjective detail: "The sand felt damp and chilly."
>
> The teacher then gives Ryan a starter sentence: "We walked across the rocks after the tide went out." Ryan is then prompted to produce an adjective detail using his vocabulary boxes. He writes, "The seaweed was slimy and slippery."

Rationale: During concept mapping, Ryan generated several related details that will guide him in producing an expanded enumerative paragraph. He has been introduced to how to add relevant facts details in a previous lesson on the detail circle. In this lesson, Ryan will make use of the adjective detail to build both cohesion and elaboration in his paragraph. This helps Ryan to learn an explicit strategy for how to integrate the facts he has gathered into his paragraph structure.

8. Discourse: Planning and Drafting the Paragraph

Ryan is provided with a planner below that scaffolds both the structure and starters for each part of the TIDE structure (see Figure 9.8).

The teacher asks Ryan to read the prompt, and then provides a starter for the topic (T) sentence. This is not a silent writing activity! If Ryan has difficulty generating a sentence for a fact in his concept map, the sentence boxes are referenced as a cue. Ryan's written productions are italicized, followed by possible teacher prompts. Later edits are reflected by crossed-out items Written scaffolds provided by the teacher are underscored.

Topic (T): *There are many ways that animals survive in tidal pools.*

Teacher: What are you thinking for your first idea?

Idea (I): *First, barnacles cling to the rocks.*

Teacher: You have an excellent first idea. What could you add to make this a richer sentence? What is available in your vocabulary box?

I: *First, barnacles cling to the rocks when the waves are crashing.*

Detail (D): ~~*The barnacles*~~ *They make cement that helps them* ~~*cling to the rocks*~~ *stick to the sides.*

Teacher: You have a wonderful relevant fact that adds information. Let's take a look at our cohesion circle. Do you have any words here that are repeated? What might work for *barnacles* the second time? [Ryan responds that *it* will work.] Are there any other words that we could change? Yes, what might be another way to say, "clings to the rocks"? [Ryan responds, "stick to the sides."] Could we add an adjective detail sentence to this?

D: *The barnacles are spiky and scrape your feet.*

Teacher: I can really picture how that might feel from your description since you have experience with tidal pools. What are you thinking for the second fact? [Ryan refers back to the concept map and states, "They hide from predators." The teacher may then prompt him to look at the cohesion circle.] What do we have at the top of our circle? Yes—the main vocabulary. What do you think we should start with?

I: *Second, snails hide from predators when the tide recedes.*

Teacher: Fabulous thinking! You used our key word from the semantic map. What are you thinking for a detail that goes with this sentence? [Ryan responds, "that the snails hide in their shells."]

D: *They ~~hide~~ withdraw in their shells so they will not be seen by the seagulls.*

Teacher: You not only remembered to use a pronoun for snails but you added another type of detail. You described why the snails are hiding. [In this case, the teacher is labeling the structures and strategies Ryan has generated.] We could use our semantic map to help with finding a word for *hiding* the second time. Do you see anything that works? [Ryan chooses to use *withdraw*.] What do you want to write for our final idea?

I: *Third, ~~animals~~ marine life in the tidal pool eat(s) food from the ~~water~~ ocean when it fills up at high tide.*

Teacher: You started with the main noun this time [*animals*]. This is great. Let's refer back to your vocabulary box to see whether there are some more specific words we could use. What might work for *animals*? Yes, *marine life* would be specific. Adding a when phrase makes this so much clearer. Let's add a relevant fact detail.

D: *~~They~~ Sea urchins and starfish eat plankton from the (sea)water.*

Teacher: Looking back at your vocabulary box, what terms might give more information to the reader? Yes, adding specific animals is a great way to do this. We could use one more adjective detail here. Thinking back to our "senses" types of adjectives, what could we say? [Ryan responds that the urchins and starfish are colorful. He also remembers that he needs to use a pronoun here.]

D: *They are brightly colored under the surface of the water and make the pool beautiful.*

Teacher: For your concluding sentence, what are you thinking? Let's look back to the prompt for ideas.

End (E): *In conclusion, marine animals living in tidal pools find many ways to survive.*

Rationale: Ryan has completed structured activities at the word, sentence, and micro-discourse level that set up his planning for writing a paragraph. The selection of a visual structure for this step is critical. Ryan is familiar with basic enumerative paragraph maps and has learned the TIDE mnemonic. He has not yet been successful in pulling the elements together to create an expanded paragraph structure, so the teacher provides a visual scaffold with sentence starters underscored. At this stage, Ryan is learning the structure, so overlearned terms (e.g., *first*, *second*) are still useful.

9. Final Draft and Editing

In this sample lesson, Ryan's final paragraph is as follows:

> There are many ways that animals survive in tidal pools. First, barnacles cling to the rocks when the waves are crashing. They make cement that helps them stick to the sides. These creatures are spiky and scrape your feet. Second, snails hide from predators when the tide recedes. They withdraw in their shells so they will not be seen by the seagulls. Finally, marine life in the tidal pool eats food from the ocean when it fills up at high tide. Sea urchins and starfish eat plankton from the seawater. They are brightly colored under the surface of the water and make the pool beautiful. In conclusion, marine animals living in tidal pools find many ways to survive.

While it is helpful to teach struggling students to edit using some type of mnemonic, generation of final drafts can be a source of frustration and should be done selectively. If the paragraph generation is accomplished through structured steps guiding students to think about their work strategically and metacognitively, there will be less need for final editing. The *process* by which students internalize strategies for accessing vocabulary, organizing their thoughts, and translating those thoughts into sentences and paragraphs is fundamental and is at the heart of the approach described here.

ACKNOWLEDGMENTS

We wish to thank Louise Spear-Swerling for her exceptional editorial advice. We are also appreciative to Sharon Vaughn for her feedback. We are grateful to the Landmark School Outreach Program and colleague Terrill Jennings for permission to adapt selected portions of *From Talking to Writing, Second Edition* (Jennings & Haynes, 2018). We express similar appreciation to the International Dyslexia Association and colleague Leslie Laud for their permissions to adapt selected portions of *Structured Literacy Approaches to Teaching Written Expression* (Haynes, Lambrecht Smith, & Laud, 2019). We also thank Kate Radville for her astute editorial and clinical contributions. Finally, we thank Natalie Smith for assistance with illustrations. We take responsibility for any errors that remain in the text.

REFERENCES

Al Otaiba, S., Rouse, A. G., & Baker, K. (2018). Elementary grade intervention approaches to treat specific learning disabilities, including dyslexia. *Language, Speech and Hearing Services in Schools, 49*(4), 829–842.

Beck, I. L., McKeown, M. G., & Kucan, L. (2013). *Bringing words to life: Robust vocabulary instruction* (2nd ed.). New York: Guilford Press.

Berninger, V. W., Nagy, W., & Beers, S. (2011). Child writers' construction and reconstruction of single sentences and construction of multi-sentence texts: Contributions of syntax and transcription to translation. *Reading and Writing, 24*(2), 151–182.

Berninger, V. W., Vaughan, K., Abbott, R. D., Begay, K., Coleman, K. B., Curtin, G., et al. (2002). Teaching spelling and composition alone and together: Implications for the simple view of writing. *Journal of Educational Psychology, 94*(2), 291–304.

Carretti, B., Motta, E., & Re, A. M. (2016). Oral and written expression in children with reading comprehension difficulties. *Journal of Learning Disabilities, 49*(1), 65–76.

Costa, L.-J. C., Edwards, C. N., & Hooper, S. R. (2015). Writing disabilities and reading disabilities in elementary school students: Rates of co-occurrence and cognitive burden. *Learning Disability Quarterly, 39*(1), 17–30.

Datchuk, S. M., Wagner, K., & Hier, B. O. (2020). Level and trend of writing sequences: A review and meta-analysis of writing interventions for students with disabilities. *Exceptional Children, 86*(2), 174–192.

Dockrell, J., & Connelly, V. (2009). The impact of oral language skills on the production of written text. *British Journal of Educational Psychology, 1*(1), 45–62.

Elleman, A. M., Oslund, E. L., Griffin, N. M., & Myers, K. E. (2019). A review of middle school vocabulary interventions: Five research-based recommendations for practice. *Language, Speech, and Hearing Services in Schools, 50*(4), 477–492. Graham, S. (2018). A revised writer(s)-within-community model of writing. *Educational Psychologist, 53*(4), 258–279.

Graham, S., Collins, A. A., & Rigby-Wills, H. (2017). Writing characteristics of students with learning disabilities and typically achieving peers: A meta-analysis. *Exceptional Children, 83*(2), 199–218.

Graham, S., Gillespie, A., & McKeown, D. (2013). Writing: Importance, development, and instruction. *Reading and Writing, 26*(1), 1–15.

Graham, S., Harris, K. R., & Troia, G. A. (2000). Self-regulated strategy development revisited: Teaching writing strategies to struggling writers. *Topics in Language Disorders, 20*(4), 1–14.

Gregg, N., Coleman, C., Davis, M., & Chalk, J. C. (2007). Timed essay writing: Implications for high-stakes tests. *Journal of Learning Disabilities, 40*(4), 306–318.

Harris, K. R., & Graham, S. (2013). "An adjective is a word hanging down from a noun": Learning to write and students with learning disabilities. *Annals of Dyslexia, 63*(1), 65–79.

Hayes, J. R. (2012). Modeling and remodeling writing. *Written Communication, 29*(3), 369–388.

Haynes, C., & Jennings, T. (2006). Listening and speaking: Essential ingredients for teaching struggling writers. *Perspectives on Language and Literacy, 32*(2), 12–16.

Haynes, C., Lambrecht Smith, S. L., & Laud, L. (2019). Structured literacy approaches to teaching written expression. *Perspectives on Language and Literacy,* 45(3), 22–30.

Hebert, M., Bohaty, J. J., Nelson, J. R., & Roehling, J. V. (2018). Writing informational text using provided information and text structures: An intervention for upper elementary struggling writers. *Reading and Writing, 31*(9), 2165–2190.

Houck, C. K., & Billingsley, B. S. (1989). Written expression of students with and without learning disabilities: Differences across grades. *Journal of Learning Disabilities, 22*(9), 561–567, 572.

Jennings, T., & Haynes, C. (2018). *From talking to writing: Strategies for supporting narrative and expository writing* (2nd ed.). Prides Crossing, MA: Landmark School Outreach Program.

Koutsoftas, A. D. (2016). Writing process products in intermediate-grade children with and without language-based learning disabilities. *Journal of Speech, Language and Hearing Research, 59,* 1471–1483.

Lambrecht Smith, S., Haynes, C., Laud, L., Larrivee, E., & Perrigo, C. (2019, November 22). *Efficacy of short-term structured intensive writing instruction for students with reading disabilities.* Paper presented at the American Speech–Language–Hearing Association Annual Conference, Orlando, FL.

Lane, K. L., Harris, K., Graham, S., Driscoll, S., Sandmel, K., Morphy, P., et al. (2011). Self-regulated strategy development at tier 2 for second-grade students with writing and behavioral difficulties: A randomized control trial. *Journal of Research on Educational Effectiveness, 4*, 322–353.

Lawrence, J. F., Francis, D., Paré-Blagoev, J., & Snow, C. E. (2017). The poor get richer: Heterogeneity in the efficacy of a school-level intervention for academic language. *Journal of Research on Educational Effectiveness, 10*(4), 767–793.

Mason, L. H., Harris, K. R. & Graham, S. (2011). Self-regulated strategy development for students with writing difficulties. *Theory Into Practice, 50*, 20–27.

Mason, L. H., Reid, R., & Hagaman, J. L. (2012). *Building comprehension in adolescents: Powerful strategies for improving reading and writing in content areas*. Baltimore: Brookes.

McKeown, M. G., Crosson, A. C., Moore, D. W., & Beck, I. L. (2018). Word knowledge and comprehension effects of an academic vocabulary intervention for middle school students. *American Educational Research Journal, 55*(3), 572–616.

Morken, F., & Helland, T. (2013). Writing in dyslexia: Product and process. *Dyslexia, 19*(3), 131–148.

Myhill, D., Jones, S., & Lines, H. (2018). Supporting less proficient writers through linguistically aware teaching. *Language and Education, 32*(4), 333–349.

Peterson, A. K., Fox, C. B., & Israelsen, M. (2020). A systematic review of academic discourse interventions for school-aged children with language-related learning disabilities. *Language, Speech, and Hearing Services in Schools, 51*(3), 866–881.

Saddler, B., Ellis-Robinson, T., & Asaro-Saddler, K. (2018). Using sentence combining instruction to enhance the writing skills of children with learning disabilities. *Learning Disabilities: A Contemporary Journal, 16*(2), 191–202.

Saddler, B., & Graham, S. (2005). The effects of peer-assisted sentence-combining instruction on the writing performance of more and less skilled young writers. *Journal of Educational Psychology, 97*(1), 43–54.

Troia, G. A., & Olinghouse, N. G. (2013). The common core state standards and evidence-based educational practices: The case of writing. *School Psychology Review, 42*(3), 343–357.

Wood, C., Schatschneider, C., & Wanzek, J. (2020). Matthew effects in writing productivity during second grade. *Reading and Writing, 33*(6), 1377–1398.

Wright, T. S., & Cervetti, G. N. (2017). A systematic review of the research on vocabulary instruction that impacts text comprehension. *Reading Research Quarterly, 52*(2), 203–226.

CHAPTER 10

Multicomponent Structured Literacy Interventions for Mixed Reading Difficulties

Louise Spear-Swerling

Mr. Goudreau is a special educator who teaches students in grades 4–6. His school serves many children who begin formal schooling with limited early literacy experiences, and most children in the school qualify for free or reduced-price lunch. Almost all of the students on Mr. Goudreau's caseload receive services for difficulties involving literacy. The reading problems of Mr. Goudreau's students tend to be broad and complex, involving both word recognition and language comprehension.

Many of these students are like Jamal, a sixth grader reading on about a fourth-grade level. Jamal's eligibility category on his individualized education plan (IEP) is other health impaired/attention-deficit/hyperactivity disorder (OHI/ADHD). After sustained phonics intervention, Jamal can decode most one- and two-syllable words accurately, but he still needs work on decoding, especially in relation to multisyllabic words. His decoding weaknesses contribute to his problems in text-reading fluency. These difficulties are further compounded by Jamal's weaknesses in vocabulary and background knowledge, which lead him to read slowly as he sometimes struggles to comprehend. Considered individually, Jamal's weaknesses are not as severe as those of some other children in special education. However, the breadth of those difficulties, combined with the escalating demands of reading in the upper-elementary grades, create many challenges for him in meeting grade-level expectations for literacy.

The most severely impaired readers on Mr. Goudreau's caseload are Terrell, who is in grade 5, and Lacey, who is in grade 4. Terrell has been identified with dyslexia and is functioning at an extremely low reading level: early grade 1. Currently he is working on decoding and spelling of consonant–vowel–consonant (CVC) words. He also still requires some practice on phonemic awareness tasks, such as phoneme blending and segmentation of words. Although Terrell's listening comprehension is far better than his reading comprehension, he has limitations in vocabulary and background knowledge, similar in nature to Jamal's, but somewhat milder. In his special education intervention, Terrell reads very basic decodable texts, so his language weaknesses are not yet having a large impact on his comprehension in reading. However, Mr. Goudreau sometimes notices these weaknesses in class discussions of read-alouds and other oral activities.

Lacey, who has been identified with a language disability, functions at an early-second-grade level in reading. Although further along than Terrell in decoding, she still needs some work on one-syllable words with vowel-*r* (e.g., *spark, thirst, word*), and currently, she has limited skills for decoding unfamiliar two-syllable words. Also, her language comprehension needs are more significant than either Jamal's or Terrell's. In addition to needs involving vocabulary and background knowledge, Lacey has particular difficulty with syntax. Texts with long, complex sentences are often difficult for her to comprehend, even when she can decode the words she is reading, and even when the text is read aloud.

Mr. Goudreau is a conscientious teacher. He has always worried about how best to meet his students' literacy needs, especially when those needs are complex or have shown inadequate responsiveness to intervention. He is also a teacher in the school district of Ms. Cuffe, the administrator mentioned in the opening to Spear-Swerling, Chapter 1, this volume. When Ms. Cuffe convinced other administrators and educators in her district to adopt Structured Literacy (SL) approaches to intervention, Mr. Goudreau was one of the first teachers trained in SL. His implementation of SL provides a good illustration of how to intervene with students who have multifaceted types of literacy difficulties, such as the three students described above.

Jamal, Terrell, and Lacey have mixed reading difficulties (MRD), involving a mixture of problems related both to word recognition and language comprehension (see Spear-Swerling, Chapter 1, this volume). Although there is some variability in each child's specific weaknesses, all three children require multicomponent interventions to progress well in reading. Multicomponent interventions address multiple components of literacy, including those related to word recognition (e.g., phonemic awareness, phonics, multisyllabic word reading) and to comprehension (e.g., vocabulary, background knowledge, syntax). The previous chapters of this book provide many examples of SL interventions for these components of reading, as well as spelling and written expression. This chapter considers the planning and design of multicomponent interventions, which involve combinations of these single-component interventions.

RESEARCH SUPPORT FOR MULTICOMPONENT INTERVENTIONS

Many poor readers require multicomponent interventions. This tends to be especially true of poor readers in the upper-elementary grades as opposed to the primary grades, and those with relatively severe as opposed to milder reading comprehension difficulties, as well as English learners (ELs) and children from low-socioeconomic backgrounds. For example, Capin, Cho, Miciak, Roberts, and Vaughn (2021) studied 446 grade 4 students who had scored at or below the 16th percentile on a group-administered reading comprehension measure. About half of these poor readers had limited English proficiency, and a majority of them qualified for free or reduced-price lunch. Virtually all of these students had a mixed profile, with weaknesses in both word recognition and language comprehension. Most of these poor readers (91%) had comparable and moderate weaknesses in both areas, similar to Jamal in Mr. Goudreau's class, but a small percentage of students had a severe deficit in one area (word recognition or language comprehension), coupled with a more moderate deficit in the other. Some other studies have identified relatively fewer poor readers with a mixed profile (e.g., Leach, Scarborough, & Rescorla, 2003; Lesaux & Kieffer, 2010), but all teachers encounter some poor readers who require multicomponent interventions.

Encouragingly, studies show that multicomponent interventions can be very effective (Fletcher, Lyon, Fuchs, & Barnes, 2019; Foorman, Herrera, Dombek, Schatschneider, & Petscher, 2017; Scammacca, Vaughn, Wanzek, Roberts, & Torgesen, 2007; Wanzek, Al Otaiba, & McMaster, 2020). For instance, Foorman and colleagues (2017) examined the efficacy of two pullout small-group literacy interventions implemented with at-risk K–2 children. Both interventions addressed language skills, such as vocabulary and syntax, as well as foundational reading skills, such as phonemic awareness and phonics. However, one intervention was a standalone intervention, whereas the other used intervention materials embedded in the core reading program employed at the study schools. Both interventions were about equally effective except for in the area of spelling in grade 2, in which children receiving the standalone intervention made more progress than those receiving the embedded intervention. After 27 weeks, children in both interventions improved, on average, 13–25 percentile points in foundational reading skills and 6–25 percentile points in language outcomes.

In addition to being highly explicit, effective multicomponent interventions use assessment to differentiate instruction for individual students, as well as to monitor progress and adjust interventions as needed (Wanzek et al., 2020). Intervention approaches that build on a foundation of strong general education (Tier 1) instruction, with intervention supplementing rather than replacing core instruction, are generally most successful. Other characteristics of effective interventions include maximizing time spent in actual reading and writing, as opposed to, for instance, memorizing and reciting phonics rules; providing adequate time for and intensity of intervention; and strong integration of interventions, both internally and in relation to core instruction (Fletcher et al., 2019). The specific programs used are less critical than adherence to these kinds of principles (Vaughn & Fletcher, 2012).

PLANNING MULTICOMPONENT INTERVENTIONS USING SL

Nature and Severity of Children's Weaknesses

Initial assessments should determine both the nature and severity of individual children's component weaknesses. Children with language comprehension weaknesses may vary greatly in the specific nature of their language problems, with potential weaknesses in an array of areas, including vocabulary, syntax, pragmatic language, inferencing, and so on. Although many children have weaknesses in multiple language areas, appropriate intervention requires a determination of specific weaknesses for individual children. Similarly, children with problems in word recognition can vary in their underlying phonemic awareness skills, their phonics skills and orthographic knowledge, automaticity as well as accuracy of word reading, and so on. The severity of the weaknesses is also important. The three children described in the opening to this chapter all had difficulties with word recognition, but they were functioning at very different levels and therefore had differing needs in terms of the focus of decoding intervention.

Sometimes it is necessary to set priorities in intervention. Terrell, the child in Mr. Goudreau's class with the most severe decoding difficulties, provides a good example of this issue. Terrell functions at an extremely low reading level because of his decoding problems, and it makes sense to prioritize his decoding needs in intervention. However, his intervention should still include some work on language comprehension, because without this kind of intervention, Terrell's limitations in vocabulary and background knowledge will almost certainly affect his reading comprehension in the future, as his decoding improves and he becomes capable of decoding more advanced types of texts. For now, since Terrell can only read very basic decodable texts, intervention for language comprehension should mostly employ listening tasks, such as teacher read-alouds with questioning and discussion. Listening tasks can use much more sophisticated texts than Terrell can read himself and can therefore be a better source for new vocabulary and background knowledge. These activities can be a vehicle for improving Terrell's vocabulary and background knowledge in ways that should transfer to his reading and writing as his decoding skills improve.

Integration of Interventions

Good integration can make interventions much more efficient and productive. One aspect of integration involves integration of Tier 2 and 3 interventions, as well as special education, with the core general education system (Tier 1). Whether they are reading in a general education class or in intervention, if poor readers receive consistent feedback about applying their decoding skills when reading passages, rather than guessing based on context cues, they will be more likely to follow through with applying these skills. If general education teachers, as well as interventionists, teach and reinforce certain spelling generalizations or specific comprehension strategies, such as summarization, poor readers will be more likely to learn them.

Another aspect of integration is internal and involves integrating the components of the intervention. This kind of integration is intrinsic to SL approaches, as discussed in Spear-Swerling, Chapter 1, this volume. For example, SL approaches have a high degree of integration between the decoding patterns or comprehension skills children are learning in intervention and the texts they read in instruction. As another example, SL approaches emphasize consistent application of skills and teaching for transfer, with instructional tasks deliberately chosen to facilitate transfer.

Teachers can use specific instructional activities in ways that increase integration. For instance, although learning to write well is important for its own sake, writing activities can also enhance reading progress in multiple ways (Graham & Hebert, 2010). Spelling words in writing tasks can help develop poor decoders' phonemic awareness skills, focus their attention on the internal details of words, and practice their knowledge of phoneme–grapheme correspondences, all skills that will aid their decoding, as well as their spelling. (See Moats, Chapter 4, this volume, for further discussion.) Teaching students about text structure in writing, or having them write summaries of what they have read, can improve their reading comprehension, as well as their written expression. Multisensory activities that involve tracing printed words while saying the letter names and the whole word aloud, and then writing the word from memory, can promote progress in spelling, as well as reading, of phonetically irregular words (Spear-Swerling & Brucker, 2004).

As another example, teaching students about morphology can improve multiple components of literacy, including word reading, spelling, and vocabulary (Carlisle, 2010; Goodwin & Ahn, 2013). If students learn to recognize and spell the root word *struct*, as well as its meaning (i.e., build) in the context of morphological word families, this can help them read, spell, and understand semantically related words, such as *structure, structural, construction, destruction, destructive,* and so forth. This kind of morphological intervention may be especially valuable for students like Jamal, who possess basic decoding and spelling skills, but who need work on decoding and spelling of longer words, as well as vocabulary development. Internal integration of interventions through these and other activities is important to increase the efficiency of multicomponent interventions and to help students transfer skills across a range of reading and writing tasks.

Grouping Considerations

Some poor readers have very severe and persistent reading problems that require a high degree of intensity of instruction for progress to occur (Torgesen, 2004); they may also have co-occurring difficulties in behavior or attention that make grouping them with other students difficult. For these children, one-to-one intervention may sometimes be required. Many students, however, can progress well in small groups of two or three children, if the groups are well constituted and homogeneous in terms of their instructional needs (Vaughn et al., 2003). Mr. Goudreau's students offer a useful example of these grouping considerations.

Mr. Goudreau initially found Jamal to be easily distracted, even in a small group. Also, especially when tasks were challenging for him, Jamal seemed embarrassed to read in front of other students, and he would refuse to attempt many tasks. Therefore, at first, Mr. Goudreau worked with Jamal one to one. However, after Mr. Goudreau implemented a simple behavior plan, and as progress in his SL intervention increased Jamal's confidence, it became easier to include him with two other students on Mr. Goudreau's caseload: Jake and Nasreen. These three students have very similar needs in literacy, involving multisyllabic word decoding, spelling, fluency, vocabulary, and reading comprehension, and they are functioning at similar grade levels, so it makes sense for Mr. Goudreau to group them together.

In contrast, currently it is difficult for Mr. Goudreau to group Lacey or Terrell with other children for instruction. Both of these students have decoding needs that are too different for them to be grouped with Jamal or with each other. However, Lacey has better decoding skills than does Terrell, and she is making excellent progress in the phonics part of her redesigned SL intervention. Therefore, it should eventually be possible to group her with Jamal or another small group of students for the word reading and spelling part of her multicomponent intervention, with her language comprehension needs continuing to be addressed one to one.

A BASIC LESSON FORMAT FOR MULTICOMPONENT SL INTERVENTIONS

Table 10.1 displays a basic lesson format for a multicomponent intervention plan that uses an SL approach. The left-hand column of the table shows the component areas of the plan, with the middle column briefly describing each area, and the right-hand column showing some sample activities.

The intervention plan has broad segments for word recognition and spelling, fluency, text reading and reading comprehension, oral language comprehension, and writing. Approximate time ranges are provided for each of these areas, with total time for the intervention plan ranging from about 45 to 90 minutes, depending on the individual student's needs. If there are scheduling constraints or other concerns, such as a child's ability to sustain attention for a long block of time, the plan could be split into two sessions—for example, a morning session focused on word reading, spelling, and fluency, and an afternoon session focused on text reading, reading comprehension, language comprehension, and writing. For children with less intensive needs, some lesson segments might also be alternated across days rather than being delivered every day. The writing segment in the plan primarily represents ways to use writing to develop and reinforce reading skills; it is not intended to represent a total program for written expression. (See Lambrecht Smith & Haynes, Chapter 9, this volume, for a detailed discussion of SL interventions for written expression.) Specific amounts of time for each area of the intervention plan in Table 10.1 should be adjusted to reflect individual children's needs. For children like Jamal, with moderate needs in both word reading and comprehension, total intervention time might be divided about equally between word reading, spelling, and fluency, on the one hand, and reading comprehension and language comprehension,

TABLE 10.1. Basic Format for a Multicomponent Intervention Plan for Students with MRD

Component(s)	Description	Sample activities
Word recognition and spelling (~15–25 minutes)	Skills for reading and spelling printed words	
• Phonological and phonemic awareness (PA)	• Key PA skills, such as phoneme blending and segmentation	• Oral practice with teacher modeling and counters
• Phoneme/grapheme, grapheme/phoneme, and morphological relationships	• Correspondences for single letters, letter patterns (e.g., *sh, ch, oy*), and morphemes	• Explicit teaching with letter cards; multisensory activities
• Generalizations (rules or strategies for decoding and spelling unfamiliar words)	• Generalizations for decoding (e.g., *-vce;* peeling-off affixes) and spelling (e.g., adding suffixes to a *-vce* base word)	• Explicit teaching of generalizations with guided practice; word sorts
• Decoding unfamiliar words	• Apply above skills to decode unfamiliar printed words	• Word-building activities with letter tiles; decoding a list of words
• Spelling	• Apply above skills to spell words	• Word-building activities with letter tiles; writing words
• Irregular (exception) words	• Read and spell words that are exceptions to typical phonics relationships	• Multisensory activities; highlight regularities, as well as irregularities
Fluency (~5–10 minutes)	Practice reading words automatically and reading text fluently	Timed flash card practice on common irregular words; timed repeated readings of text; phrase-cued texts
Text reading and reading comprehension (including text-specific vocabulary; ~10–25 minutes)	Application of word recognition skills to reading an unfamiliar text and reading with comprehension	Guided reading of instructional-level text with immediate teacher feedback to decoding errors; teaching comprehension strategies, such as summarization; question writing (by students); comprehension questions (from teacher) and discussion of text students have read; turn-and-talk routine as part of explicit teaching of target vocabulary words
Language comprehension, including general vocabulary development (e.g., Tier 2 vocabulary words; ~10–15 minutes)	Development of important areas of oral language comprehension	Teacher read-alouds of listening-level text with comprehension questions and discussion; explicit teaching to help students understand potentially confusing syntax; explicit and extended vocabulary instruction with child-friendly definitions and contextual examples
Writing (~5–15 minutes)	Using writing to teach or reinforce important components of reading, both foundational skills (e.g., phonemic awareness, decoding, spelling) and higher-level language skills (e.g., reading comprehension, text composition)	Write and spell dictated sentences; answer questions about text that students have read or listened to; sentence-combining activities; use of graphic organizers; writing a summary of a text

on the other. However, for students like Terrell, with much more severe needs in one component area than the other, more time should be devoted to the weaker area. Writing activities can be used to develop children's skills in a variety of areas involving both foundational skills and higher-level skills and can be targeted accordingly depending on students' needs. Teachers should use regular progress monitoring assessments to inform decision making about whether time allocations require adjustment.

Some details in the content of Table 10.1 should be highlighted. The section of the plan involving word recognition and spelling includes multiple subsections, which are bulleted in the table, beginning with phonemic awareness. Not all of these subsections are relevant for an individual student. For example, Terrell still requires some intervention in phonemic awareness skills, whereas Jamal and Lacey do not. Nor will new skills be taught in every subsection for every lesson. Generalizations for decoding, such as *vce*, or for spelling, such as adding suffixes to a base word, often take some time and repetition for students to learn and apply consistently. Therefore, a teacher may teach a new generalization on one day, then review it and have children practice it for several successive lessons (or longer) before teaching a new generalization.

Vocabulary is addressed in two places on the plan. In the section on text reading and reading comprehension, teachers should address unfamiliar text-specific words whose meanings children need to know in order to comprehend the text they will read. (See Stevens & Austin, Chapter 8, this volume.) The most important word meanings should be taught prior to children's reading of the text, whereas other word meanings may be addressed in context, as they come up during reading. Vocabulary may also be addressed in the oral language comprehension section of the plan, through read-alouds or other oral activities. (See Coyne & Loftus-Rattan, Chapter 6, this volume.) Because these oral activities are calibrated to children's listening rather than reading levels, they can target relatively sophisticated vocabulary words. These often include the kinds of words used in a broad program of vocabulary development—that is, more advanced words found across a range of texts and domains, like *significant*, *remorse*, and *suspicious*—what Beck, McKeown, and Kucan (2002) term "Tier Two" vocabulary. In some cases, these words could also include "Tier Three" words, domain-specific vocabulary from the grade-level curriculum, such as science, that children are currently unable to decode independently (e.g., *photosynthesis*) and that are being taught orally. Depending on individual children's needs, the oral language comprehension segment of the plan can be used to teach other aspects of language, such as syntax or narrative language, that can also improve children's reading comprehension (Clarke, Snowling, Truelove, & Hulme, 2010; Snowling & Hulme, 2012; see Zipoli & Merritt, Chapter 7, this volume), as well as their written expression (see Lambrecht Smith & Haynes, Chapter 9, this volume).

SAMPLE INTERVENTION LESSONS FOR JAMAL, TERRELL, AND LACEY

After Mr. Goudreau began participating in professional development related to SL, he became aware of several steps that might improve the reading progress of his students.

First, although he had been using state standards to guide his teaching, he recognized the value of a more detailed scope and sequence for teaching literacy, especially for foundational skills, such as phonemic awareness, decoding, spelling, and basic writing skills. He began using this kind of scope and sequence in different areas. He also adopted a synthetic-phonics approach at the grapheme–phoneme level in his initial decoding and spelling instruction with students like Terrell. He made greater use of assessment, both in identifying his students' specific difficulties, and in monitoring their progress. He continues to use assessments, such as oral reading fluency and maze probes, criterion-referenced decoding assessments, embedded comprehension checks, and observational procedures, to adjust his instruction on an ongoing basis with all of his students, including the three described in more detail below.

Jamal

Table 10.2 shows a sample intervention lesson for Jamal that applies the format discussed above. Time allocations reflect approximately equal emphasis on skills for word recognition and comprehension, with a total intervention time of about 60 minutes. The plan would be implemented in a small group with the two other students mentioned previously: Jake and Nasreen.

The initial segment of the lesson focuses on morphology. Mr. Goudreau begins by eliciting from the students how morphemic knowledge is helpful (e.g., it provides important clues for reading, spelling, and understanding families of interrelated words). He uses flash cards to review previously taught affixes, such as *non-*, *mis-*, *re-*, *-able*, *-logy*, *-ist*, and *-ity*. He also reviews previously taught strategies for decoding long words, such as peeling-off affixes and the need to be flexible in trying different possible ways to pronounce a long word. (See Kearns, Lyon, & Kelley, Chapter 3, this volume, for a detailed discussion of these strategies.) Then Jamal and his group mates are explicitly taught two new morphemes—*bio* and *geo*—as well as how to apply them in reading, spelling, and understanding unfamiliar words. In modeling sample words and in choosing practice words for students to read and spell, Mr. Goudreau selects several words from a text on climate change that the students will read later in the lesson (e.g., *geology, geologist, biodiversity, renewable, nonrenewable*). All of the students need vocabulary development, and many of the words are important content vocabulary, so Mr. Goudreau consistently discusses the meaning of the words, as well as their spelling and how to read them.

The students' text reading on climate change was chosen in part to help prepare the students for an upcoming unit on climate change in their science classes. However, because the students cannot read the grade 6 science textbook, Mr. Goudreau has selected a lower-level text, written at a grade 4 level, which also addresses climate change. Although this text is at the students' instructional levels, given their difficulties with word reading, Mr. Goudreau still wants to monitor their accuracy of text reading. Therefore, for this part of the lesson he has two of the students read in a pair, while he listens to the third student read aloud. The third student is rotated across sessions; for today's session, Mr. Goudreau will listen to Jamal. After Jamal reads the text the

TABLE 10.2. Sample Intervention Lesson for Jamal (with Jake and Nasreen)

Component(s)	Activity
Word recognition and spelling (15 minutes)	
• Decode, spell, and learn meaning of two new morphemes (e.g., *bio*, *geo*) related to curriculum words	• Teacher elicits from students how morphemic knowledge is helpful (i.e., helps you read, spell, understand related words). • Teacher uses flash cards to quickly review previously learned morphemes (affixes; e.g., *-logy*, *-ist*, *-ity*, *-able*, *non-*, *un-*, *re-*); introduces new morphemes, their spelling, and their meaning (e.g., *bio* = *life*, *geo* = *earth*) with sample words.
• Review strategies for breaking up and decoding a long word (peeling off, every syllable has at least one vowel [ESHALOV], be flexible)	• Teacher briefly reviews previously taught strategies orally by asking students questions about how to approach a long, unfamiliar word, with modeling on sample words, as needed.
• Decode and spell unfamiliar multisyllabic words with the above morphemes	• Students read a list of words with the new and review morphemes, including several from today's text on climate change; teacher and students discuss meanings. • Students write several multisyllabic words with the new and review morphemes dictated by the teacher (e.g., *biology*, *geology*, *biologist*); teacher provides feedback on spelling, as needed.
Text reading and reading comprehension (20 minutes)	Students orally read text selection about climate change (unfamiliar text)—grade 4 level; "turn-and-talk" routine on new vocabulary (*renewable* and *biodiversity*); practice writing gist statements in a gist log, with teacher feedback and discussion.
Fluency (5 minutes)	Teacher does timed repeated reading with Jamal (student is rotated each session), with goal setting, as well as charting and discussion of results.
Language comprehension (10 minutes)	Teacher reads aloud from grade 6 science text; discusses two important content words from the curriculum (new vocabulary: *glacier* and *habitat*). With teacher guidance, students write words in their notebooks, correctly spelled with a brief definition, for future study.
Writing (10 minutes)	Students respond in writing to a question about climate change related to today's readings, include at least two of the new vocabulary words, edit response for spelling and basic writing skills. Complete for homework.

Lesson objectives for Jamal

- Decode at least five out of six multisyllabic words with taught morphemes correctly.
- Spell at least four out of five multisyllabic words with taught morphemes correctly.
- Read the unfamiliar grade 4 text aloud with at least 95% decoding accuracy and at least 75% accuracy on comprehension questions.
- Reread the grade 4 text selection with no more than one error, appropriate prosody, and an increase of at least five words correct per minute (WCPM).
- Write appropriate gist statements for the text read in the lesson.
- Spell and use both new vocabulary words correctly in the written response.
- Write at least a five-sentence response with appropriate content.
- Apply previously taught spelling and basic writing skills correctly in the written response, with no more than one error.

first time, he will also do a timed repeated reading of a portion of the text as a fluency activity, including setting of a goal and charting of the results (see Hudson, Anderson, McGraw, Ray, & Wilhelm, Chapter 5, this volume). These fluency procedures will be repeated with the other two students in Jamal's group in subsequent sessions.

Before students read the climate change text, their teacher briefly previews the text and asks them to be alert to some of the new vocabulary words in the text, especially *renewable* and *biodiversity*, which are key science curriculum words. He lets them know that after reading they will do a "turn-and-talk" routine with these words (see Stevens & Austin, Chapter 8, this volume). Students have already been introduced to writing gist statements about what they have read—today Mr. Goudreau wants to provide them with more practice writing gist statements, in preparation for a future lesson on using gist statements to write summaries. Students will write gist statements in a log that will be used for feedback and discussion with the teacher at the end of this lesson segment.

For the oral language comprehension segment of the lesson, Mr. Goudreau uses a variety of texts and activities across his lessons. Sometimes he uses read-alouds and oral activities to help develop Tier Two vocabulary and background knowledge, similar to those described for Terrell and Lacey below. At other times, he uses this segment to help students with content learning. This week, because he wants to prepare Jamal, Jake, and Nasreen for the unit on climate change, he will read aloud from the grade 6 science curriculum materials. Today's focus involves explicitly teaching two important content words: *glacier* and *habitat*. After discussing the words, Mr. Goudreau has the students write the words in a notebook kept for this purpose, with the correct spelling and a concise definition of each word, for ongoing study and review. The lesson concludes with a writing activity that involves responding to a question about climate change, as well as applying some specific foundational skills that students have been taught.

At the bottom of Table 10.2 are some specific objectives for this lesson, which are tied to Jamal's (as well as the other children's) IEP goals. Mr. Goudreau includes these kinds of objectives for all of his lessons. During and after each lesson, he quickly checks off lesson objectives that students met and notes any specific difficulties they had next to the ones that were not met. These objectives help inform his planning of subsequent lessons. In conjunction with regular progress monitoring assessments, they also help him gauge his students' progress and adjust his instruction, as needed.

A couple of points should be made about the lesson objectives, which also apply to the other students discussed in this chapter. First, objectives are embedded in lesson activities and do not require a separate series of assessments. If students need support or scaffolding to meet an objective, Mr. Goudreau provides it; however, he makes a note of this need, because it usually indicates that he should continue working on the same objective in the next lesson. Also, although Mr. Goudreau often makes use of timed repeated readings to develop text fluency, he is cautious about timing in text reading, especially when the students are reading a new or challenging text. He does not want to give students the implicit message that they should focus primarily on reading text quickly, because he is concerned about a possible trade-off between reading speed and comprehension. A potential trade-off is a particular concern for these students, who all have a comprehension component to their reading difficulties. The use of regular oral reading fluency probes enables Mr. Goudreau to assess whether his instruction is translating into rate gains in text reading for his students, whether or not he uses timed repeated readings in his fluency activities.

Terrell

Table 10.3 shows a sample lesson for Terrell, delivered one to one, with a total time of about 75 minutes. Because of Terrell's severe needs in word recognition and spelling, more time is devoted to this first segment of the lesson plan than for Jamal and his group mates. Also, lesson segments for fluency and writing are focused primarily on improving Terrell's foundational skills, such as building automaticity in reading irregular words, applying decoding skills to accurate text reading, and applying previously taught spelling skills in writing.

The specific skills taught in the first segment of the lesson focus on reading and spelling CVC words, which have short (lax) vowel sounds. Mr. Goudreau begins by providing Terrell with some brief practice, just a minute or two, on oral phoneme blending and segmentation tasks. He then moves quickly into the phonics part of his lesson, in which Terrell will receive more practice in phoneme blending and segmentation, in the context of a word-building activity that requires him to decode and spell CVC words.

Mr. Goudreau has avoided teaching all short vowel sounds at once, because he knows they are highly confusable. Instead, he has taught short sounds for one vowel letter at a time. Terrell now consistently knows short sounds for all vowel letters except for *u*, to be introduced in today's lesson, and *y*, which has not yet been taught because it is uncommon in CVC words. After the sound has been introduced, Mr. Goudreau has Terrell practice decoding and spelling CVC words with short *u* in the word-building activity, and then he includes review words with previously learned short vowels. Mr. Goudreau also addresses reading and spelling of common phonetically irregular words, using a multisensory activity. This activity involves tracing the printed words with a pencil, while saying the letter names and the whole word aloud, and then writing each word from memory.

For fluency development, the teacher does a quick flash card review of previously taught irregular words. Then Terrell rereads a familiar decodable text (i.e., a text read in a previous lesson) to build fluency, with timing. Before this reading, Mr. Goudreau helps Terrell set a goal for his reading; after the reading, he and Terrell graph and discuss the results, similar to what he did with Jamal.

Terrell then reads an unfamiliar decodable text that he has not read before. This reading is not timed, and the focus is primarily on reading accurately while monitoring comprehension. Like the text used for fluency practice, this text mainly includes CVC word patterns, as well as phonetically irregular words that Terrell has learned. (The texts Terrell reads are Mr. Goudreau's first source for the irregular words that he teaches Terrell.) Mr. Goudreau asks questions during this part of the lesson and addresses CVC words whose meanings Terrell may not know (e.g., *vat, lug*). He wants to ensure that Terrell reads for meaning and that he uncovers any sources of comprehension difficulty.

TABLE 10.3. Sample Intervention Lesson for Terrell

Component(s)	Activity
Word recognition and spelling (25 minutes)	
• Oral phoneme blending and segmentation	• Teacher uses oral tasks to provide Terrell with brief practice blending and segmenting three-phoneme words orally, including words with stop consonants, which are harder to blend and segment.
• Learn new letter sound, short vowel sound for the letter *u*	• Teacher quickly reviews previously taught single consonant sounds and short vowels (*a, e, i, o*) with letter cards, teach short *u* with multisensory activity and key word (*up*).
• Decode and spell CVC words, all vowels	• Teacher uses word-building activity to have Terrell practice decoding: first, CVC words with *u* (e.g., *sun, run, rug, tug, tub*), then CVC words with other vowels (e.g., *tab, tap, tip, hip, hop, hog, log, leg, let*). Teacher forms words with letter tiles. • Reverse word-building activity to practice spelling of CVC words, first with *u*, then with other vowels (teacher dictates words; e.g., *bun, but, hut, hit, hat, mat, met, men*; Terrell spells them with letter tiles).
• Learn to read and spell two new irregular (exception) words with similar spellings (e.g., *come, some*)	• Teacher introduces new irregular words, pointing out similarities between them, followed by multisensory tracing activity; then Terrell writes the new words from memory along with several review words.
Fluency (10 minutes)	Teacher does flash card review of 15 previously taught irregular words (e.g., *the, to, do, of*), with timing. Teacher then helps Terrell set a goal for a timed repeated reading of a previously read decodable text (CVC words) at his instructional level. After the timed reading, the results are graphed and discussed.
Text reading and reading comprehension (15 minutes)	Terrell reads a new (unfamiliar) decodable text (CVC words). Before Terrell reads, teacher reviews any difficult-to-decode words, such as names. During reading, teacher provides appropriate scaffolding if Terrell has difficulty reading a word or makes a decoding error; teacher also asks questions frequently to ensure Terrell monitors comprehension while reading and to catch any misunderstandings promptly.
Language comprehension (15 minutes)	Teacher reads aloud from *Shiloh*, a chapter book that he has been reading to Terrell on a regular basis, with discussion of new vocabulary and background knowledge. Teacher explicitly teaches meaning of two Tier Two words from the text: *impatient* and *flustered*. After reading, teacher asks Terrell to use each word in a sentence orally.
Writing (10 minutes)	Teacher dictates three sentences that apply spelling skills that Terrell has learned (CVC words with *a, e, i, o, u*, and irregular words), as well as other previously taught basic writing skills (e.g., ending punctuation; capitalization of the word *I*, names, first word of sentence). Terrell writes each sentence with proofreading for basic writing errors.

(continued)

TABLE 10.3. *(continued)*

Lesson objectives for Terrell
• Give short vowel sounds for vowel letters *a, e, i, o, u* correctly. • Decode at least nine out of 10 CVC words correctly (all five vowels). • Spell at least five out of six CVC words correctly (all five vowels). • Read irregular words correctly, including both new and review words, with no more than one error. • Read all review irregular words from the timed flash card activity within 30 seconds. • Read the unfamiliar decodable text with at least 90% decoding accuracy and at least 80% accuracy on comprehension questions. • Reread familiar decodable text with no more than one error, appropriate prosody, and an increase of at least three WCPM. • Answer comprehension questions about the read-aloud text, including questions aimed at vocabulary and background knowledge, with at least 80% accuracy. • Correctly use in a sentence the two new vocabulary words from the read-aloud. • Apply previously taught basic spelling and writing skills in dictated sentences, with no more than one error across the three sentences.

For the most part, however, these texts are very easy for Terrell to comprehend, and the main focus in this part of the lesson is his application of decoding skills to text reading.

Terrell's needs involving vocabulary building and teaching of background knowledge are addressed mostly in the language comprehension segment of the lesson. During this segment, Mr. Goudreau reads aloud to Terrell from *Shiloh* (2000), by Phyllis Reynolds Naylor. This is a chapter book, approximately at Terrell's grade placement. Terrell greatly enjoys *Shiloh* due to his strong interest in dogs, as well as the engaging plot line of the book. During the read-aloud, Mr. Goudreau asks questions and discusses relevant background knowledge and vocabulary that are unfamiliar to Terrell, including two specific Tier Two vocabulary words: *impatient* and *flustered*. After the reading, he asks Terrell to use each of these words orally in a sentence, to see whether he remembers their meaning and can use them correctly. He also records the words in a notebook for use in future vocabulary activities. The final writing segment of the lesson involves dictated sentences that provide Terrell with additional practice in spelling and basic writing skills.

Lacey

Lacey's sample lesson plan is shown in Table 10.4. The plan involves about 75 minutes of intervention time in total, currently delivered one to one, with about 30 minutes devoted to word reading, spelling, and fluency, and about 45 minutes to skills contributing to reading comprehension and language comprehension.

The first segment of Lacey's lesson focuses on vowel-*r* letter patterns. Prior to this lesson, Lacey has already learned sounds for the vowel-*r* patterns *ar, er, ir, or,* and *ur*. In this lesson, Mr. Goudreau teaches a slightly less common vowel-*r* pattern: *wor* (as in *word, work, worst, worm*). He draws Lacey's attention to the fact that *wor* has a different sound (i.e., /wer/) than does the pattern *or* (i.e., /or/ as in *fork* or *storm*). He also briefly

TABLE 10.4. Sample Intervention Lesson for Lacey

Component(s)	Activity
Word recognition and spelling (20 minutes)	
• Review sounds for previously taught vowel-*r* and vowel team combinations (letter patterns)	• Teacher uses flash cards to quickly review sounds for previously learned vowel team (e.g., *ai, ay, oo, ee*) and vowel-*r* letter patterns (e.g., *ar, er, ir, or, ur*), as well as other patterns, such as consonant digraphs.
• Learn sound for new vowel-*r* pattern: *wor* (as in *work, word*)	• Teacher uses a multisensory activity and key word (*work*) to teach the *wor* pattern; teacher draws child's attention to the different sounds for *or* and *wor*.
• Review previously taught generalizations for determining the vowel sound of a one-syllable word; apply to decoding words	• Teacher briefly reviews previously taught generalizations by showing a sample word (e.g., *spot, time, go*) and asking for the relevant generalization (e.g., closed, *-vce*, open). • Lacey sorts closed, *-vce*, open, vowel team, and vowel-*r* words into five separate piles, with teacher feedback and coaching as needed. • Lacey reads sorted words aloud.
• Learn to spell two new irregular (exception) words with similar spellings (e.g., *does, done*)	• Teacher introduces new irregular words, pointing out similarities between them, followed by multisensory tracing activity; then Lacey writes the new words from memory, along with several review words.
Fluency (10 minutes)	Teacher does 1-minute flash card review of 25 previously taught irregular words (e.g., *the, to, do, of*), with timing. Lacey rereads a phrase-cued selection from a familiar, early grade 2-level text, with an emphasis on accuracy and prosody of reading.
Text reading and reading comprehension (15 minutes)	Lacey reads from an unfamiliar, early-grade 2 text. Before Lacey reads, teacher preteaches any key vocabulary words that are unfamiliar, as well as any difficult-to-decode words. During reading, teacher provides appropriate scaffolding if Lacey has difficulty reading a word or makes a decoding error. Teacher asks questions frequently during, as well as after, reading to ensure Lacey monitors comprehension and to catch any misunderstandings promptly.
Language comprehension (15 minutes)	Teacher reads aloud from early grade 3 trade book (*Julius, the Baby of the World* by Kevin Henkes), with discussion of new vocabulary and background knowledge. Teacher explicitly teaches the meaning of two Tier Two words: *extraordinary* and *disgusted*. After reading, teacher asks Lacey to use each word in a sentence orally.
Writing (15 minutes)	Sentence-combining activities with word patterns and irregular words Lacey has been taught. Teacher introduces sentence combining, telling how it is useful both for understanding what is read and for writing. Teacher then explains and models sentence combining with a few sets of kernel sentences. Lacey completes several items with teacher guidance, edits for previously taught spelling and basic writing skills, finishes additional items for homework.

(continued)

TABLE 10.4. *(continued)*

Lesson objectives for Lacey
• Give sounds for all taught vowel-*r* letter patterns correctly. • Sort 15 word cards into closed, *-vce,* open, vowel team, and vowel-*r* categories, with no more than one mistake. • Decode at least five out of six vowel-*r* words correctly. • Decode at least eight out of nine other words in the sorting task correctly. • Read irregular words correctly, including both new and review words, with no more than one error. • Read all review irregular words from the timed flash card activity within 30 seconds. • Reread the phrase-cued text with no more than one error and appropriate prosody. • Read the unfamiliar text with at least 92% decoding accuracy and at least 75% accuracy on comprehension questions. • Answer comprehension questions about the read-aloud text, including questions aimed at vocabulary and background knowledge, with at least 75% accuracy. • Combine kernel sentences to make grammatically appropriate sentences in at least four out of five sets of items. • Apply previously taught basic spelling and writing skills in sentence combining, with no more than two errors across all five sets of items.

reviews one-syllable generalizations that Lacey has previously learned, such as closed (a syllable with one short vowel that ends in a consonant) and *vce,* which are useful to determine the vowel sound of the syllable. In his review, he avoids asking Lacey to provide lengthy recitations of rules. Instead, he focuses on Lacey's ability to recognize letter patterns in words and to use them to aid in decoding unfamiliar words. He employs a sorting task that requires Lacey to apply her recognition of all the patterns she has learned thus far. He provides coaching as needed, but Lacey does well with this task and needs help only with categorizing one word. Lacey then reads all of the sorted words aloud. Next, Mr. Goudreau does some work with Lacey on spelling phonetically irregular words. Lacey's ability to read common irregular words accurately is relatively good, but she continues to require work on spelling many of these words.

Although Mr. Goudreau has sometimes used timed repeated readings to develop Lacey's text-reading fluency, more recently he has begun using phrase-cued texts like those described by Hudson, Anderson, McGraw, Ray, and Wilhelm, Chapter 5, this volume. He has found this approach especially helpful for Lacey, given her difficulties with syntax. Lacey is already familiar with phrase-cueing annotations, so today's fluency activity emphasizes having Lacey practice with a familiar text that she enjoyed and that contains phrase cues. Unlike Terrell, Lacey does not require a highly controlled decodable text. However, Mr. Goudreau ensures that the texts used both in fluency practice and in the text-reading/reading comprehension part of Lacey's lesson (i.e., reading of unfamiliar text) are at her instructional level: early grade 2. Also, because Lacey has a more significant language comprehension component to her reading difficulties than does Terrell, Mr. Goudreau puts more emphasis on reading comprehension in this part of the lesson than was the case for Terrell.

In the language comprehension segment of the lesson, Mr. Goudreau does a read-aloud to help develop Lacey's vocabulary, using a more challenging text than Lacey can currently decode. The read-aloud text is Kevin Henkes's *Julius, the Baby of the World*

(1990), a book that Lacey enjoys because it is very funny. This book has a relatively simple sentence structure that Lacey comprehends easily, but rich vocabulary (e.g., *lullaby, extraordinary, disgusting*) that Mr. Goudreau uses to build Lacey's knowledge of new word meanings. Mr. Goudreau selects two Tier Two words for explicit teaching and extended activities, using procedures similar to those he used for Terrell.

The final writing segment of the lesson focuses specifically on Lacey's needs in the area of syntax. Mr. Goudreau uses sentence combining, an activity that can be helpful not only in improving students' sentence structure in writing but also in enhancing their reading comprehension. (See Zipoli & Merritt, Chapter 7, and Lambrecht Smith & Haynes, Chapter 9, this volume, for more detailed discussion.) In sentence-combining activities, a teacher gives students a set of short kernel sentences, and students combine them into a grammatically correct sentence. For example, two sentences, such as "The cat is black" and "The cat has long, thick fur," can be combined as "The black cat has long, thick fur." Given Lacey's decoding and spelling weaknesses, her teacher is careful to use kernel sentences that she will be able to read and spell correctly.

Lacey has been identified with a language disability, and she receives services from a speech–language pathologist (SLP). Although not shown in her sample lesson, Mr. Goudreau and the SLP coordinate their work to ensure consistency of services, as well as to integrate and reinforce Lacey's language and literacy learning. This is an important aspect of Lacey's program that is helping to improve her progress.

Features of SL in These Lessons

The sample lesson plans for Jamal, Terrell, and Lacey exemplify many features of SL. Key skills and concepts—both in relation to foundational skills and higher-level areas, such as vocabulary and comprehension—are explicitly taught, explained, and modeled by the teacher. Mr. Goudreau's use of a scope and sequence in various skill areas has helped him make his instruction more systematic. For example, Lacey was taught sounds for vowel-*r* letter patterns before being expected to read words with those patterns. The use of a synthetic-phonics approach at the grapheme–phoneme level is evident in Terrell's word-building activity for decoding and spelling, which focuses on grapheme–phoneme (and phoneme–grapheme) correspondences, not word families or onsets and rimes.

Each lesson provides an ongoing review of skills. Equally important, instruction is organized to provide practice and application of previously taught skills in multiple ways. For instance, the texts that children read, and the writing activities in each lesson, provide practice on important skills that children have learned; there is teaching for transfer. Instruction is also organized and sequenced to minimize confusion, as when Mr. Goudreau avoided teaching Terrell all short vowel sounds at once, and when he avoided using any words that Lacey could not read or spell in his sentence combining activities with her. Mr. Goudreau provides prompt, targeted feedback not only in the decoding and spelling segments of the lessons but also in his use of questions during children's reading, his feedback to oral reading errors, and his feedback to writing activities.

SUMMARY

Students with MRD require multicomponent interventions aimed at both word recognition and comprehension. Multicomponent interventions based in Structured Literacy approaches can be very effective for these children. These interventions have the key features of SL discussed in Spear-Swerling, Chapter 1, this volume, including explicit, systematic teaching of important skills and concepts; the provision of prompt, clear, corrective feedback; planned, purposeful selections of instructional examples, tasks, and texts; teaching for transfer; and data-based decision making. Important considerations in planning these interventions include the nature and severity of individual poor readers' word-reading and comprehension difficulties; grouping decisions; and ensuring integration of interventions, both internally and in relation to core (Tier 1) instruction. Internal integration of interventions is intrinsic to SL approaches and can be further enhanced through the use of specific intervention activities—for example, using writing to develop specific reading skills.

Application Activities

Activity 1

Samantha is a second grader who has been receiving tiered reading interventions for the past 6 months. Initial concerns about Samantha's reading, near the end of grade 1, highlighted problems with decoding and text-reading fluency. Her current intervention has addressed phonemic awareness and phonics, as well as application of those skills in reading basic decodable texts. Spelling skills are also taught systematically and are reinforced through dictated sentences that incorporate learned word patterns. Her interventionist says Samantha is making good progress, and that comprehension is not a problem in texts that Samantha is able to decode.

Recently, Samantha's parents had an independent evaluation done. Samantha's scores on subtests from the Woodcock–Johnson IV Tests of Achievement (WJ IV ACH; Schrank, Mather, & McGrew, 2014a) and the Woodcock–Johnson IV Tests of Oral Language (WJ IV OL; Schrank, Mather, & McGrew, 2014b), are displayed in Table 10.5. Average range for standard scores on these subtests is from 90 to 110.

Based on the preceding information and the scores in Table 10.5, answer the following questions.

1. Explain why Samantha's patterns of performance suggest a mixed profile of reading difficulties.
2. Why do you think Samantha's interventionist has not seen comprehension as an area of difficulty?
3. Discuss some additional assessments that could be useful in planning a multicomponent intervention for Samantha.

TABLE 10.5. Samantha's Scores on the WJ IV ACH and WJ IV OL

WJ IV subtest (brief description)	Samantha's score
Letter–Word Identification (reading a list of real words)	82
Word Attack (reading a list of nonsense words)	87
Spelling (writing words dictated orally by the examiner)	80
Sentence Reading Fluency (silent sentence reading requiring a basic level of comprehension, under timed conditions)	75
Passage Comprehension (reading comprehension measure with most items using a cloze task)	72
Oral Comprehension (similar task to Passage Comprehension except that the examiner, not the child, reads all items aloud)	82
Picture Vocabulary (naming pictures, an expressive vocabulary measure)	78
Segmentation (segmenting spoken words into syllables and phonemes, a phonological awareness measure)	95
Sound Blending (blending syllables and phonemes into spoken words, a phonological awareness measure)	99

Note. Average range = 90–110.

ANSWERS

1. In addition to below-average performance on multiple subtests related to word recognition (i.e., Letter–Word Identification, Word Attack, Spelling), Samantha demonstrates below-average performance on two oral language subtests: Picture Vocabulary and Oral Comprehension. A comparison of her performance on Passage Comprehension and Oral Comprehension is especially informative. These two subtests use a similar cloze (fill-in-the-blank) format for most items; their primary difference is that on Oral Comprehension, the examiner reads all items aloud to the child, whereas on Passage Comprehension, the child must read the items. Samantha's performance on Oral Comprehension was below average with a standard score of 82. Her score on Passage Comprehension was even lower, 72, probably due to the additional influence of poor word reading. This pattern suggests MRD.
2. Currently, Samantha reads decodable text in her intervention. Although this type of text is appropriate to her present level of decoding, it likely does not place heavy demands on comprehension. Therefore, Samantha's comprehension weaknesses would not be as evident in this type of text as in grade-level materials. Moreover, Samantha's language comprehension weaknesses are relatively mild, and even in relation to second-grade texts, might not be as striking as her decoding and fluency problems.

3. Many assessments could be useful, but it would be particularly helpful to obtain further information about the nature of Samantha's language weaknesses—for example, in areas such as inferencing, syntax, and narrative language (see, e.g., Zipoli & Merritt, Chapter 7, this volume).

Activity 2

At a meeting to discuss the results of Samantha's evaluation, her interventionist was reluctant to adjust Samantha's program to include the area of comprehension. She says that, during her sessions, Samantha comprehends decodable texts very well. She is demonstrating good progress in decoding and has mastered decoding several new word patterns during intervention, including closed syllables with blends and digraphs, *vce* syllables, and those syllable patterns with inflectional endings (e.g., *-ed*, *-ing*). Her decodable texts focus on those patterns, and her fluency in these texts is good. The interventionist does not see the value of addressing comprehension in her work with Samantha.

1. How would you convince the interventionist of the value of a multicomponent intervention?
2. What are some specific ways that Samantha's intervention should be adjusted?

ANSWERS

1. First, it is important to highlight the significance of the work that the interventionist has done in the areas of phonemic awareness, phonics, spelling, and text-reading fluency, because those skills form a vital foundation for reading comprehension and written expression. However, those skills are necessary, but not sufficient, for Samantha's continuing progress. As she advances to reading more difficult texts and grade-level materials, her language comprehension weaknesses will almost certainly impact her reading comprehension (as well as her writing), even if she can decode well. Addressing those needs in intervention certainly does not mean abandoning work on foundational skills and does not necessarily require large amounts of time. Including an oral language component to her intervention, with teaching of key language skills using SL methods, could greatly benefit Samantha's literacy development in the future.
2. Samantha's intervention should be adjusted to include a segment addressing oral language comprehension, using activities such as teacher read-alouds and oral discussion. These activities should employ more difficult texts that Samantha is currently unable to decode, calibrated to her listening level and including grade-level materials with appropriate teacher scaffolding. Oral language activities should focus on vocabulary and perhaps on other areas as well (e.g., syntax), depending on information from additional oral language assessments. Writing

activities, such as dictated sentences, should be adjusted to include areas such as vocabulary and other language areas that have been taught, as well as foundational skills, such as spelling.

REFERENCES

Beck, I. L., McKeown, M. G., & Kucan, L. (2002). *Bringing words to life: Robust vocabulary instruction.* New York: Guilford Press.

Capin, P., Cho, E., Miciak, J., Roberts, G., & Vaughn, S. (2021). Examining the reading and cognitive profiles of students with significant reading comprehension difficulties. *Learning Disabilities Quarterly, 44,* 183–196.

Carlisle, J. F. (2010). An integrative review of the effects of instruction in morphological awareness on literacy achievement. *Reading Research Quarterly, 45,* 464–487.

Clarke, P. J., Snowling, M. J., Truelove, E., & Hulme, C. (2010). Ameliorating children's reading-comprehension difficulties: A randomized controlled trial. *Psychological Science, 21,* 1106–1116.

Fletcher, J. M., Lyon, G. R., Fuchs, L. S., & Barnes, M. A. (2019). *Learning disabilities: From identification to intervention* (2nd ed.). New York: Guilford Press.

Foorman, B., Herrera, S., Dombek, J., Schatschneider, C., & Petscher, Y. (2017). *The relative effectiveness of two approaches to early literacy intervention in grades K–2* (REL 2017-251). Washington, DC: U.S. Department of Education, Institute of Education Sciences, National Center for Education Evaluation and Regional Assistance, Regional Educational Laboratory Southeast. Retrieved from *http://ies.ed.gov/ncee/edlabs*

Goodwin, A. P., & Ahn, S. (2013). A meta-analysis of morphological interventions in English: Effects on literacy outcomes for school-age children. *Scientific Studies of Reading, 17,* 257–285.

Graham, S., & Hebert, M. A. (2010). *Writing to read: Evidence for how writing can improve reading. A Carnegie Corporation Time to Act Report.* Washington, DC: Alliance for Excellent Education.

Henkes, K. (1990). *Julius, the baby of the world.* New York: Greenwillow Books.

Leach, J. M., Scarborough, H. S., & Rescorla, L. (2003). Late-emerging reading disabilities. *Journal of Educational Psychology, 95,* 211–224.

Lesaux, N. K., & Kieffer, M. J. (2010). Exploring sources of reading comprehension difficulties among language minority learners and their classmates in early adolescence. *American Educational Research Journal, 47,* 596–632.

Naylor, P. R. (2000). *Shiloh.* New York: Atheneum Books for Young Readers.

Scammacca, N., Vaughn, S., Roberts, G., Wanzek, J., & Torgesen, J. K. (2007). *Extensive reading interventions in grades K–3: From research to practice.* Portsmouth, NH: RMC Research Corporation, Center on Instruction.

Schrank, F. A., Mather, N., & McGrew, K. S. (2014a). *Woodcock-Johnson IV Tests of Achievement.* Rolling Meadows, IL: Riverside.

Schrank, F. A., Mather, N., & McGrew, K. S. (2014b). *Woodcock-Johnson IV Tests of Oral Language.* Rolling Meadows, IL: Riverside.

Snowling, M. J., & Hulme, C. (2012). Interventions for children's language and literacy difficulties. *International Journal of Language and Communication Disorders, 47,* 27–34.

Spear-Swerling, L., & Brucker, P. (2004). Preparing novice teachers to develop basic reading and spelling skills in children. *Annals of Dyslexia, 54,* 332–364.

Torgesen, J. K. (2004). Lessons learned from research on interventions for students who have difficulty learning to read. In P. McCardle & V. Chhabra (Eds.), *The voice of evidence in reading research* (pp. 355–381). Baltimore: Brookes.

Vaughn, S., & Fletcher, J. M. (2012). Response to intervention with secondary school students with reading difficulties. *Journal of Learning Disabilities, 45,* 244–256.

Vaughn, S., Linan-Thompson, S., Kouzekanani, K., Bryant, D. P., Dickson, S., & Blozis, S. A. (2003). Reading instruction grouping for students with reading difficulties. *Remedial and Special Education, 24,* 301–315.

Wanzek, J., Al Otaiba, S., & McMaster, K. L. (2020). *Intensive reading interventions for the elementary grades.* New York: Guilford Press.

Index

Note. Page numbers in *italic* indicate a figure or a table.